Tales of an Uncommon Man:
Uncle Ort's Keepsakes

To Joe Hall

Tales of an Uncommon Man: Uncle Ort's Keepsakes

Janice Feagin Britton

Slow Loris Press
Fairhope, Alabama

Published in October 1994 by
The Slow Loris Press, Fairhope, Alabama

ISBN No. 0-9643940-0-6
Copyright © 1994 Janice Feagin Britton

All rights are reserved. No part of this book may be reproduced or transmitted in any form or by any means, electronic or mechanical, including photocopying, recording, or by any information storage and retrieval system, without permission in writing from the Publisher.

First Printing

Copies of this book ($14.95 postpaid in USA) may be ordered from:
Ms. Janice Feagin Britton
500 Spanish Fort Boulevard, Spanish Fort, AL 36527

Dedication

My late husband, Francis Richard Britton, was a vital source of support and understanding during the five years of writing this book. He took calls and protected me from interruptions. When I declined invitations, totally altered our daily life, and devoted days to research rather than companionship, he never complained. Once when I thought the task was beyond my reach, he encouraged me. This book is dedicated to him.

Acknowledgments

To acknowledge by name every relative and friend who contributed to my writing this biography is impossible. I hope the people I failed to mention will be forgiving. I am indebted to every person who was helpful. An asterisk signifies ten accommodating people who died before the book was published.

Those who share their memories and experiences with Uncle Ort included Charlie Bodden, J. B. Blackburn*, Jimmy Faulkner, Bob Hodgson–kingpins in Bay Minette, Alice Duck*, Mickey Wentworth*, Leon Leak*, Bob Seidentopf*, Gladys Woolsey*, and Floyd Williams* each shared their Uncle Ort reflections and experiences. The ladies who chatted enthusiastically with me in the Presbyterian church parlor in 1989 gave me a good start–Edith Bodden*, Garner Godwin, Geraldine Stanford, Florence White*, and Inez Zehner.

Significant others who enriched this book are William Belk, Ella Chandler, John Crowell, Willard Dahlberg, Luella Ferguson, Voncille Lackey, Pauline Logue, and Morton McMillan. Their stories are true. Names of real people have been used throughout. Early in the process Grace Terney graciously gave me two classic books on writing style.

Without the cooperation of relatives many colorful incidents would have been omitted. The Lindseys–Eloise, Walter, Gaye, Donald, David, and Walter's brother Jimmy and his wife, Betty–and kinfolks far and wide dug out old clippings, memories, and pictures, as did Dorothy Dill in Ohio, George Ertzinger* in Missouri, his brother, Paul, in Maryland, and his sister, Ruth Shanahan, in Indiana.

I am especially indebted to those who read the manuscript and made invaluable criticisms, namely Charles Blackledge, Shirley Bolton, Gaye Caffee, Rhea Lewis, Agnes Mason, and Henrietta Wilkinson. Especially important to me are the innumerable people who during the many years listened attentively to my endless palaver about the vicissitudes of writing.

Preface

This is a biographical love story about my uncle, a man with the strange name Ort Ertzinger. In his own high-spirited Ortish way, he did unheard-of things, such as going on rattlesnake shoots, celebrating two birthdays in one year, and recording the rabbits smashed on an Idaho highway.

After completing high school in Huntington, Indiana, he moved to Bay Minette, Alabama, in 1909 with his family. Too young to establish a business in his own name, he resourcefully named his title and abstract business J. A. Ertzinger & Son. A many-faceted person, he at one time wrote for five publications, including the Baldwin Times and the Mobile Register. A prolific writer of rhymes, he scribbled on whatever paper was at hand.

He played the horn in a band, the organ at church, and the piano wherever needed. His strong tenor voice was a passport to singing groups from Sunday School to the role of Escamillo in Carmen. A devoted churchman whose love of fishing ranked second only to his family. He lived a life overflowing with merriment and accomplishment.

Attracted to young people as a piece of steel is drawn to a magnet, Uncle Ort is still talked about in these parts. His name is in the recently established Baldwin County High School Hall of Fame–not as a player but as a coach and advocate. He led the high school girls' basketball team to win the state pennant. He didn't let his fellow school board members renege on their responsibility to maintain a credible sports program. When necessary, he umpired baseball games and carried the lineman's stick and chain for football games. Outgoing, friendly, and humorous, he worked with young people for twenty-six years as an Presbyterian youth advisor.

Before it was mainstream talk, he avoided cigarettes–even the smell of their smoke–protected the environment, was a tree farmer and a recycler. His impeccable integrity, business acumen, and ability to listen and communicate earned him the admiration and respect of others.

People young and old will enjoy reading this American success story about an ordinary Yankee who made good in the South when the world was discovering the use of electricity, automobiles, and the telephone. I am not familiar with any published work that depicts, in a lighthearted manner, the life in Baldwin County, Alabama, during the first part of the Century of Progress.

Uncle Ort died in 1959. I always intended to write about him. When it dawned on me that he had been dead over thirty years, I got to work. I never dreamed I would spend seven years collecting data and writing. Nor that the task would be so enriching.

Contents

	Prologue	1
1	Trek into the Unknown	7
2	New Beginnings	15
3	Man about Town	24
4	Marriage	31
5	An Organizer in Euphoria	39
6	Satsumas and Hampers	49
7	A Man in the Middle of Things	57
8	A Man and His Money	67
9	Education Makes Sense	77
10	AAA–An Athletic Achiever	88
11	Music, Music, Music	97
12	A Special Place in His Heart	104
13	Reaching Out	115
14	The Automobile	124
15	The Communicator	134
16	Fun and Frolic	141
17	Relationships	148
18	The Family	156
19	Orange Beach	165
20	More about Orange Beach	177
21	Gramp	187
22	A Nonconformist	195
23	Leader Extraordinaire	203
24	A Boy and a Man	212
25	Trip of a Lifetime	221
26	A Time to Reap	233
27	Southern Exposure	243
28	Western Arena	251
29	Autobiography	258
30	Crescendo	265
	Epilogue	273
	Illustrations follow page 150	

Prologue

M Y COUSIN ELOISE AND I stood close to each other beside Uncle Ort's silver-grey casket. We gazed at the man we both loved lying amid the shiny satin. Grief oppressed us.

Eloise looked pensive. Finally she spoke: "You were closer to Daddy in some ways than I was." I agreed.

The bay window in the living room where we stood now embraced Uncle Ort. He'd hosted many parties and happy gatherings in this house he built for his bride. He'd planted the trees just outside. Now I could see they were laden with pecans ready to burst from their pods.

I looked across the room to the brass plaque he had cherished. It was seven or eight feet away, affixed to the mantel. My eyes flooded. Hot tears flowed down my face as I read the words engraved underneath the Celtic cross:

WELL DONE THOU GOOD AND FAITHFUL SERVANT

ORT HARMON ERTZINGER

YOUTH ADVISOR 1926—1952

The past twelve hours had been frantic for me, but I had made it. The reality of Uncle Ort's sudden death numbed me.

A hand touched my shoulder, and Cly Smith, the postmaster and a Masonic brother of Uncle Ort's, greeted me. His brown eyes behind pince-nez glasses looked sad. As usual he wore a bow tie and was impeccably dressed.

"I'm glad you are here." Cly's voice was genuine. "Ever since Florence heard of Ort's death in Indiana, she tried to contact you. New York City is a heck of place to find someone with so little to go on."

"I went ahead to visit friends for the weekend before a nursing conference," I explained. "I never dreamed there would be reason for anyone to contact me." Cly had been mother's right-hand man in trying to locate me.

1

"We were determined to leave no stone unturned to find you. We knew you would want to be here. Last night when Florence learned you'd canceled your reservation at the Barbizon Plaza, she felt doomed.

"That's when I asked Florence if you two had any mutual friends in the Big Apple. I was thinking you might give them a call while you were there. Florence remembered the Blassingames. They were our last chance."

"That did it!" I chimed in, eager to pick up the story. "Miracle of miracles, Count Blassingame and I had talked on the phone only half an hour before Mother called him." He and Peggy, his wife, were native Alabamians. Peggy, a third-generation friend of my father's, was not at home. That's why I had given Count my phone number.

"I was afraid you would not have time to get here for the funeral." Cly's voice was sad and slow.

"I barely made it! The last plane left Newark in less than an hour and a half after I heard of Uncle Ort's death. It was a close shave. The midtown bus to Newark pulled away just as my taxi drove up. The driver wasn't used to driving outside Manhattan Island and got lost driving to the airport—those cloverleaf turns had us going around in circles.

"The plane was taxiing out to the runway when I picked up my ticket. After my hysterical pleas, the Eastern attendant radioed the pilot to wait for me.

"They piled me into a jeep, and I was swished through the night to the plane—barely paused on the runway—and literally thrown aboard with my baggage." A sense of shock pervades me even now, thirty years later. I clearly recall the entire episode.

"It's time to go to the church," someone said. The flowers were being removed from the foot of the casket. In blank submission I turned and followed. Mother, close beside me, clung to my arm.

I wanted very much to be in control of myself, a shoulder for her to lean on, but I wasn't sure I could be. All her life Mother had looked up to her older brother. He had been a reliable strength and helped her keep sane during a crisis in her life. She would feel insecure without him around.

As soon as our car was parked outside the church, I heard the organ music. Music had been a vital part of Uncle Ort's worship of God. Several years earlier, when the new sanctuary was nearing completion, Uncle Ort had selected that organ with special care and given it to the church. In 1956, when it was installed, Uncle Ort's longtime friend and pastor Hunter Norwood had made a special visit to Bay Minette to dedicate the electronic wonder.

The music dissolved my control. I sobbed and my muscles quivered in grief as I walked down the aisle to sit in the family pew. Now, in the fullness of time, in this church Uncle Ort had hallowed in his soul, his physical body was making a final visit.

After Uncle Ort's burial, I made one of the most important decisions of my life. I took time out to grieve. My personal life took priority over my professional responsibilities.

My recent appointment as Administrator for Nursing at Pensacola Junior College in Florida had resulted in an invitation to a nursing conference at the headquarters of the National League for Nursing in New York City. Developing a curriculum for students of nursing in a junior college, in those days, was controversial. We were moving into uncharted territory long dominated by Florence Nightingale's precepts of nursing education.

This adventure of preparing students to become R.N.'s in less than three years attracted the attention of the Rockefeller Foundation. The Foundation funded the establishment of eight programs strategically located across the United States. The purpose of the conference was to set national guidelines for this radically new type of education called Associate Degree Nursing. Directors of the eight pilot programs would be there.

The opportunity to meet with these key leaders was extremely important to me. I'd stuck my neck out and was establishing the first Associate Degree Nursing Program in the state of Florida. Furthermore, this was being done with precious state tax money; no federal or private funds were being used. The work I was doing was being carefully and critically watched by countless observers in the South. Gleaning ideas from other trailblazers like myself was crucial to the success of the Pensacola Junior College Nursing Program. Until the death of my uncle, *nothing* could have kept me away from this exciting conclave.

In the darkness of a wakeful night, I decided not to return to the New York City meetings. I was in shock and needed time to pull myself together. Uncle Ort was my Rock of Gibraltar. He was the epitome of stability among the things that really counted. He understood me.

News of Ort Ertzinger's sudden fatal heart attack sent shock waves to his friends all over. His death, while he was preparing to go fishing, was as he would have chosen. Being among those who loved him was the right place for me. Grieving for a week at home was for me a luxury.

Uncle Ort was on people's minds. We laughed, cried, and talked about Uncle Ort as we adjusted to life without him. This was a golden opportunity to talk with a few of Uncle Ort's special friends. I made notes with the thought of writing about him.

People I knew, and some I did not know, talked eagerly and gladly about Uncle Ort–about his baseball playing, fishing camp, or a Shocco Springs adventure. Some recalled his delight in showing his movies and talking about seeing the great sequoia trees. As though by magic, his spirit was among us as we talked on the sidewalks and porches and in the living rooms of Bay Minette thirty years ago.

The stories I collected from townsfolk and relatives, plus my own experiences, especially of going fishing, were the basis for an article I wrote with the hope of selling it to the *Reader's Digest* for its monthly feature, "The Most Unforgettable Character I've Ever Known." I asked my friend Count Blassingame, a literary agent many of whose clients had been published in the *Digest*, to read the article and advise me about getting it published.

Count advised me that I had not described in a specific and convincing way why Uncle Ort was unforgettable to me. In other words, the article needed rewriting. Reluctantly I decided not to proceed. If I wrote about Uncle Ort as Count suggested, I feared I would offend my father. I shelved the idea for then, but kept the article and story in my files.

Now, three decades later, I have returned to the task of writing about Uncle Ort, more aware than ever of the importance of relationships. As Jonas Salk puts it:

> The meaning of life is felt through relationships
>
> ...Relationships with others and with one's own self.
>
> From what it is at birth to whom we become as child,
>
> Adult, parent, grandparent and ultimately, as ancestor.
>
> The meaning of life flowers through relationship
>
> Parenting, teaching, serving, creating.
>
> Learning from nature, the sages, our peers,
>
> From our emerging selves in a state of becoming.

Many reservations and several questions assailed me as I sat down to write. How could I reduce my dynamic uncle to words on paper? For those who did not know him, how could I express who he really was? Why was Uncle Ort such a fabulous giant in my life?

Using a wealth of his keepsakes–printed materials, his diary, and others–along with the recollections of friends and relatives and my own recall, I have reconstructed Uncle Ort. The relationship of names, dates, and facts has a fascinating way of producing real stories–the whole is larger than the sum of its parts.

I knew I was headed in the right direction when a friend in her nineties, Floy Williams, telephoned me in January. My Christmas card had told of how engrossed I was in writing about my uncle. She telephoned. "You're writing about your mother's brother, Uncle Ort?" she asked. "He worked with young people. I met him once, at Christmas. I want to read about him." She had met him only once, back in the thirties when he visited Mother in Graceville, Florida, yet after all those years she still remembered him and wanted to read about him!

To laugh often and love much

To win the respect of intelligent persons and the affection of children

To appreciate beauty

To find the best in others

To give of oneself

To leave the world a bit better, whether by a healthy child, a garden patch, or a redeemed social condition

To have played and laughed with enthusiasm and sung with exultation

To know that even one life has breathed easier because you have lived

This is to have succeeded.

Ralph Waldo Emerson

1

Trek into the Unknown

ELOISE CAME TO LUNCH with her arms full. Her husband, Walter, followed close behind with a box brimming with papers. "These are Daddy's things we talked about, just as Mother kept them. I haven't read them all."

She laid the things on my table. I noticed that her trim figure and curly chestnut hair were as attractive as ever. I'd always envied the fact that my petite cousin could eat anything she wanted without gaining weight. She is the nearest thing I have to a sister, and we have always been close–different, but close.

As we sat down in my Westminster Village apartment, Walter spoke up. "Mr. Ort was the kind of man who impressed others." His dreamy green eyes had a faraway look as he contemplated the past. Uncle Ort's son-in-law thinks before he speaks. I was particularly interest in what this quiet-mannered man had to say.

> "He was friendly, with an outgoing personality. He was quick about everything he did. I remember when I first started working at the office, I would be waiting to ask him something, and he would finish typing, get his hat, and walk out of the office. The next thing I knew I would see him driving off. And I was still sitting there waiting for him to finish what he was doing.

"Did you ever watch him type?" Walter asked, looking directly at me. "He beat anything I've ever seen. He could really make that typewriter talk with just three fingers." Pictures of him sitting in a straight chair pecking away flashed in my mind.

Before me on the marble-topped table lay a surprising array of history about a man I deeply loved. Uncle Ort had a healthy respect for himself but loved to poke fun at his unusual name. Webster's defines *ort* as "a scrap or fragment of food left from a meal." In jest my uncle said that he was a "worthless leaving."

The paper trail about him included a murder trial, an account of the fire at the tar plant which nearly took my uncle's life, clippings of the South Alabama baseball league when Uncle Ort played catcher, and more. I was eager to read every word.

Wordsworth wrote of the "inward eye/Which is the bliss of solitude." I was alone and truly blissful as I gazed at Uncle Ort's mementos. My inward eye saw more than what was on the page as I looked at the letters, clippings, and diaries. These memorabilia enticed me; every piece yearned to be read and interpreted in terms of the world in which he lived–the same world as Harry Truman's.

During the first decade of the twentieth century, excursion trains came south from Chicago to the Alabama county whose southern tier is on the Gulf of Mexico–Baldwin. Enticed by the advertising schemes of land developers, hundreds of people came looking for a new place to settle.

One day in 1907, Grandpa and his son, Ort, boarded the train in Huntington, Indiana, and went down for a look-see. A journey of discovery. They were all eyes and ears. A fellow train traveler advised them that Bay Minette was the best and most promising town in the Baldwin County.

A majority of people were migrants fleeing the hardships of Europe. Some came directly, while others first located in the northern midwest, then moved south. These people were looking for a desirable climate and place to earn a living, build a home, and raise a family. The John Adams Ertzinger family was considering a move for an entirely different reason.

They had roots and a comfortable home and a good lifestyle in Huntington. Their exploration was due to Uncle Ort's health. His doctor had recommended a warmer climate as a cure for his chronic catarrh (a condition we now refer to as "sinus trouble").

Baldwin County, the Ertzinger men found, was not a typical Southern county. Unlike so much of Alabama, cotton was not king. The county had come into existence in 1809, ten years before Alabama became a state. In another way the cart came before the horse. In 1901, when the seat of government moved from Daphne, Bay Minette was an unincorporated settlement on the railroad line. Six years later, the year the Ertzingers first visited, the town was incorporated.

The Ertzinger men were impressed when they first set foot on the sandy clay soil. Building was taking place everywhere–streets, houses, office buildings. The county government created and generated new jobs. People were needed to do such things as hold court, do land assessments, levy taxes, enforce the laws. Each train from the north brought new settlers. The doors of promise were wide open. There was only one drawback.

No industry. My grandpa, the primary wage earner in the family, was a master mechanic and a foreman in a railroad shop. The likes of his skills were not in demand in Baldwin County; therefore the move would split the family. Grandpa would have to keep his job in Indiana while his wife, son, and daughter made a home in Bay Minette. This fact certainly put a damper on the move idea.

The whole thing was a wild idea–family members trekking off to a faraway, unknown part of the country. That is the way they thought of Alabama. The very notion of a move that would separate the family and force them to live hundreds of miles apart seemed too much.

Under any circumstances, even if the entire family stuck together, the move would break up the Bartmus and Ertzinger clans. They would find themselves in a totally different environment–from the small Indiana city they loved to a rural town with unpaved streets and no electricity. That was a downright daring thing to do. Such a move into the unknown required self-confidence and courage.

Uncle Ort's health problems did not abate. So in 1908, immediately after graduating from Huntington High School, my uncle chaperoned his sister and mother to Bay Minette. The family females wanted to check out the southern exposure for themselves. They returned from Bay Minette with a glowing enthusiasm about life way down South.

As pessimistic as the family was about their move, they did concede that doing what was best for the health of this promising young man was the paramount concern. Ort, their fair-haired prince, was eager to start his own business–and make his fortune. As it happened, my grandparents led the way for other members of both clans who came south later.

During the early part of the Century of Progress, the Wright brothers made their initial flight. The Atlantic and Pacific Oceans were connected by the Panama Canal. The American railways were binding the country together. In Alabama the pot was boiling with change and progress.

The Louisville and Nashville railroad was opening up Baldwin County to the outside world. The Union Station in Bay Minette was in the center of it all. Settlements up to that time had been along the coastline. Lack of roads and access to the interior curtailed inland development. Then came the silver rails and the great iron horse. Bay Minette was leading the way in progressive changes in this great country.

Certainly there was plenty of room for growth. In 1901, the *Baldwin Times* reported that "the most thickly populated county in Alabama is Jefferson County, which has 133 people per square mile. At the foot of the list comes Baldwin, with only eight people to the square mile."

Delegates to the 1901 Alabama Constitutional Convention gathered at the state capitol in Montgomery. This legislative body endorsed the movement of the county seat from Daphne on Mobile Bay inward to Bay Minette. Located geographically in the center of the county and situated on a 269-foot plateau, the highest location anywhere on the Gulf Coast, Bay Minette was thought to be a more accessible seat of government.

The town was planned around the public square. The location of the future Baldwin County courthouse was to be the junction of Hand Avenue and Second Street.

As might be expected, there was plenty of opposition to this momentous decision. The details of how and why the county seat was moved are debated to this day. Eyewitness accounts of the move of the courthouse records are contradictory. According to historian Kay Nuzum, Mr. James D. Hand led the clandestine removal of court records from Daphne to Bay Minette. James Hand had brothers, all of whom had sons. I do not know exactly how many Hands in all worked to make the settlement into a county seat, but a century later Hand Avenue remains a main street.

In 1901, the year of the Constitutional Convention in Alabama, Uncle Ort was a twelve-year-old Huntington schoolboy. As far as he was concerned, Baldwin County and Bay Minette might as well not have existed. The big news printed in the *Baldwin Times* and vital to Uncle Ort's future business was this:

> On July 4, 1901, Bay Minette held the greatest celebration ever– the laying of the cornerstone for the courthouse.
>
> People came from all around. There was speech making, a grand barbecue, and at night a real old time country dance for the young people. [Don't you wonder what an "old time" dance was like in 1901?] Local citizens formed the welcoming committee and greeted the guests, most of whom arrived by train.
>
> A passenger coach was attached to the regular freight train leaving Mobile in the early morning. [The use of one engine for both passenger and freight service was an efficient method commonly employed.] Quite a number of Mobilians took advantage of this opportunity to visit Baldwin's new capital. They brought along a brass band to furnish music during the entire event.
>
> Visitors also came from Montgomery. Upon arrival of the southbound local passenger train bringing several hundred people from places north, the parade was formed at the Masonic hall. They marched to the court house square, a 300 foot square plot. [Likely there were more visitors than residents in this small community for this occasion.]
>
> Several dignitaries spoke prior to E. B. Smith, the court house architect. Mr. Smith thanked the city fathers for the authority they invested by having him design their court house.

The corner stone was laid with an array of mementos inside–a copy of the *Baldwin Times* and *Mobile Register*, a letter from Governor Jelks, the story of the founding of Bay Minette in 1861, a silver dollar, Hoo Hoo pin #7375 [a political pin] and a key ring. Judge Hall presented the key ring which for thirty years carried the keys to the court house and jail.

At the conclusion of the on-the-square ceremony the parade re-formed and marched about a half-mile to the grove. They rested before proceeding to enjoy the barbecue dinner. Beef, corn and other edibles in plenty was served to a jovial crowd.

That night the Mobile orchestra provided music for the young folks who danced until a very late hour. Their frivolity and gaiety climaxed a memorable day.

The story of the founding of Bay Minette put in the cornerstone will be interesting reading. On the celebration of the hundredth anniversary I hope the cornerstone will be opened and its contents made public.

Many years later when we fished together in Bay Minette Creek Uncle Ort pointed out the place where, according to tradition, early explorers came ashore. The original settlement was on Minet Bay near an estuary of the Blakeley River. A community, so this story goes, was founded in the early 1700s by a French surveyor, Henri Minet. Minet traveled with Sieur de Bienville, the famous explorer.

A look at a detailed map of those swamps confirms how this could happen. During the railroad boom in the latter part of the nineteenth century, the L&N laid tracks across Baldwin to a point north of that settlement. This brought about a change.

Mary Byrne, the postmistress, moved her home from the bay closer to the rails that brought the mail. Other residents followed her, and the town relocated itself in its current location. Uncle Ort doted on telling this story because it was a woman who had, in effect, been the "founding mother" of the town. His stories often highlighted women, whom he considered intellectually equal to men.

Draw your own conclusions about the young man described in the *Huntington Herald* in 1907.

MOTHER AND SON GO SOUTH

> Ever since passing through a serious siege of typhoid fever last summer, the health of Ort Ertzinger, a reporter for the *News-Democrat,* has been on the wane. The family physician has ordered that he go south for the purpose of recuperating. This will be news of an unpleasant nature for his many friends about the city. Few could tell it by his jovial disposition and happy-go-lucky manner. He is quite a philosopher, realizing that others have their troubles and do not care to hear about his.

There is not a harder working news-gatherer in the city than Ort and the rest will do him good. He will be missed by the local force, but in the meantime some interesting southern letters will be expected. When he returns next spring to resume his position he will be well equipped with a southern dialect.

The person who wrote this perceptively sized up my uncle, putting in a nutshell the qualities that stood him in good stead with others. Uncle Ort never talked about his troubles.

Newspapers in Indiana and Alabama were a part of the warp and woof of Uncle Ort's life. As soon as he was old enough, he delivered newspapers in Huntington. In high school he became a reporter. Several excerpts give a reality check on the weekly newspaper in the first decade of the nineteenth century. The *Baldwin Times*, which until 1901 had been published in Daphne, described its new home:

> The first brick business house is being erected in Bay Minette. It will have offices upstairs and stores downstairs. This is the first two-storied building in town and is being erected by the *Baldwin Times*. It adjoins court square and will be completed in about three weeks. Squire Frank Racine has the contract.

Several years after the completion of the building, the paper issued this invitation:

> Our friends are invited to call on the *Baldwin Times* to see in operation a most wonderful piece of machinery, the newly installed Simplex type setting machine. The demand for fresh news in full detail

right up to the hour of publication makes it imperative to keep up with the great developments in the newspaper business.

The *Baldwin Times* and my uncle both entered the world circa 1889, Uncle Ort in Huntington, Indiana, and the *Times* in Daphne, Alabama. The *Times* played an important role in community affairs and the development of the county. So did my uncle. He and the *Times* intertwined, each devoted to Baldwin County and its progress.

2

New Beginnings

In BITTER COLD WEATHER on the eleventh day of 1909, Ort Ertzinger left Huntington, Indiana, to begin a new life. Accompanied by his mother and sister, he boarded a train and headed for Bay Minette. His father stayed behind to earn a living.

With his high school diploma carefully packed, imagine how this ambitious twenty-year-old must have felt as he waved good-bye at the train station. He left ice and snow, a multitude of family and friends, the tried and true of the only home he'd ever known. He was fast becoming a man.

A long, slender three-by-eight-inch hardback booklet was among his keepsakes. The words printed in coal-black letters read, "TALLY BOOK." Designed for tallying columns of numbers, it had a few figures entered on the back pages. But there was a surprise inside, for my resourceful uncle had used the lined pages primarily to tally events–to keep a journal. On the inside cover, penciled in Palmer-style script are the words "Ort Harmon Ertzinger, 119 First Street, Huntington, Indiana." The journal of his adventure, like any journal or diary, gives a rare insight into the person who writes it:

Monday, Jan. 11–Left Huntington 4:30 en route to Bay Minette. On time, Train No. 8. Arrived in Cincinnati at 6:17, engine 166, seventeen minutes late. A break in the baggage car detained us for some time. Twenty-five minutes late at Columbus, Ohio. Train heavy.

Tuesday, Jan. 12–Our car No. 1051 arrived Bay Minette 3:30, five minutes late. Weather cool. John Schumacher was waiting at the train. He was planning a wild cat hunt for Wednesday night. Cutting wisdom tooth, hurts awfully bad.

Wed. Jan. 13–Got up at 6:30. First up in the whole house. Breakfast at 7:30, dinner at 12:30 and supper at 7:00. Fixed rooms for light housekeeping. Put up stove. Visited a number of men I had met while here last March. Took pictures of nine views of the town. All very good negatives. Was invited to a party but could not go. Stirred up several old tennis players and expect to get to play in a few days.

Thursday, got up at 7:05, fooled around for some time and wrote four letters home. Visited the land agent and had a long talk. The three acres of town land Papa and I looked at are still for sale, he held them for us. Split some wood in the afternoon. Printed a lot of pictures in the evening. Results bum! A pile of girls and boys were in to see the process. After I finished they wanted me to play and sing for them. Florence did too. A large audience gathered in front of the house before we finished. Turned in 10:45.

Fri. got up 7:20, walked around some, wrote a lot of letters and sent post cards home. Attended murder trial in the afternoon. Went to a party in evening.

Sat. loafed most of the day, split wood and played crokinole downstairs in the parlor. Went calling a short time in the evening.

Sun. Jan. 17, went to Sunday School and church. Went out driving in the afternoon and took Miss Stanmeyer, also Mama. Enjoyed first ride very much. Mother too big for the buggy seat, she sat uncomfortably. Called on Mrs. Trammel [the hotel owner] in the evening. Cold out.

Mon. gee! this was a BIG day. Went to fair grounds this morning with two other fellows. Cut a cord of pine tar wood. Blisters on my hands as the work progressed. Am proud of them. This afternoon Dr. Dahlberg and I began work on the tennis court; finished at six. Four fellows helped us. We took all the sod off and tomorrow will line it and play a few games. It was hard work, but I liked it.

What a beginning! During the first week he took a lady riding in a rented carriage with his five-foot-tall overweight mother as a chaperone. He was the catalyst in building a tennis court and was in the swing of social events. He blistered his hands doing manual labor and was proud of it. How macho! This young city Yankee, now in the rural South, was open to whatever.

Two of Uncle Ort's characteristics emerge from the journal–his innate capacity to enjoy life and the importance he placed on his night's rest. He made note of the time he retired each night and often when he got up. His healthful lifestyle bore witness to the respect he had for his body. Taking care of himself is each person's own responsibility. Failure to do so was a kind of debauchery in my uncle's eyes.

The journal continues:

> Wednesday, got up at 7:15. Made a trip to the P.O. Split a pile of wood. Put up ten hens' nests for the hotel lady. Fixed a broken grind stone and ground two axes. Built a new wash stand for the ladies of the place [boarding house]. Played catch at noon. Called on Mr. Mix and the new Presbyterian preacher in the afternoon. Played catch in the evening. Had a date with Miss Stanmeyer for Prayer Meeting, afterwards we played and sang. Had a grand time.

As far as I ever knew, the Ertzingers never raised chickens, so he was doing anything to make money!

The day after he made the hens' nests for Mrs. Trammel, something special happened. A package arrived for him from Hammond, Indiana. It was from his father. Imagine how ecstatic he must have been when he opened it and found a photograph of his handsome, broad-shouldered father and a brand-new catcher's mitt and breastpad–man-to-man gifts. Perhaps Uncle Ort had a lonely-in-the-heart instant; his paper wasn't there to play catch with him. I'm sure he found a baseball buddy to play pitch with him and break in his fine new mitt.

The hotel parlor where they lived temporarily was the scene of cozy evenings. Florence played the piano and sang alto. Ort sang tenor. "A crowd gathered to listen." Sometimes Alice joined them and others as they played parlor games–dominoes, caroms, krokinol, etc. He always won, according to his journal.

The young Presbyterian church in Bay Minette was newly organized. Uncle Ort and his mother and sister became active in the white frame church from their first Sunday in town. The family adjusted, made friends, and soon felt at home. They moved from a boarding house to a suitable house on Hand Avenue less than a year after they came to town.

One Sunday in February, two ordinary events occurred: "Mother and I called on Mr. and Mrs. Mix after dinner and remained until 3:15. Afterwards I went to church where a Presbyterian youth group was organized." Both events had extraordinary consequences in Uncle Ort's life.

His own experience as a member of this neophyte youth organization was bedrock for his many years of leadership with young people. The visit with Mr. and Mrs. Mix was something else.

Walter Lindsey, who bought out my uncle's business, shared with me what he deduced about the beginnings of J. A. Ertzinger & Son. Walter's comments and my own investigation brought me to this understanding.

On their exploratory trip to Bay Minette, he and his father had met with Mr. Mix, an attorney who did abstracts. Uncle Ort knew nothing about abstracts, but the work had an appeal and he a future.

The wave of settlers streaming into the area bought land. Land transactions required titles and abstracts, and the possibilities for increased sales due to the settlement of the land intrigued Uncle Ort. If Mr. Mix would teach him the trade, my uncle figured, he could open his own abstract business–there was business enough for both.

After their move to Bay Minette, my uncle followed up. Mr. Mix was cooperative and helped Uncle Ort learn the business. In due time, things got rolling.

- Monday, the day after he and his Mother called at the Mix home, Uncle Ort saw Mr. Mix in his office.
- A couple of weeks later, Grandpa was down from Hammond, Indiana. Uncle Ort took his Papa to talk specifics with Mr. Mix.

- A week later, Uncle Ort wrote, "Called on Mr. Mix and did a little business talking."
- A few days after that, "Mama and I went to Mr. Mix's office. We transacted a little business, then got some papers off to Papa.
- On Saturday, March 10, he went to Mr. Mix's office and filed corporation papers. J. A. Ertzinger & Son was born!

The name was forever being explained. No, it is not an error: there was only one son. No. J. A. Ertzinger was never in any way a partner in the business; the name came about because Uncle Ort established the business before he was of age.

The business's birth was definitely a family affair. Grandmother did the proper thing: in the absence of her husband, she presented herself with her young son when he talked serious business. Grandpa made the business possible by lending his name. The title and abstract business gained strength and prospered with a single parent, Ort Harmon Ertzinger.

The establishment of his own business marked the demise of Uncle Ort's journal. His daily notations for four months ended without explanation–simply no more entries in the tally book.

Uncle Ort located his abstract office midway between two places central to life in the Bay Minette community, the depot and the courthouse. One side of his office faced the main entrance of the courthouse.

Uncle Ort's title and abstract business fed on records in the probate judge's office as a bee feeds on nectar. An abstract is a kind of genealogy of the land–a precisely written history of changes in ownership. Records of land transactions kept under the care of probate are vital.

Easy access to the probate judge's office, where land transactions were recorded, was a real advantage to my uncle. His route there became well known. He moved, usually at a trot, out his back door, through a short outside passage between the variety store and Stacey's Drug Store, across the street, up the stairs, and into the courthouse suite at the right, the probate court and record room. I wish I had a penny for every trip he must have made from his office to the courthouse.

Soon after coming to town, he was cast in a leading role in *Married Life*, a three-act play. For weeks he practiced. Each night he escorted a lady or two through the dark streets of the town to play practice. He described his role in the play as that of a man with a wife, sometimes. After the performance he wrote, "I was declared the star of the bunch."

Uncle Ort looked out for his mother, Alice, and Florence, his sister. They were a closely knit threesome. His hail-fellow-well-met nature eased the tension and built bridges in their new habitat. He wrote: "After practicing a lot of music with the quartet at the Palmeto Club, I went to Mrs. Carrol's. Mama and Florence were there. I acted the fool with them until 11 o'clock, then we came home together."

Uncle Ort had musical talent oozing out his pores. He played wind and string instruments, sang solo and with all kinds of groups, appreciated good music, and, in more ways than I can count, brought pleasure to others with his music. For the life of me, I can't find out anything about his formal training in music other than one semester in public school. Self-education was his hallmark. He earnestly developed and used his talent as though it were a sacred trust from Almighty God.

In no time after coming to Bay Minette he was singing in a men's quartet and arranging their music, while his sister served as the accompanist. They were popular entertainers at the Palmetto Club, the social gathering place near the depot. The young singers filled Florence's music cabinet with sheet music. A few years later the quartet sang at her wedding.

In appearance Uncle Ort fit the stereotype of German people–fair-skinned and blond-haired. He had a large frame and a commanding presence. His eyes, I think, were green, but they were not outstanding. His thin lips and broad smile dominated his long, oval face. As one would expect, this handsome young man had an eye for young ladies. Meeting, mixing, and partying with girls in Bay Minette was as natural for him as needles on a cactus.

The damsel he took for a carriage ride that first Sunday became a favorite. Their growing friendship is evident in the way he addressed her. At first he referred to her as Miss Stanmeyer; as he knew her better he wrote of Mary Belle Stanmeyer, then Miss Mary Belle, and finally simply Mary Belle.

Comments about many young ladies pepper this journal: "Went to church late, but the lady I was looking for was not there. Worked in tax collector's office with a pretty girl, Miss Abbie Hall."

Two pretty young ladies at the ballpark attracted his attention: "One day following practice, another fellow and I were joined by two ladies. The four of us ate a whole box of the ladies chocolates. The girls are pretty but some of their looks is attributed to powder." He definitely had standards.

Bay Minette was not the only place he had girlfriends. One February day he wrote of "longings for 311 North Jefferson Street." This was the address in Huntington of a young lady, Ottilla Stahl, who had been his lady friend before he moved.

A couple of days after this confession, he "sent camelias North." Likely he was hoping these colorful beauties he had picked would impress his lady love. They were indicative of the mild climate and a pleasant contrast to the ice and snow of her Indiana winter.

His longings were short-lived. The evening after mailing the flowers to Miss Stahl, he went to a "select" party at the Carrolls' down by the railroad track. Mable Beasley was his partner.

The day after he arrived in Bay Minette he developed pictures. That's mind-boggling when you think about it. Where did he find the needed equipment and a suitable place to develop film and print snapshots? I guess he ingeniously improvised the necessary containers; perhaps he brought the developing chemicals and paper from the North. Without electricity there was plenty of dark after the sun went down, so finding a "darkroom" in the boarding house would have been easy. Being able to develop his own film put him in a special category.

On another occasion he wrote that "a pile of boys and girls around the hotel watched me develope and print pictures." I have a suspicion this was the first time they had seen anyone perform this magic." Doing something spectacular was Uncle Ort's trademark.

One Monday night at a party at Orpha Hall's, he snapped a bunch of pictures, then immediately dashed home and developed the negatives. "Up until the wee small hours," he reports. The next evening after work, he printed 72 postcards. Wednesday he got up at nine (that is the latest hour he ever recorded getting up), distributed (gave away) the snapshots, then "loafed the rest of the morning." (He didn't spend much time loafing, either.) His hobby of photography was a handy adjunct for a man who was into everything.

Played crocket, went fishing down by the railroad track and took pictures. [His hand-held camera was a distinguishing feature in contrast to earlier ones that had had to be mounted on a tripod.] After boat riding on the pond with Miss Carroll Sunday afternoon, came home in a wagon, stopped to get some misteltoe and flowers–took pictures.

Michael Shipler, who is collecting a pictorial history of Bay Minette, says that 80 percent of the pictures in his collection were taken by Ort Ertzinger. People did not engage in photography as a hobby then as now. At the time he took the pictures, the keen young man little realized the import they would have. With a fresh eye for what was going on around him, he took pictures of the depot, water tower, courthouse, businesses on the square, streets, fishing and hunting bounty, and many other scenes, ordinary in their time.

The business, born in the spring of 1909, provided a livelihood in the same family for eighty years before it was sold. Uncle Ort had other irons in the fire in 1909 besides the title and abstract business. A Huntington newspaper kept tabs and wrote about him in 1910:

> Who do you suppose is in the city? Not Ort Ertzinger. Yes. He came this morning looking as fit as a fiddle and as brown as a berry, with a muscle as though he was about to enter the prize ring. No change much in the old scout, except that he had grown better looking.
>
> Ort, you know, is something of a professional ball player, having played with semi-professional ball teams in the south. He bears marks to show that he has been in some "foul" games. His fingers

are stove up. [His double joints and rearranged knuckles were like a trademark. He showed them to me with pride and explained in detail how each injury came about.]

The drey business he owns is going well as is the abstract and land office. He is the possible director in a new bank to be organized. He is special correspondent for the *Montgomery Advertizer, Mobile Register,* and *Birmingham Age Herald.*

Young Ort was a "newsmaker" in more than one way. He wrote the news stories as a reporter, but, besides that, in some of the things he did he made news. Before radio and television were popular, newspapers were *the* news medium.

Reporting news for three or four publishers kept Uncle Ort's ears tuned to what was going on and his fingers busy at the typewriter. The most curious story he ever reported began in the summer of 1911.

> The marshall, James W Smith, was shot Tuesday. He saw two negroes whom he regarded as suspicious and dangerous so he arrested them. Barely had the two men been put under arrest when one whipped out a gun and shot the marshall three times. The marshall died instantly.
>
> Keyser Brown was run down and arrested a few hours after the shooting. His companion made his escape. The escapee is described as 5'8" tall, black, and of small frame. An intensive search is underway in Baldwin County and throughout the state.

This must have been the strangest case Uncle Ort ever reported. He dispatched his report from the depot telegraph office to Mobile, Birmingham, and Montgomery. The search for the second man at the murder scene continued, but no clues were found as to what had happened to him. At the trial, Mr. Hawkins, the attorney appointed by the court, made the best defense possible, according to the Mobile and Bay Minette newspapers. Both white and black people testified against Keyser Brown.

On December 7, 1911, Keyser Brown was sentenced to be hanged.

On January 5, 1912, the sentence was executed at the Bay Minette jail near where he lived.

Twenty-five years intervened before the full truth was known about this shooting.

3

Man about Town

HELLZAPOPPIN, the title of a once-popular Broadway musical, described what was happening in Uncle Ort's life and new hometown between 1909 and 1913.

The church in Bay Minette was a child, a four-year-old, when the Ertzingers added their names to the roll. The book of church history shows that Alice, John, Florence, and Ort Ertzinger were "admitted" to the Burkett Memorial Presbyterian Church on October 20, 1912. Although the Bay Minette Ertzingers were active in the white frame church from their first Sunday in town, Grandpa continued to live and work in Indiana, and therefore their membership was not immediately transferred. The Ertzinger four made an imprint in the membership roll of fewer than fifty.

All churches in this growing town were small, sometimes fewer than forty souls, but Christian commitment was great. The Presbyterian pastor preached once a month for a salary of $2.50. When there was no preaching at the Presbyterian church, Uncle Ort attended the Methodist service.

The Methodist, Episcopal, Baptist, and Presbyterian churches in Bay Minette were located within three blocks of one another. One year the

Sunday School leaders united in doing what they called a "town canvass." I suspect Uncle Ort was the initiator of the canvass of residents, for among his keepsakes is the questionnaire he used in the survey. The questions as to whether or not the person attended a church, how long he or she had lived in the town, and so on, are timely now, as is the need to canvass the town. He was a change agent in the swing of things.

A red, white, and blue keepsake from this era of his life is telling. On the cover of this patriotic-looking program is printed in red, "HEED THE CALL for training for YOUR PLACE in the Sunday School Army." The leaflet gives the motto for the two-day event in Garland, Alabama: "Childhood the hope of the world." A picture of a young bugler represented a Christian military man, dressed in a Navy uniform, reflective of World War I. Uncle Ort gave a ten-minute talk at this statewide Sunday School convention in July 1918. His topic was "What We Are Doing and What We Need."

About the time he was setting up his office, front-page news in the Times announced:

> Workmen are engaged in constructing the Bell Telephone System in Bay Minette. The Bell System has never been known to do things by halves. It will operate the telephone exchange in rooms on the second story of the Baldwin Times building on Court House Square.
>
> 'Hello, Central, give me No. 315.' That's what you're going to hear, right here in Bay Minette in a few days.

Undoubtedly Uncle Ort was one of the first Southern Bell customers in town.

Newspaper advertising and Uncle Ort's business were incessantly linked. The weekly Baldwin Times teemed with all sorts of news about the progress of the town, county, and state. From the very beginning, when his business was brand-new and his office was described as being on Court House Square, the Times was peppered with ads about Uncle Ort's business.

> April 6, The Bay Minette Literacy Society held another meeting Tuesday evening in the home of Mrs. Lambert. Much interest is being manifest in the studies they have taken up. Mr. Ort Ertzinger

made a business trip to Loxley Tuesday....Ladies apparel at the Elite Millinery Shop hats, ribbons and laces...J. A. ERTZINGER & SON LIFE AND FIRE INSURANCE, REAL ESTATE

June 15, The members of the Bay Minette Tennis Club are playing some fast games since their grounds are in playing condition. Ort Ertzinger is on a winning streak....A moonlight supper was very much enjoyed by a jolly crowd of young people on Godbolt's Creek. Ira Thompson and Ort Ertzinger were hosts.

August 15, J. A. Ertzinger of Hammond, Indiana visited his family here last week. He states the flow of migration from northern Indiana will be heavy this winter with many new settlers for Baldwin County...ORT H. ERZINGER NOTARY PUBLIC Near Depot, Board and Lodging_ Meals 30¢...Ham and Eggs with coffee, 25¢...Coffee & cake 10 cents...For those who use night trains, the restaurant will be open midnight 'til 3 a.m.

RAILWAY SCHEDULE CHANGES: The evening train from the Fort Morgan Branch gets here at 5:30 instead of 6 p.m. No. 4 connects with Selma and Pensacola trains in Flomaton....J. A. ERTZINGER AND SON REAL ESTATE, LIFE AND FIRE INSURANCE

It seems strange now, but back in those days the growth and vitality of a town was measured by the volume of mail that went through the post office.

March 12, 1911, A good indication of the growth is furnished by the increased business at the post office. The total number of pieces handled during May were 86,797. There were 67,748 first class letters besides a large number of newspapers, magazines and circulars. There were 1,517 pieces of registered mail and 74 foreign letters.

The exact influence of newspaper advertising on Uncle Ort would be impossible to calculate, but advertising, then as now, influenced attitudes and perceptions about almost everything. It pays its own way, for without ads most newspapers would be insolvent. Beyond question, this is the way money talks and shapes public opinion.

In a sophisticated manner large companies like L&N and Southern Bell advertised regularly. Full- or half-page advertisements were bound to attract one's attention. The significant role of the Louisville and Nashville Railroad is obvious. Examples from a snippet or two explain themselves. The provocative title "What Thinking Men Think" was the topic of an entire full-page ad. It quotes a member of Teddy Roosevelt's cabinet as saying:

> Our railroads are without parallel in the world, because we are a united nation. That accounts in part for the wonderful efficiency of the American system. In Europe they live as a divided community.

The advertisements for Southern Bell had a more practical gist.

> The telephone aids the busy farmer. It enables him to keep in touch with neighborhood affairs. He can call his neighbors in the evening and discuss events of the day. Send a postal card and ask for a free booklet about telephone installation on your farm.

Most local people who advertised were more direct and simple. The "Personal and General" in the *Times* was *must* reading–gossip, news, and advertising blended together.

> A. Kahalley's now handle Butterick patterns. They have just received a new supply of the latest and most up-to-date....See a new shipment of silk and organdie waists and crepe-de-chine handkerchiefs at the Elite Millinery Store, Elizabeth Simason....J. A. ERTZINGER & SON, REAL ESTATE, LIFE AND FIRE INSURANCE....The Ladies Aide Society held another meeting Tuesday, much interest is being manifest....The Bay Minette Tennis Club have their court in playing condition. The members are playing some fast games. Ort Ertzinger is on a winning streak.

I glared at one item written in 1911:

> Mr. Ort Ertzinger presented us with a copy of his latest song, "I dont want to be a tightwad." It is a well written song and shows that Mr. Ertzinger possesses great talent as a composer.

This complimentary note surely gave my twenty-two-year-old uncle a plug. Surprise, then amazement hit me when I saw that he'd composed music *and* lyrics. I never knew he wrote lyrics. A thought struck me.

An envelope containing shreds of paper torn into pieces the size of my thumbnail was among Uncle Ort's keepsakes. Only bars and notes of music were distinguishable. My husband patiently pieced the thumb-sized scraps together and constructed a large, ten-by-fourteen-inch sheet of music.

Guess what? The title, "I Don't Want to Be a Tight Wad," appears on the cover in large blue letters, followed by the name of the composer, Ort H. Ertzinger. The name and address of the publisher were in smaller print: Kirkus Dugdale Co., Washington, D.C. On the back were instructions to "Send 15 cents for a complete copy of this popular number." The words are as follows:

I

They say I'm a big tight wad,
They call me 'tight wad-do,'
But still I'm always with the gang
No matter where they go.
I guess they'd like my bank account.
It's really quite a sum.
And when they ask about my pile,
I'll manage to keep mum.

II

Now it's a cinch that I'm not tight,
Tho' every one thinks so,
Because I've always some dough left,
No matter where I go.
They often try to break my pile.
Of schemes they're never done.
But I'm the chap whose motto is,
Look out for number one.

Chorus

I don't want to be a tight wad.
'Tis true I've got a pile,
But let me say in my behalf,
I earned my chunk of gold.
And if I keep it when I'm young,
I'll have it when I'm old.

Copyright 1911 by Ort H. Ertzinger, Bay Minette, Alabama

The reconstructed sheet of music reveals a phase in his life that I'd never known about. One out of character.

A flood of questions came to mind. Who tore up the music? Why? And a more probing question: If it was torn up, why was it kept? No one I can find knows anything about it! Thinking back to my uncle's bachelor days, I pondered what would cause my footloose, fancy-free uncle to write such a song. Some composers write from fiction, others from fact.

Hank Williams came to mind. When we were children, he and I both lived in Georgiana, Alabama. Hank's father was gassed in World War I and was not able to work enough to provide a decent living for his family. My father, the local Commander of the American Legion after World War I, worked with Hank's mother to see that the Williams family got every penny from the government that was due them. Hank and his sister, Irene, often came with their mother to our house.

Many who knew Hank then think that the lyrics "take a cold tatter and wait" came out of Hank's real experience–times when his mother told him to do just that. She worked at a boarding house, and the paying guests came first.

Was Uncle Ort influenced, like the famous Hank, writing from his personal experience? What was going on in his life to cause my ambitious bachelor uncle to write, "It's a cinch I'm not a tight wad, tho' everyone thinks so"? Sounds as though his pride were hurt.

Bonnie (Voncile Lackey), a protégée of Uncle Ort's and now a grandmother, remembers Uncle Ort well. I looked over her shoulder as she played his composition. The tune is lively and "Uncle-Ortish," but the lyrics?

I could tell by the expression on Bonnie's face that she, too, was perplexed. "He never was a tightwad," she said. "I can't imagine him writing a song like that. The part about saving–'If I keep it when I'm young, I'll have it when I'm old'–rings true." She spoke quite emphatically. "He was a cinch on that. He lectured us young folks, when we got a job, to give a tithe to God and save some for our own future."

Bonnie folded the music and got up from the piano bench. "A bunch of us were talking about him the other night. He surely meant a lot to us when we were growing up."

I walked away with the tune ringing in my ears. The pathos of the lyrics sent me searching for an explanation. If not writing from personal experience, why would he have written so defensively? There's hurt in the lyric words.

He wrote this song at a time when he was involved in many community activities–playing tennis and baseball, singing in a quartet, playing in an orchestra and the band. On the other hand, he'd been in business for two long years but was still living with his mother and sister. I'm sure he wanted to be married, to have a family and his own home. That took money. He was in a bind–a true case of laughing on the outside and crying on the inside!

His bank account was slow in building, though he was working like a beaver and thriftily managing his money. Being a jolly good fellow was in conflict with his other ambitions. Starting a business from scratch was tough.

4

Marriage

In 1913 GOOD THINGS WERE BUSTIN' OUT ALL OVER the new hemisphere in ways that affected my young uncle's life. Several colossal events explain what I mean.

The building of the Panama Canal was the *news* of the century. This great achievement dramatically affected the entire world of transportation. The city of Mobile was the most important seaport near the amazing new canal and therefore was chosen to host the Pan American Congress in October 1913. Celebrating this truly unexcelled engineering achievement was the function of this congress. To top it off, one of the biggest things that had ever taken place in Mobile occurred. Woodrow Wilson, the twenty-eighth president of the United States, attended. This historic event was called the greatest gathering ever held in the South.

Construction of the canal had started back in 1904 against seemingly impossible odds. Connecting the Atlantic and Pacific oceans created gigantic problems. "Sea level" for the Atlantic and Pacific was different, posing an engineering challenge. In addition, canal workers were plagued by yellow fever, which took many lives. The leaders who masterminded the solution to these problems were William Gorgas, an army surgeon, and George Goethals, an army engineer. Dr. Gorgas is credited with ridding the canal of mosquitoes, those worrisome little insects that carried the yellow fever virus. Only after conquering this little devil were the men able to build the canal. Then Goethals' genius engineered and built the canal that joined the oceans.

President Woodrow Wilson had a special place in the hearts, minds, and souls of Southerners, Presbyterians in particular. The son of a Presbyterian minister, he was born in Virginia and married a lady from Rome, Georgia. During his first year in office, news that the president was to travel to Alabama thrilled Southerners.

Boundless enthusiasm in Mobile and its environs marked the summer of 1913 as citizens prepared for the coming of the president of the United States. A welcoming parade was planned in which every town's band was invited to participate.

Bay Minette was proud to be included, but there were problems. There were more men who could play instruments than there were instruments to play. No one had uniforms. To become a real band, they needed financial backing.

Bay Minette's Agriculture and Civic League, the pulse of the town, responded to the invitation by appointing a band committee with Uncle Ort's bachelor buddy Ira Thompson as head. Uncle Ort already wore two hats in the League–secretary as well as publicity chairman. As secretary, he knew the inside workings and plans of the League; as publicity chairman, he passed on the proper information to the newspapers. On September 14, 1913, the Times reported:

> Ira Thompson has drawn up a constitution and by laws for the band. As soon as Ort Ertzinger is back from the North he will incorporate the band. [Uncle Ort was in Huntington for a special reason.] Merchants are being solicited to contribute money for the uniforms and instruments needed.
>
> Bay Minette hopes to send a band to Mobile in October for President Wilson's visit to the Pan American Exposition. The band will be there. We want to let everyone know Bay Minette is on the map.

Just then Uncle Ort's life was on the fast track. He resisted his temptation to squander his money, so his bank account was growing, and his business, too. As we know, he'd played the field in Bay Minette. For almost three years he'd dated numerous young ladies. But none of the Southern belles won his heart. On the other hand, his courtship by correspondence was encouraging. So one day he rode the train to Huntington, went directly to 312 North Jefferson Avenue, and proposed to Ottilla Stahl. She accepted, so they made immediate plans for a wedding.

Most of what his lady love knew about the South was what he'd told her. Her promise to marry him and move away from her parents and friends must have inspired him. Their bonds of love were strong. After he returned home, they wrote each other every day of their engagement.

Uncle Ort returned to Bay Minette and started building their house. I do not know where or how he gained skill as a carpenter. I do know that their house was well planned and soundly constructed.

J. B. Blackburn, his attorney in later years, told me that when he was a little boy he used to go watch my uncle building the house. "I especially remember climbing up on the roof when he was putting down the shingles. I thought it great fun to watch him."

The large two-story house Uncle Ort built was later pictured in a promotional booklet. His house measured up to the best in Baldwin County. Many special features were built to his future wife's specifications: a built-in china cabinet with a mirror back, a cedar-lined closet, and a leaded-glass door, to name a few.

The unusually large, sixteen-by-thirty-two-foot living room was Uncle Ort's idea. He wanted a passel of children and liked to entertain–two good reasons for having a large living room.

The lady with whom he had fallen in love was very refined and intelligent. Her calm, cool collectedness was always a model for the way I'd like to be. She was stately and thin, and her brunette hair complemented Ort's blond tresses; they were a handsome pair.

True to his character, he had chosen a lady whose courage and aptitude for adventure matched his. Their courtship was a very special time in their lives, as attested by the trinkets of their romance and marriage that they carefully kept. I recall seeing pictures and hearing their stories of those happy days.

My popular aunt and uncle were widely entertained. One of the many prenuptial parties was described by a *Huntington Democrat* writer as follows:

> Miss Ottilla Stahl was the honoree at a delightful gathering announcing her engagement to Ort Ertzinger of Bay Minette, Alabama. Guests who were members of the Eu Ki Sans crowd gathered soon after eight o'clock and were entertained with games and contests for about two hours.
>
> At ten o'clock they were ushered into the dining room where a delicious two-course lunch awaited them. The table was very tastefully decorated with a wreath as the center piece; green smilax extended to each guest's place. Numerous pink candies helped to brighten the scene. Underneath the dainty pink rosebud place cards were hidden hearts. When the guests lifted the cards, they found one heart which read "Ort" another "Ottilla," and a third "September 10."

Congratulation of the happy couple was accompanied by regret because the bride-to-be was "leaving for a home in such a s distant place." The writer goes on:

> Miss. Stahl is the daughter of Mr. and Mrs. E. M. Stahl. Since graduation from the local high school Miss. Stahl has been a teacher in Huntington township. She also took several years Normal School training at Winona College. Her kind way made her devoted to all her scholars.
>
> Mr. Ertzinger was formerly a Huntington boy, a graduate of the local high school and is popularly known as a young man of jovial disposition and great ability to make good at whatever he attempts. He is now engaged in a thriving real estate business in Bay Minette. The couple will be united in marriage at Miss Stahl's home.

It was while Uncle Ort was in Huntington being married that the *Baldwin Times* announced that he would incorporate the band upon his return. Imagine! As soon as he brought his bride to their new home, the pressing matter of organizing a band to play for President Wilson awaited his attention!

The first time Ottilla Stahl laid eyes on the town of Bay Minette was on her honeymoon. She must have been very proud of her new husband, who was so active in the affairs of the community where she had come to make her home. Obviously her husband did more than whisper sweet nothings in her ear as they got settled.

Ottilla Stahl Ertzinger was no helpless clinging vine. Soon after arriving in her new hometown, she was busy–unpacking wedding presents, putting up curtains, being entertained, and getting acquainted with people in this thriving new community.

Newspaper advertising, which mirrors its times as surely as the fashion shows on Fifth Avenue, gives some idea of how different a world my aunt and uncle lived in. In the early years of their marriage, some of the ads were for horse breeding, Rhode Island Red hens, and pure cane syrup at ten dollars for a 27-gallon barrel. Times have certainly changed!

One of the greatest lifestyle changes was brought about by the introduction of the automobile. Privately owned cars changed the very fabric of society, and the impact of their novelty is shown by an item in the weekly Personal & General column, which reported that "five autos of the Ford make were unloaded at the L&N station this week. One was for sheriff Richardson, another belonged to Dr. J. C. McLeod, one for Ort Ertzinger, and the other two went to Stockton." Although the arrival of new cars from the factor would hardly warrant such publicity today, it was typical of my uncle to be among the first to have anything new.

Meanwhile, Uncle Ort had innumerable things to do to whip the band into shape. From what I gather, young lads with musical know-how had been making music together, just for fun, but had not organized themselves into a band. It took the invitation to play for President Wilson to bring the official band into being. Getting sheet music and learning to march as well as play marching songs took some doing. Photographs show smiling band members in uniform.

In mid-October, while Uncle Ort and the band members were feverishly getting in shape, they were inspired by news of what was going on in Washington, D.C. From the nation's capital city the president set off a signal that connected the Atlantic and Pacific oceans.

"Is the cable ready?"

"Yes," came the answer.

The operator at the White House made four distinct dots, twenty seconds before 2 o'clock. On the dot President Wilson closed the keys which sent the current into the dynamic apparatus. President Wilson sent the magic electric current more than 4,000 miles over land and under sea to blow-up the Camboa dike, the last practical obstacle in the great inter-oceanic waterway.

The Pan American Congress had much to celebrate!

What excitement the Bay Minette band members must have felt traveling together on the train with their spanking new uniforms, drums, and shiny horns. They carried with them one other important item, a newly made banner, which proved to be the right stuff.

Bay Minette merchants were pleased to read in the Mobile papers about their band attracting much attention as they carried the banner down Mobile's paved streets at the Pan Am shindig. "'Look Out for Bay Minette,' read the banner with the lively music and the Bay Minette band," reported the *Mobile Press Register*. The *Mobile Post* put it this way: "Frank Stone carried the banner that read, 'Look out for Bay Minette.' The music and the band made a splendid showing and added a lively tune to this great event in Mobile."

I have a hunch that one reason for Uncle Ort's wholehearted support for the band was the inner satisfaction it brought him. Lively band music made people feel good. No music he ever had anything to do with was played very slowly. That went against the grain with him.

After that big bash for the president of the United States, the Bay Minette band played for all kinds of events. Ball games, Fourth of July celebrations, and other civic happenings were made more enjoyable by their spirited music. One band trip was to Georgiana, three stops north on the fast train. They were invited to play for the opening of a new addition to the town.

The publicity the band brought the city was another reason Uncle Ort must have appreciated being a part of the band. He wanted the town to grow and prosper.

The Agricultural and Civic League was editorialized as "the important organization in the development of Bay Minette." The town was sadly in need of lights for the streets at night, especially in the business section of town. The January 1914 meeting of the League, held in the courthouse, was attended by an enthusiastic crowd awaiting a report of the committee formed to handle this matter. I have a hunch Uncle Ort and Aunt Tillie were there.

The democratic process took time. At a League meeting the task force reported discussions with people on the county commission, etc. After several reports, Mr. L. T. Rhodes finally summarized remarks to a loud round of applause: "The town and county will get together next week to formulate a plan for installing a lighting system."

The League was responsible for all sorts of good things as the little village grew. One event they sponsored was the Chautauqua. There was a problem one time when Lolla Trax, a famous woman's suffrage organizer from Baltimore, was scheduled to speak. A school entertainment was planned at the courthouse at the very same time. So Lolla and her followers held an open-air gathering in the bandstand outside the courthouse. The Times reported that Lolla Trax "seemed to be a logical thinker who based her claims for women's suffrage on democratic and economic grounds."

I'll wager Uncle Ort found a way to attend both meetings. He attended all school entertainments as a token of his support. As an advocator of women's right, he supported women's right to vote, too.

In 1916, the Literacy Council in Bay Minette–another organization sponsored by the League–stated its goal:

> Let's remove illiteracy in Bay Minette. We can do it! Every citizen should give his support to this laudable undertaking.

Aunt Tillie and Uncle Ort gave their full support although the Literacy Council was a women's group, and so Uncle Ort could not technically be a member.

One of the largest annual events sponsored by the Agriculture and Civic League was the Baldwin County Fair. A month after he married, in addition to helping organize the band and playing for President Wilson, Uncle Ort chaired the publicity committee for the fair. The full-page advertisement published by the *Baldwin Times* announced the fair on November 5, 6, 7, and 8, 1913.

> The Foley train will be held over each day. The fair will feature horse racing, band concerts, speaking, a public womanless wedding, and other attractions of all kinds. And *something different* from anything ever attempted before. [I've never found out what that was.]

As publicity chairman Uncle Ort was gearing up for the following year when he was to head the whole Fair committee.

Uncle Ort and his young bride joined forces intent on making Bay Minette an ideal place to live and raise their family. They were married not only to each other but also to the town of Bay Minette. Aunt Tillie and Uncle Ort forged a bond with the town that lasted as long as they lived.

5

An Organizer in Euphoria

THE CLEAR BLACK-INK DRAWING on the warm brown cover attracted my attention. The artistic figure was not a flower but an unusual cluster of five beautifully shaped pecans. I opened this booklet the color of a pecan shell. The Sibley Land Company had published this material, which took me back to the early part of the century in Bay Minette. Inside, the stated purpose: "To inform the home-seeker about the extraordinary opportunities in and around Bay Minette."

Uncle Ort was head over heels promoting progressive growth of the county seat. The booklet is undated but was likely printed when he was newly married and his home freshly built, in 1913—14. The features highlighted mimic Uncle Ort's notion of what was ideal about his hometown–good-tasting soft water, soil without stones, growing temperatures all year.

The old-fashioned vernacular of this brown nugget of propaganda is resplendent with hope and promise. This mover and shaker in the community surely had a hand in this prospectus intended to sell land–fodder for the abstract business. The booklet makes this pledge to the reader:

> We, the following businessmen and citizens of Bay Minette, extend a sincere greeting to the home-seeker and investor. We invite you to Bay Minette, a town with a most delightful climate, unexcelled advantages for farming, dairying, stock and poultry raising. We believe there is no section in the United States that equals the opportunities here. Come and see!

The booklet's centerfold listed over fifty sponsors. Among them were the Power and Ice Company, Hill Brothers Haberdashery, Elite Millinery, and Irvin and Perry Livery and Feed Stable. Individual professional sponsors were J. C. McLeod, M.D.; S. A. Y. Dahlberg, Dentist; J. H. H. Smith, Probate Judge; and J. A. Ertzinger and Son, Title and Abstract. The booklet described the land of milk and honey as follows:

> Bay Minette is the largest city in the county and is located on the mainline of the Louisville and Nashville Railroad, twenty-four miles north of Mobile, Alabama. The town is the highest place on the gulf coast, with an elevation of 268 feet. Water wells have an average of only 70 feet and the water is remarkably pure. A water analysis is available to those who request it.
>
> The evenness of the climate accounts for the healthfulness of the residents. Located on the southern extremity of the state, Baldwin County benefits from its geography. It is bounded on three sides by navigable waters. In the summer these waters absorb the rays of the sum and prevent high temperatures. In the winter the warming influence of the gulf stream is felt along the shores. Cold weather is almost unknown.
>
> The climate is never too cold or too hot but moderate to permit outdoor work all year around. There is no reason why a farmer should permit his soil to lie idle at any season. Droughts are unknown, so irrigation is unnecessary. Our soil is easily worked and quickly cultivated with the least amount of labor. Top soil has an average depth of six to ten inches. The settler coming here comes to a prosperous and progressive county.

Practically all the new residents were farmers. There was a dispute over the exact increase in the population of the county. Most agreed the figure quoted by the census takers, 24,000, including farmers and those engaged in filling the needs of the farmer, was too low.

Of course, there were also those filling the needs of farmers; that is where Uncle Ort fit in. In today's parlance, he was a "significant other" in the growth and settlement of Baldwin County. The following excerpt gives a glimpse of the quality of the people and the nature of the community.

> No man need feel that in coming to Baldwin County he is a solitary pilgrim to a strange country. Many thousands have come ahead of him and many thousands will follow. There are no factions or clans, seeking to build up self at the expense of the town folks. The spirit of co-operation prevails to the advantage of the new settlers who find sociable neighbors ready and willing to assist them in every manner possible. Newcomers are assisted in making their new home comfortable, prosperous and happy. Neighbors are happy in the cosmopolitan and companionable neighborhood.
>
> In Bay Minette the ladies have a Town Improvement Club aimed at improving the appearance of the community in every possible way. The School Improvement Association is another valuable social asset and the methods of education are in keeping with the progress and intelligence of the entire nation.

The booklet assured the reader, "We are more than an advertising scheme put out by shyster developers." Comments from a list of successful dairymen, progressive farmers, and fruit growers were straightforward and honest.

> Jacob Yoder is a substantial German settler, who came from Kansas two years ago, and purchased a farm two miles from Bay Minette. He is farming in a general way, raising corn, hay, potatoes and satsuma oranges. [This different kind of orange was never called merely a satsuma.] He raises hogs and cattle for market. He is perfectly satisfied with his new home and surroundings.
>
> C. A. (Mac) Aylin owns a farm two miles east of Bay Minette. In addition to raising general crops he raises watermellons, onions, and poultry for the home market. From 15 year old pecan trees he gathered 100 pounds of nuts per tree, sold them wholesale for 15 cents a pound, and collected $15.00 per tree.
>
> Aylin came from Illinois, with stomach trouble. He claims the water and climate have completely cured him. His farm of 160 acres cost him $5.00 an acre. Recently he had an offer of $5,000.00 for 80 acres. He refused to sell.

L. T. Rhodes is one of the progressive and scientific farmers. He pushes diversity in farming. His sugar cane crop from three acres made 1,500 gallons of syrup. [A syrup-making plant was located in Bay Minette at that time.] His sweet potatoe yield from 250 acres made a profit of $2,500.00. After the potatoes are gathered this land is sown in cow peas which produce a ton and a half per acre.

J. M. Stover, of the Stover Nursery and Orchard Company, came to Bay Minette about twelve years ago from Pennsylvania. He avers that from his first visit to the present time, he has been thoroughly pleased with this section. He is engaged in the promotion and development of fruit by adapting them to our soils and climates. Due to his efforts, today there are many farmers growing pecans, satsuma oranges, Japanese persimmons and figs. His company specializes in the care-taking of orchards for non-residents.

J. M. puts it plain: "All this community needs is more good earnest home seekers. This section is a veritable garden of plenty waiting for people who are not afraid of working in their own behalf. *The fellow without any money and no energy will do well to stay where he is."*

The farmer was the top dog. The unity of purpose of the community was indeed heartwarming, and the land companies worked hand in glove with the farmer. The heterogeneity of the population made it strong. The crowning nugget in the booklet:

If this material deviates from the true picture, then it is on the side of conservatism. It is preferred to leave something good for the newcomer to discover for himself, rather than to hold out to him promises that cannot be made good.

New people moved in from various European countries. Some came by way of Midwestern or Northern states before finally settling in Baldwin County. Uncle Ort used to brag about Baldwin County, where Swedes, Germans, Italians, and other nationalities were developing the land. Fondly and with respect, he told me of the Lutheran Church in Elberta where the services were held in German.

New settlers kept up with relatives and friends back in the old country. They knew what was going on back where they were born, as shown by this quotation from a *Baldwin Times* article:

Statistics show that Germany and France are getting crops nearly three times as large as those grown in America from every acre of land. The Europeans have surplus money to invest in securities, but they do so at a far less percent of interest than we get in Baldwin County.

The most striking illustration the world has ever seen is furnished by Denmark. What they have accomplished in farming, by using improved methods of stock raising and dairying is outstanding. This little country with a population of three million, where for many months in every year the temperature is much colder than it ever is here, has climbed from a state of almost destitution, after World War I, to one with the highest average prosperity ever existing in a country. All from farming!

We can do even better. The citizens of Bay Minette challenge the world to show a section that will enable the home-seeker possessing some means, industry and ambition to earn more on his money investment, muscle and mind than he can in this wonderful country.

Uncle Ort listened to what these men said. He believed with all his heart in the potential of the land and the people who cultivated it.

He boasted about the rich mix of people and cultures, the mild climate and the crop experimentation in Baldwin County. He worked along with many others who were making a living and laying away money for their nest-egg.

Baldwin, the extraordinary county, inhabited by Scandinavians, Italians, Germans, Greeks, Poles, Czechoslovakians, Quakers, and Mennonites, was moving ahead. This 1,585-square-mile county, larger than the state of Rhode Island, was referred to not only as an "empire" but also as a "commonwealth." A *commonwealth*, by definition, is a group united in purpose, an apt term indeed.

The role and predominance of the two major land companies in the area bears mention. In a way, each complemented the other, but their approaches to development were different. The Bay Minette Land Company cleared and fenced many tracts of land as well as built homes for purchasers. The advancement of agricultural development came about by encouraging the development of acreage the size for the farmer to grow and market produce in train carload lots.

Planting potatoes, cucumbers, and strawberries in carload lots was practical since all that was grown went to market by rail. The Bay Minette Land Company worked in cahoots with the L&N railroad.

In contrast, the Sibley Land Company sold undeveloped land. This unimproved, "cut-over" land (on which the trees had merely been cut) was sold for as little as five dollars an acre. Sibley claimed their undeveloped soil equaled in productivity any land in the county. Many farmers bought undeveloped land on which they planted pecans, satsuma oranges, or other fruits without removing the stumps.

Later, when Newport Industries was established, the first industry in Bay Minette, they bought and dug up the rich stumps and extracted rosin and oil from the pine wood at a profit. Cash paid for the stumps motivated the farmer to clear his land, an arrangement profitable to both buyer and seller.

The prestigious Agriculture and Civic League sponsored the biggest event of the year, the county fair. With farming as the principal occupation, this was naturally a big event. Mr. F. C. Hall, president of the League in 1914, had a fine stock of pigs to exhibit. The success of the fair was important to him.

Young Ort Ertzinger, then twenty-five years old, was a jovial young man who had great tact in handling people. He was energetic, resourceful, and a good organizer. Though Ort was not a farmer, Mr. Hall chose him to head the committee for the October fair.

Horse racing, baseball, and other amusements were a part of the fall extravaganza. But the farmers and their wares were the nucleus of the fair. The term farming (now we would call it "agribusiness") at that time included raising poultry, stock, and swine and growing pecan and fruit trees as well as vegetables and grain.

The central focus and most talked-about feature was the exhibits. Farmers and their wives entered the best of what they had produced. Canned goods, quilts, and all kinds of ladies' handwork were displayed in colorful ways. Nationally known Mr. R. C. Carey came to town especially tow work with the exhibitors.

Uncle Ort undoubtedly injected some new ideas into the 1914 fair. In addition to Mr. Carey, he procured the services of Mr. William James, an L&N agricultural expert. Both were known far and wide for their expertise in managing successful country fairs.

The fair brought into play several forces important to the economy. The L&N Railroad's bread was buttered by promoting farming. Farmers were the backbone of their shipping customers. On the other hand, the farmer respected and praised the railroad company, which provided essential transportation. Cooperation among people with common interests pays off. The fair offered an opportunity for them to learn to know each other.

An air of excitement prevailed as people from various ethnic groups and farming customs gathered at the Bay Minette fairgrounds. Fairgoers traveled from every corner of the large county over terrible or nonexistent roads. Trails were often the only connectors between the farm and the sandy clay roads to town.

As never before, people came to display the success of their own efforts, to show off their fowl, fruit, swine, vegetables, dairy stock, beef cattle, and so on. Equally important, they came to socialize and to share ideas. Mr. Carey was quoted as saying, "Exhibitors in Baldwin show greater progress than in other places in the country. Baldwin exhibits are amazing in substance and in variety." The spirit of comradeship was strong within the Commonwealth, and the fair was proof of it.

Official Carey's special attention was on the pig exhibit. He pointed out that all these porkers were raised and fattened for less than one cent per pound–a remarkable achievement. The Duroc Jersey boar of Oak Hill Farms captured the sweepstakes. Hog owner F. C. Hall bragged that his pigs never tasted any rations. A Berkshire boar owned by L. T. Rhodes won second place.

Chickens were exhibited, too, segregated by sex and age. They were judged in the categories of cocks, hens, and pullets. The farmers knew their chickens. The names of the breeds were exotic and colorful–Golden Wyandottes, White Leghorns, Rhode Island Reds, and Bronze Turkey. Ribbon winners for poultry were first-family Baldwin Countians–the Byrnes, Hands, and Edmundsons.

New species of plants as well as new varieties of old ones made the agricultural exhibits delightful and surprising. A new velvet bean, used for forage and to improve the soil, made a big show. C. E. Watkins of Foley proudly showed a prolific Dasheen plant. This tuber vegetable resembled an elephant ear. Some thought it was destined to surpass the Irish potato. Exhibitors showed the titillating results of experimentation being done with cucumbers, sweet potatoes, and eating corn.

Canned fruits were attractively arranged in glass jars–plums, figs, strawberries, and blackberries. Fresh Japanese persimmons, the size and color of an orange, purple-skinned stalks of sugar cane, and satsuma oranges all took their place in the exhibits.

Japanese persimmons had a notable delight for my uncle. He bragged on the size and sweetness of his fruit to his Indiana friends. They did not believe there could be a persimmon the size or color of an orange. The common variety they knew is slightly larger than a grape.

Uncle Ort was repeatedly guffawed at by the Indiana folks when he bragged about the persimmons on his tree–their sugar-sweet taste and large size. Friends were skeptical, and this tantalized him. One season he picked the largest and best of the crop, carefully wrapped them, and mailed them to Huntington. His friends saw and tasted persimmons as he'd described them. Uncle Ort's boast about Baldwin County persimmons, they agreed, was not exaggerated. His were the best persimmons they'd ever tasted.

Back to the fair. Surely Uncle Ort, a believer in healthy competition and recognition for achievement, was delighted with the press notices.

> The judges completed their work on Friday, the last day of the Fair, EDUCATION DAY. Prize ribbons were placed on the winning exhibits, then cash premiums, liberal and numerous, were promptly distributed. This year the prizes surpassed those given in former years.

The Sunday edition of the *Mobile Press* declared the Baldwin County Fair the most successful in history. The youthful countenance of my newly married uncle beams from the front page. Underneath his picture is the caption, "Ort Ertzinger, a factor in the success of the Fair."

His experience with the fair and the farmers was a catalyst, I believe, for a business venture Uncle Ort made a few years later. Uncle

Ort kept abreast of developments in agriculture–motivated by his healthy appetite and inquiring mind. This news article, which appeared in 1914, may well have provoked some thought for my uncle, who was constantly looking for ways to make money:

> The satsuma orange is a highly profitable product. The light open soils and climate of this section are perfectly suitable for growing this particular satsuma orange. There are a number of bearing groves in this section; a great many acres in young trees and new settings are constantly being planted. The fruit stands shipping exceedingly well. The first carlot of these oranges is being sent from Baldwin County this season.
>
> The satsuma tree is hardy and thornless. It hardens in the Fall and lays dormant until spring, eliminating the danger from frosts. The trees have withstood a temperature as low as seven degrees without injury. This makes their growing a safe proposition in this section. The trees are dwarf and do not grow above eight feet.
>
> Picking their fruit is a pleasant occupation. It can be done with leisure. The fruit clings to the tree for eight to twelve weeks. Better shippers or sellers are not grown anywhere. The fruit ripens early when there is no other orange competition on the market.
>
> These satsuma oranges are unexcelled in flavor, and bring splendid prices at near-by markets. They are a favorite for the reason that they are not high in acid, and can be peeled and eaten without difficulty or without losing its juice. Sometimes they are referred to as the "kid glove" orange.

When Uncle Ort first moved to Bay Minette, a front-page story pointed out the need for a box factory. No one had built one. The seed germinated in Uncle Ort's brain.

Seven long years after his family moved South, from 1909 to 1916, Grandpa Ertzinger had worked in Hammond, Indiana, and commuted to Bay Minette. He visited his family at every opportunity he had, made friends, and was eager to stay for good. On November 16, 1916, the *Baldwin Times* announced: "J. A. Ertzinger from Hammond is expected to arrive the latter part of the week to remain permanently with his family here." I wager there was much rejoicing among the Ertzingers when Grandpa arrived, bag and baggage, at the Bay Minette depot.

Now the seed idea in Uncle Ort's mind was ready to sprout. The organizer, euphoric over his father's reunion with the family, began to make plans.

6

Satsumas and Hampers

NINETEEN-SIXTEEN WAS THE YEAR the Ertzinger population in Bay Minette doubled, and life from then on had a different pace. Eloise Arline Ertzinger was delivered to the arms of Ort and Ottilla in their home on White Avenue. The new parents were overjoyed with their cuddly baby daughter. A few months later, John Adam Ertzinger moved from Hammond, Indiana, to live next door to his granddaughter. The Ertzinger influence in Bay Minette was assured for some time to come.

When Alice and John, now 56 years old, could sleep together every night, there was a new satisfaction in living. At long last their family was together! Uncle Ort proudly showed his father the Commonwealth of Baldwin County. Baldwin County land developers used the word *empire* when they wrote:

> In the northern section are picturesque wooded hills and valleys with thousands of acres of primeval pine and oak forests. Poplar, cedar, sweet-gum, and magnolia thrive. In the spring the woods are a riot of dogwood blossoms and yellow jasmine. In the winter red holly and yaupon brighten the woods. Vivid rose clay ravines lend relief to the varied hues of green foliage–the pine, magnolia, and smilax.

The long stretches of snow white sand which line the southern border are unexcelled. Miles of shoreline offer the sportsman boating and swimming in the tranquil waters of many bays and bayous along with the Gulf of Mexico. Palmettos border the shores of the lagoons and rivers. The southern area is a sharp contrast to the promising agricultural areas in other parts of Baldwin. All together there is an EMPIRE.

The fact that Uncle Ort showed his father around and introduced him to his friends all around the county did not go unnoticed.

> Ort Ertzinger was in Fairhope yesterday with his father J. A. Ertzinger whom he was taking on a tour of South Baldwin. Mr. Ort is a real estate and insurance man, newspaper correspondent, baseball and basketball expert and President of the Baldwin County Sunday School Association. He is one of the live wires in his city and county.

That report in the *Fairhope Courier* was later reprinted in the *Baldwin Times* with this additional comment.

> Our friend Mr. Gaston, editor of the *Courier*, is not familiar with all of Ort's endowments. We want to mention, for his enlightenment, some others. Such as orchestra leader, tenor soloist, fruit grower, secretary of the Burkett Memorial Presbyterian Sunday School. He is the daddy of little Eloise Arline Ertzinger, the coming queen of Baldwin County.

As the two men drove through the South Baldwin countryside talking with people, Uncle Ort pointed out crops that were unfamiliar in Indiana–sugar cane, pecan and persimmon trees, and the satsuma orange tree. Ideas were swirling around in their heads as they talked.

The low, squatty half tree with dark-green leaves, sometimes growing in orchards, was of special interest to Grandpa. Many people, including his son, had a few of these satsuma orange trees in their yards for their own use. Everyone loved this "kid glove" fruit with a tantalizing taste. It was sure to be in demand. My uncle and grandfather talked about a way to profit from its popularity.

First introduced in the United States in 1898 by the American ambassador to Japan, this outstanding fruit made its way to the Battles community on Mobile Bay via Sammuel White, a man from Boston.

This nucleus of trees the New Englander planted spread.

Dr. W. H. Ludwig of Foley is credited with making the first commercial shipment of the satsuma orange in 1913. Soon afterward, the Gulf Coast Citrus Exchange was organized by the growers. They developed standard packs and grades for distributing the fruit. Sixty carloads were shipped from Baldwin in one year. Marketing centers–Chicago, St. Louis, Buffalo, and Philadelphia–were readily accessible by rail.

Grandpa and Uncle Ort talked about a proper shipping crate for this new orange. Other fruits and vegetables that the innovative farmers were bound to supply would need boxes, too. Back in 1908, a front-page article in the *Times*, "What Bay Minette Needs," had declared that a nursery, a laundry, and a box factory were at the top of the list. Eight years later, there was still no box factory, although the need for one had increased.

Dr. O. F. E. Winberg, a scientist, was an authority on satsuma oranges. He lived in Silverhill, where he grew fruit and wrote. Following a cold spell in 1917, the year after Grandpa moved down, Dr. Winberg wrote:

> I have carefully examined the Satsuma trees and declare only 10% damage and that only to the young trees. the ability of the Satsuma to resist cold makes Satsuma culture in Mobile and Baldwin Counties as safe as the orange industry in Florida or California. This is the consensus of conservative horticulturists.
>
> Wherever our fruit has been introduced and sold, a demand for more has been created. We have no fear of overproduction. From a climatic point of view, there is only a limited geographic area suitable for Satsuma Orange culture. Along the coast of the Gulf of Mexico and inland for about 65 miles. That includes Bay Minette and South Baldwin.

These assurances from an expert probably encouraged the Ertzinger men in their ideas about becoming a part of the agricultural explosion around them.

In the meantime, Uncle Ort kept close contact with his Indiana connections. The clouds of war brought gloom to the country but did not impair Uncle Ort's sense of humor. Uncle Levi, Grandpa's brother, was a butcher and co-owner of the Brill-Ertzinger Meat Market in Huntington. One day, out of the blue, he received a telegram. Immediately Uncle Levi knew his nephew who sent it was up to some tomfoolery. The *Huntington Press* quoted the telegram and put it this way.

"Am expressing highly perishable package to you today. Hound express office until it arrives. Unpack immediately. Divide with Stahls." This cryptic message from Ort H. Ertzinger, of Bay Minette, to his uncle, L. A. Ertzinger, of this city, aroused the Huntington man's curiosity to high pitch. What was what the writer evidently intended.

Wednesday morning the package, or rather the box, arrived. It was about five feet long and labeled, "Lay Me Down, Do Not Stand On End, Rush, Perishable." Handlers were warned. The entire package was covered with highly explicit messages.

The box was hustled to Ertzinger's meat market on East Market Street. It yielded a four foot catfish, weighing 49 pounds. Its head was about one third the length of the fish. Right away Levi called friends to see it and entertained them. He bragged that he'd seen even larger fish taken from the waters at Bay Minette when he visited there about a year ago.

The fish was put on display for a time and then cleaned and divided with Mr. and Mrs. E. M. Stahl, parents of Mrs. Ertzinger.

My two uncles had fished together on the Wabash River when Uncle Ort was a little boy. In retrospect, I think Uncle Levi was a kind of role model for his nephew. His character and morality were exemplary, plus the fact that Uncle Levi was a successful businessman–in a business he himself had founded. The two men admired and loved each other. Soon after the armistice of World War I was signed, Uncle Ort wrote:

Bay Minette, Alabama, May 25, 1919

Dear Uncle Levi,
Papa and I have made the big plunge. The rumors you heard about us starting a new business are true. We have opened the Bay Minette Manufacturing Company referred to as the hamper factory.

You liked the Satsuma Oranges we sent you last year; everybody likes them. Marketing boxes for the fruits and vegetables grown in our fine soil and climate has great promise. Our plant makes shipping containers, mostly hampers.

We got a break when the Chicago Mill & Lumber Company in Hurricane was put up for sale. Papa examined the mill which originally made wooden veneer, thin slats of wood. He thought the machinery could be used and added to to make shipping crates.

Papa and I got our heads together. My ideas for labor saving and his knowledge of machinery are working together. I'll spare you the details, come to see it.

The big challenge was the money to get started. I persuaded ten local businessmen in Baldwin County to invest. They are the Directors. I'm the President and General Manager with an office in Bay Minette. Papa is the superintendent at the mill in Hurricane.

As soon as people got wind of our plan potential customers contacted us. That was encouraging. Baldwin County farmers now get hampers and crates from Mississippi.

The mill is in Hurricane about 10 miles south of Bay Minette. We cut virgin trees, pine and gum from nearby forrest to make the slats. Some are four foot in diameter, a pretty big tree, but we can handle it.

Papa keeps his eye on the massive turning lathe designed to slice a continuous quarter inch layer from the log, and cut it up into boards about six inches wide. Then the boards are ready for kiln drying. The machine is complicated and can cause trouble. That's Papa's baby. I keep busy with the hiring and selling end of the business in Bay Minette.

We are off and running. Sixty people are employed when we are operating to full capacity.

Thanks for remembering my birthday. The 33rd year of my life promises to be a great one.

Love Ort

What a delightful treasure his keepsakes provide when one takes the time to delve into them! A yellowed clipping from the Vanity Book editorializes:

Last week the editor [then Bob Vail] had the great pleasure of going with Ort Ertzinger to Hurricane where he saw the big hamper factory of the Bay Minette Manufacturing Company in full blast.

To the uninitiated the first trip to the plant is an eye-opener. About fifty persons are employed under the capable direction of "Chief" John A. Ertzinger.

Ort's genius as an organizer and inventor stands prominently before one at every turn. A do-dad here and a thing-a-ma-jig there. Bearing distinctly the Ort Ertzinger earmarks. These are seen in all parts of the establishment. And nearly every idea is a money saver, enabling one man to take the place of two. Ort claims, "It's just a case of using your old bean." He has long been a shining light in doing just that.

The hamper factory is running full tilt. Ort is President, General Manager, all round overseer. We started to write a little item about the mill and find ourselves writing nothing but about Ort–and Ort glorified. But, then, any story about the former is just naturally a story about the latter. Seldom does a business reflect its guiding genius so emphatically as does the Bay Minette Manufacturing Company reflect the genius of Ort.

A visit to his factory will be an interesting trip. It will open your eyes, if you have never been there. Go see it!

The operation of the Hurricane division of the Bay Minette Manufacturing Company met the demands of the increasingly large orders for wooden boxes, crates, and hampers. One account records: "The mill was running at capacity every hour of the day in order to finish the 200,000 lot order of orange box contract with Gulf Coast Citrus Exchange. Carloads of these boxes leave the mill every few days."

Three years after the hamper factory opened, new equipment arrived for the enlargement of the mill. The expansion was to include improving the premises at the Hurricane Mill where the fifty mill employees lived. The thick woods near the plant had been cut down and measures taken to kill the mosquitoes and do away with malaria. The company planned to lay out new streets and build better houses with up-to-date sanitary facilities. Each family was to have a house and garden plot.

With an expanded line of containers came the need for additional personnel. One newspaper advertisement states: "The company plans to keep pace with the growth of the county by expanding as rapidly as necessary. The best seller is the Baldwin Hamper. Quotations will be cheerfully furnished on any product of the company."

The business expanded, and there was a new letterhead:

> BAY MINETTE MANUFACTURING COMPANY (Inc.)
> the new baldwin hamper, cabbage crates, orange boxes
> various kinds of vegetable shipping
> containers, box hooks
> and egg cases

The new stationery also indicated a change in personnel. Originally Uncle Ort was the President, Grandpa the Vice President and Treasurer, and Herbert Weston the Secretary. With the growth of the company a new name was added–H. L. Porter, Manager. Naturally, Mr. Porter had access to the company's bank account.

No one would have guessed what Mr. Porter would do to this thriving business. He had a nice wife and home. Eloise recalls their children at school. One day he wrote a check for the entire account, cashed it, and left town. The new manager had absconded with the company's entire bank account.

Suddenly the mill closed down.

The plant was open from 1919 to 1927. A dishonest man, not mismanagement or bad times, caused the downfall of a thriving mill. Bankruptcy laws did not protect the owner then. Dreams and hopes for economic success were dashed.

Surely Uncle Ort must have experienced anger and frustration at this tragedy, but to me that never showed. I never remember hearing him talk about the "bad guy," Mr. Porter. My uncle's greatness overshadowed Mr. Porter's dirt.

I was totally unaware of the gravity of the situation at the time. Uncle Ort made good in a bad situation. To me he was a man in shining armor.

Every worker was paid the wages owed him. The tone of family talk about him was pride. He paid the indebtedness of the company although it was not his personal responsibility to do so. Time and personal sacrifice for my uncle and his family were required to do the right thing. The Ertzingers did what their conscience, not their pocketbook, dictated. That is about all I know about the devastating event that affected so many people's lives.

This loss was tragic to both father and son. My grandfather lost his life's savings, which he'd invested in the plant. I think Uncle Ort always felt a special obligation to his father because of that.

Ironically, the closing of the Bay Minette Manufacturing Company came at a time when "the bloom was on the rose" in...

It is sad even now to read about this promising business that went awry. But the chief organizer used this tragedy as a stepping stone. He pressed on. The evil behavior of another did not devastate him. Uncle Ort, like Saint Paul, put all things behind and pressed forward to the high calling of God. For uncle Ort, there were other fields to conquer, other worlds to explore.

7

A Man in the Middle of Things

MY MEMORY BANK IS FULL OF UNCLE ORT. My only brother and I loved to go to Bay Minette, as something appealing was always going on wherever Uncle Ort was.

Back in the flapper days of the twenties, when women were first exercising their vote, I was a little girl. We lived in Georgiana, Alabama, about 175 railroad miles north of Bay Minette. My father was a locomotive engineer for the L&N, so we had free passes to ride on the railroad. My family visited in Bay Minette more than the Bay Minette relatives came to Georgiana.

After all, there were two Ertzinger families to visit in Bay Minette–Eloise, Aunt Tillie, and Uncle Ort in one house and Grandpa and his wife, whom we called Aunt Hattie, next door. Both households made us feel welcome and wanted.

Jack and I made many weekend visits during the school year, but on holidays and during the summer we stayed longer. Uncle Ort is in the middle of my memories and visits. So is Eloise. Because she was five years older, I looked up to her. I thought she had everything in the whole wide world she wanted–life on a silver platter.

Her father built her a Ferris wheel that had support posts buried in a deep hole filled with cement. Riders went way up in the air. It was the most bedazzling contraption. I'd never seen anything like it. The giant wheel, in a class by itself, had bars with tires around them. It took two people to make it go. Jack and I thought it was great fun. We hung onto the bars and went high up into the air, then came down and around again. Around and around we went.

Children from all over town came to Eloise's yard for a ride. None of the other children had a father who made them such unique playthings as the Ferris wheel. My father had built me a fine playhouse where I had played for years, but other children had playhouses.

Those were the days when dinner was the noon meal. We ate outside under the high, sturdy scuppernong arbor Uncle Ort had built. It ran from the roof of the back porch over the back door, providing shade and coolness during the hot months of summer and fall. Eating under the green grape leaves was pleasant, a sharp contrast to the heat in the kitchen, where the burning wood stove scorched temperatures. The bronze ripened scuppernongs in late summer were a bonus to the high umbrella of shade the vine provided.

Those days are vivid in my memory. Eating summer vegetables fresh out of Uncle Ort's garden while the bluejays in the pecan trees squawked at the cat. Bantam corn-on-the-cob, which he called "roasting ears," were Uncle Ort's favorite. The field corn sold in local markets was for the stock and not fit for human consumption, according to my uncle.

Popcorn was something else he grew, or tried to grow. Only after many failures did he concede that the climate was not cold enough to grow popcorn. The first popcorn ears I ever saw were the ones he brought from Indiana. If I was around when he was shelling it to store, he let me help. Shelling kernels from the cob for storing was a treat. Popcorn was stored in blue fruit jars in the pantry.

Uncle Ort's was the only place I ever had the chance to shell the grains from those tiny ears–another unique Uncle Ort experience. Many friends did not know what I was talking about when I told them I shelled popcorn. They thought popcorn came in a can.

Uncle Ort was up front with many wonderful things such as a popcorn popper. He had the first electric one I ever knew anything about. Mother made good popped corn in a pan on top of the stove for a long time before we (in my eyes) caught up with my uncle and bought our own electric gadget.

Uncle Ort's time to serve popcorn was after a bounteous meal on Sundays. Almost everyone ate second helpings at the table. Then, while the women were doing the dishes, Uncle Ort would pop a huge bowl of corn and pass it around. His popcorn was always eaten as easily as one drinks a pleasing cordial.

Disastrous fires in Bay Minette were not uncommon in those days. Houses and businesses were totally destroyed. This *Times* clipping highlights the results of Uncle Ort's awareness of the danger of smoke and flames.

> There might have been a disastrous fire in the school house had not Mr. Ort been quick to act. He was showing a visitor around town when he passed the school and noticed a flame through the window. He got out of his car and went in to investigate. He put out the fire in the waste paper basket of Miss. Eleanor McMillan's classroom, deserted at the time, and went on his way.

In September 1925, the Mobile newspapers carried a front-page story of two fires in Bay Minette. The burned-down plants were a $200,000 loss in Bay Minette. Uncle Ort was the fire chief who fought those fires.

> Monday afternoon the B&M Lumber Company roared in a furious flame for hours. The Volunteer Firemen worked in the torrid heat to contain the blaze. Volunteer Firemen dug trenches as they watched 250,000 feet of lumber burn. The twisted wreckage of one of the town's two important manufacturing plants lay smoldering.

On top of this, the next morning the wildcat whistle blasted through the calm morning air. Another fire alarm challenged Uncle Ort as no other fire ever had. The shrill code–one long blast followed by three short ones–indicated a fire on the south side of town. The tar plant was on fire.

Fire was the most dreaded thing that could happen to this Newport Industries plant. The highly flammable products being manufactured, turpentine and pine oil, came from pine rosin. Rosin-rich pine stumps and roots were dumped into a hopper where they were ground into chips. These chips were run into a retort where the oil was extracted by a steam process. People's lives were at stake if and when a fire broke out.

The fire came suddenly. Before the person in the retort plant knew what was going on, the building was wrapped in flames. So quickly did the fire develop that one man lost $133 he had left in his locker; the fire beat him to it. Others lost their clothes and valuables. This is the way the *Press Register* told of the disaster:

> Some of the finest amateur fire fighting ever done was exhibited in holding the fire to one unit of this extensive plant. Sparks threatened to ignite several adjoining buildings, but the Volunteer Fire Fighters braved the flaming scourge, stood their ground, and successfully fought it back.
>
> Several prostrations were reported: Fire Chief Ort Ertzinger, and the Chief Engineer of the Newport Company, J. H. Hansen, were in serious condition. There were others, too numerous to mention, who helped in holding the terrific blaze to one building.
>
> The most effective work was in preventing the fire from spreading into the storage tanks about 200 feet away from the retort plant. These storage tanks hold about 1200 gallons of flammable pine products.
>
> The negro employees rendered yeoman service in fighting the flames. White persons were dropping out on all sides from sheer exhaustion and prostration, but the negroes held their ground and faced the very hottest part of the work without flinching. Their work was highly commendable.
>
> The fire fighters were able to save not only the storage tanks and their contents, but the tremendous piles of "lighter wood" and the thousands of barrels of rosin which were in another section of the plant.

People all over town were talking about the tar plant fire for a long time. The Baldwin Times gave a full account of the calamity. Even the column "Personals," usually devoted to tidbits of social news, had a comment.

> No one was out for glory in the fight on the big blaze, but many won generous helpings of it. The work of Fire Chief, Ort Ertzinger, Ralph Carrol, Cly T. Smith, Mac Aylin, "Mutt" Ray, L. J. Hooper and others stood out and contributed generously to holding the fire to one building. Bay Minette's Volunteer Firemen cannot be improved on: They respond and they deliver the goods on every occasion.

Uncle Ort was my fire chief hero. One of the cardinal rules of fire fighting was getting to the fire quickly. The manner in which he parked was an expression of his commitment. He always backed into a parking place and was careful to leave his car where it was not likely to be obstructed, putting into practice the Boy Scout motto, "Be Prepared." Frequently, even now, when I back into a parking place, Uncle Ort flits across my mind.

Amid all other kinds of noises, volunteer fire fighters have a sixth sense for hearing the fire alarm. The Newport plant whistle was the town's fire siren–the same whistle that blew regularly morning, noon, and night to signal starting and quitting times. Different combinations of long and short blasts gave the fire alarm. The whistle also indicated the section of town where the fire was burning. Many times Uncle Ort let Eloise and me go to fires with him. He drove in the direction of the fire and found it by following either the smoke or people.

Oddly, I remember going to the fires, but for the life of me I cannot remember what I did after I got there. The red-orange flames pale in comparison to the excitement I felt at the sudden action taken at the toot of the whistle. I wonder how many volunteer fire fighters allowed their nieces to accompany them to fires. Going to fires with Uncle Ort was as exclusive to me as shelling grains of corn from the tiny popcorn cobs.

Once the fire alarm blasted just as Uncle Ort was going to bed. The noise of his giant steps coming down the stairs before the whistle stopped blowing is clear in my head. He was buttoning his shirt, but his eyes showed that his mind was listening to the whistle's signal, not looking where he was going. Eloise and I jumped into his car. The fire, naturally more spectacular at night, blazed. A few pieces of household goods had been dragged from the house and sat amid the curious gathered on the edge of the flames.

Something gradually connected in my consciousness. I became aware of how being a fire fighter and selling fire insurance was related–a harmony, which made for a unity of purpose.

As a fire fighter he was cognizant of how often fires occurred and the inherent tragedy they caused. Businesses and homes in Bay Minette, built of very flammable heart pine, burned like a tinderbox. That tragedy and destruction also produced an opportunity. His title and abstract business branched out in a new direction–selling fire insurance.

This type of insurance, a new idea then, would provide the fire victim with money for refurnishing and rebuilding. And there was profit in it for him. Fire prevention was something he consistently practiced and preached.

Victims of a fire often saw Uncle Ort as a V.I.P.I. (very important person indeed). As fire chief, he was the leader of the fight to save their property. To those who bought fire insurance from him, he was Johnny-on-the-spot to survey the damage and make payment for their loss. Each Bay Minette fire was a significant event to him; each warranted an entry in his line-a-day diary.

In a good-humored way the *Times* editor wrote about my uncle:

> Nearly every town has them, the Ort Ertzingers. They are mighty fine people to have around. Ort is Bay Minette's handy man. He is a member of the City School Board, a Sunday School worker, Worshipful Master in the Masonic Lodge, manager of a splendid business–taking part in everything, and always in good spirits. He is a valuable asset.
>
> The writer will never forget the first few days he was in Bay Minette. Went to a ball game and Ort was catching, and doing a fine job too. Went to a Lodge meeting and Ort was taking a leading part. Went to Sunday School next morning and Ort was President of the class.
>
> We have been sorry that we did not get to take in the Ladies Aide so we might further check up on Ort. Ort is a good citizen!

The Masonic Hall near the courthouse was familiar to Uncle Ort. The first and third Saturday nights of each month were meeting nights for the A M No. 498. If he was in town, he was there. Again, Bob Vail, the Times editor, wrote:

> Last Saturday night we enjoyed the privilege of sitting in on the meeting of the local Masonic Lodge. And did we enjoy it–every minute of it.
>
> Never have we seen a finer set of men, and every man there seemed to be alert to the real meaning of Masonry, which as we see it, is to make good men better men. The Masonic Lodges of this country are agencies for the creating of the finer things of life, and a good Mason is always a splendid citizen. A community possessing a live Masonic Lodge has a vital force for right and decency in its midst.
>
> The Bay Minette Lodge, under the inspiring leadership of Master Ort Ertzinger, has developed into a power for good in this section. Today we find A M No. 498 is one of the liveliest and fastest growing Masonic organizations in the state. Its generosity as disclosed in its many charities despite the fact that it is paying for its Temple, is enough to make every member choke with pride over his affiliation with such a fine body.

The use Uncle Ort made of his time–volunteer fire fighting, his achievements as a Mason–were a few drops in the bucket depicting his love and concern for others. The issues he supported likewise were just. Some Christians believe the true Church–the body of Christ–is out in the world, not in a building. Uncle Ort's keepsakes document his active embodiment of the Church in the world.

One cold Sunday afternoon in January, circa 1932, Uncle Ort and Dr. Marlette (the Baldwin County Health Officer) drove up to Monroeville to a union service at the Baptist church. Every mile of the forty-mile journey was bumpy and cold. I'm sure they dressed in their long handles, sweaters, and woolen clothes, as car heaters had not been perfected then, and the trip itself was a rugged one.

The two men had accepted the Alabama Council of Christian Education's invitation to speak as part of the state campaign against *religious illiteracy*. Both speakers had the ability to get their point across. Their plea was for people to get busy–parents, schools, and churches.

To surround the boys and girls with a loving environment and an opportunity to develop four-square for God–physically, mentally, morally, and socially. These dedicated men were well received by a large group of Monroe Countians and spoke by invitation in three counties.

Uncle Ort's stand against alcohol and cigarette smoking was legendary. He was the secretary-treasurer of a group called the dry forces that opposed the sale of alcoholic beverages. Cigarettes really bothered him. Something about cigarettes made them more evil than a pipe, probably because his father was an ardent pipe smoker. The association of air pollution and sinus congestion was not well established then, so I don't think he realized smoke irritated his sinuses–a physical reason to justify his disdain.

This man in the middle of things had a hand in many a pie. Those who remember the Civilian Conservation Corps know what C.C.C. stands for. This part of Franklin Roosevelt's New Deal was to create meaningful jobs for people who had none. The C.C.C. camp on the outskirts of Bay Minette had Uncle Ort's attention. A watermelon cutting was given by the young people of four churches. The town crier picked up on this expression of friendship toward the C.C.C.

> They consumed sixty, high quality watermelons, the kind only Baldwin County growers can produce. First there were games of all kinds after which, just before dark, some six tables laden with melons were devoured by the young people. Approximately 300 young people enjoyed the watermelon cutting at the high school campus one Saturday evening. Much credit for the success was given to "reliable Ort Ertzinger." He's always willing and ready.

I have no notion by whom or how the idea of a shirt factory in Bay Minette was started. The man in the middle of things and a number of other patriotic citizens worked diligently to bring this business to Bay Minette. Uncle Ort's efforts to bring jobs and business to the town he loved are shown by his own words, extracted from his diary for October 1937:

> Oct. 5 Owl Creek 'till noon, five fish; office in p.m. Left at 10 p.m. for Maryland. Ham Hall, B. O. Hendrickson and W. R. Stuart form party.

Oct. 6 Reached Montgomery at 12:30 a.m. Drivers alternate. Nearly ran off bridge at 3:00 a.m.

Oct. 7 Drove to Richmond for breakfast, reached Easton, Maryland at 4 p.m. Visited factory, back to Washington. Spent night at a place his bachelor nephew, Paul Ertzinger, suggested. Cold.

Oct. 8 Left Washington D.C. at 11 o'clock, drove to Wytheville for night, drove over the skyline drive.

Oct. 9 Drove to Montgomery through rain, to bed at 12:30 a.m. Stopped en route in Chattanooga, Knoxville and Birmingham.

Oct. 10 Sunday. Up at Seven. Attended Sunday School, home at 4 p.m. Young People's meeting in evening—42 present.

Oct. 11 Office all day. Mass meeting at night to report about trip to shirt factory in Easton, Maryland.

The *Baldwin Times* also covered the story.

Report on shirt plant is 100% good. A telegram to the *Times* this afternoon relayed the good news from a group who went to Maryland this week to investigate the shirt factory planning to locate in Bay Minette. It will eventually employ 500 girls.

The diary continues:

Oct. 12 Office till six. Cottage Hill to lead singing at the revival meeting. Drive for factory money began today.

Oct. 13 Abstracted until late. Cottage Hill at night.

Oct. 14 Office all day, no fishing trip. [This was a Thursday, the day he always left the office at noon to go fishing.] Factory meeting at night.

Oct. 19 Spent all day hunting money for the shirt factory. Football—Bay Minette 3, Century 0. Uncle Lewis, Ada, Ella and Warren came today.

The shirt factory never materialized. Bay Minette could not raise the necessary capital. One does not have to stretch one's imagination to know that the men who worked to bring the factory to Bay Minette were disappointed.

I have no idea what prompted this article in the *Times* a few weeks after the demise of the shirt factory project.

Ort H. Ertzinger is a man of many personal activities. In business he is a concentrated specialist in Baldwin County Realty Titles. Abstracts also occupy much of his study, thought, time, and attention and have done so for the past twenty eight years. He and his father organized the business in 1909. Since that time he has collected records which form a most valuable county asset.

Many resident and non-resident land owners have come to depend upon Ort Ertzinger to keep their titles clear; look after the payment of taxes, keep squatters off their lands and otherwise protect their property rights and interests.

The firm has offices centrally located, next to the Western Union Office and separated only by an alley from courthouse square. [Western Union rented office space in his building.] Their most important records are safely kept, in duplicate, so that their destruction by fire or other disaster is guarded against.

Mr. Ertzinger has been active in civic affairs since he came to Bay Minette and his activities in church and Sunday School matters began in Huntington, Indiana. Still young enough to play baseball [48], he is deeply interested in Young People's movements, organized the boy's band, and coaches the state championship girl's basketball team.

Mr. Ertzinger is active in the Bay Minette Lions Club and other movements of an altruistic and progressive nature.

Uncle Ort was in the middle of things. Even the shirt factory failure had winning ways for this man of boundless energy and intellect. His experience with the town's inability to get the necessary capital led him into the financial arena.

8

A Man and His Money

UNCLE ORT'S MIND was actively figuring out and implementing money-making schemes. As a small boy in Huntington he had pulled horseradish out of the ground and grated, packaged, and sold it. He captured a queen bee on the courthouse square, started his own beehives, and sold honey—enough to have a Bee account in the bank. He respected the power of money, the security it provided, the good deeds he could do with it. The love of money did not create evil in Uncle Ort's heart.

Immediately after World War I in the United States, free enterprise was flourishing in an unprecedented manner. In 1920 women paid poll taxes and began casting their vote. Uncle Ort was president and manager of the expanding Bay Minette Manufacturing Company. The entire nation was growing like a mushroom. This was the state of affairs the year I was born.

A few months before my birth in 1921, the Ertzingers were saddened by the death of Alice Bartmus Ertzinger. My grandmother died of diabetes mellitus (a malfunctioning pancreas). That was before Banting discovered the use of insulin in the treatment of the disease. Tragically, my grandmother literally ate herself to death. The lady who had rocked the cradles of my mother and Uncle Ort was memorialized thus:

> A cloud of sorrow swept over the community last Sunday morning when the message came that one of the most esteemed and honored neighbors, Mrs. J. A. Ertzinger, passed away. There are few who are more faithful and devoted to their church. No chair in the Sunday School will be noticed in its vacancy more than hers. Even in the agonies of intense suffering she would inquire about prayer meetings and Sunday School. How great is the influence of a good life!
>
> Her good voice brought joy and gladness to many. The writer knows of one time when the song she sang at a religious service was the means of turning to a new life for a very sinful man. As she has gone to her reward in heaven we trust the influence of her beckoning hand will be an inspiration to us all.

Uncle Ort was certainly a "chip off the old block." He and his mother shared a close, loving relationship with each other. Both loved the church and had a talent for singing. Maybe he inherited from her his ability to sing and his healthy appetite. Are there such genes?

The Bay Minette Manufacturing Company was going well. Uncle Ort donated a pipe organ for the Burkett Memorial Presbyterian Church. To me, this gift affirmed his love for music and for his church. In 1926 Uncle Ort first became the adult advisor for the church's young people. The Adult Bible Class that year held a social on Tuesday night, April 20. The Times reported: "Socials in the home of Mr. and Mrs. Ort Ertzinger are pleasant. Every member was expected to be present."

A glance at the world scene in 1927 gives us insight into Uncle Ort's world. A brand-new six-cylinder automobile sold for $875, Charles Lindbergh flew nonstop from New York to Paris, and coins minted that year included 47,144,000 Indian head and buffalo nickels. In that year men in Baldwin County waked up to the opportunity to feather their own nests and benefit their communities.

On January 19, 1927, Uncle Ort gathered with the leading businessmen at the Hotel Norden in Silverhill, Alabama. The mayors of Fairhope, Bay Minette, Robertsdale, Foley, Daphne, Loxley, and Elberta were also in attendance. The purpose of this meeting was to organize the Building & Loan Association.

The plan was for the association to collect funds through membership fees and savings deposits and to lend money for the financing of homes in Baldwin County. A state charter was issued by the Alabama Banking Commission. Shortly thereafter, at the kickoff banquet, fifteen directors and an advisory board were elected. Listed among the directors were Winberg, Randall, Cummings, Haupt, Baldwin, and Ort H. Ertzinger. (At that time, in addition to being owner of J. A. Ertzinger & Son, Abstracts and Insurance, he was the president of the Bay Minette Manufacturing Company, manufacturer of produce containers.)

When the Building & Loan Association went public, a half-page ad in the *Baldwin Times* explained its purpose.

> We are a mutual cooperative financial institution. The members save money together, they lend money together. We divide the profits with each other.

The Building & Loan precepts were so American, and so in line with his own ideas. Had this organization been in place, Bay Minette would probably have been able to secure the shirt factory. The Building & Loan was a way to help individuals enrich their community, own their homes and farms, and perhaps at the same time add money to their own bank accounts.

Application forms to purchase shares were printed in the newspaper. Membership in the Association was $50.00, and shares sold for $2.50 each. Letting everyone buy stock and share in the profit was a concept that excited Uncle Ort. He talked it up to city employees, beauticians, farmers, church friends–anyone who would listen.

Profit sharing from the lending of money was equitable and fair, a way of letting your money work for you. The Building & Loan was Uncle Ort's cup of tea; he was proud to be a part of it and help it grow. He emphasized that it was not necessary to own stock in the Baldwin County Building & Loan Association in order to have a savings account; a person with five or ten dollars could save there. The sales of land made possible by loans from the Building & Loan were like fodder to the cow. They fed Uncle Ort's abstract and insurance business. This is another dimension in my uncle's life–another example of the harmony of his pursuits.

Bay Minette, Alabama
September 12, 1934

Dear Boze,

The organization of the new Baldwin County Building & Loan Association this year offers a way to help Baldwin County grow and prosper. I am a member of the Board of Directors. I quote what President Hoover writes.

"Building & Loan Associations are engaged in a type of financing which is pre-eminent for its low overhead and general efficiency. The association encourages systematic saving, and the lending of funds to home builders and buyers within the same community.

"Through the properly conducted and well regulated Building & Loan Association it is possible to invest regular sums of money, in smaller amounts with greater safety and at a higher interest return than through any other investment medium known...." The Magazine of Wall Street August 2, 1934

Promoting Building & Loan goes well with my business. Last week I was near Foley to write an insurance policy for Mr. Corley, a farmer. He rotates his crops and is making money growing gladiolus, sweet potatoes and soybeans on a 150 acre farm.

I told him about the new Building and Loan organization and mentioned the coupon in the paper, an application for membership and shares. He thought this sounded too good to be true–to own shares and get dividends from the profit made in lending money while at the same time getting a better rate of interest on his savings than he could at the bank. After our conversation he decided to buy shares.

Several days later Corley was at a Masonic funeral I conducted in Foley. [Uncle Ort knew the Masonic funeral service by heart.] Corley told me he'd bought 50 shares and figured in a few years the interest from the shares would be enough to build a better barn. He liked the idea of being a part of something that let his money work for him.

I think you will be impressed with Baldwin County's pine forests and the good farm land when you see them.

Cordially, your ole pal
 Ort

Uncle Ort, a lifetime member, did not miss a single meeting of the board of directors as far as I know. Aunt Tillie, with her typical grace, went along with her husband's commitment. In 1949, when he was recovering from his heart attack, the board met in his home. In later years, the Ertzingers' travel trips were planned around board meetings.

In 1952, they left home in the morning packed to travel to Cuba. The first stop was in Robertsdale to attend a B&L board meeting. They drove on to Florida, spent the night in Fort Walton Beach, then went on to Miami and the Caribbean. Similarly, when they went to Europe, they planned their itinerary so as to return the day before the board met.

The B&L headquarters were in Robertsdale, so on our way to Orange Beach he would always stop–to leave or pick up a paper, or maybe just to say hello to George Page, the manager. The next stop was at the bakery to buy spiced raisin bars–the very best. The fragrance of those warm spice bars lingers in my head.

Uncle Ort educated me about saving. He made it sound exciting and fun. The lyrics to "I Don't Want to Be a Tightwad" shocked me, but they were consistent with his ideas about saving.

"You don't have to be rich to save, but you get rich by saving." This was almost like a creed. This poem elaborates on his saving philosophy:

> Save with a purpose, save with a plan,
> You'll be surprised how easy you can.
>
> It don't take a million, to start an account,
> You can start it here with any amount.
>
> Wherever you live, whatever you do,
> It's smart to have money working for you.
>
> You'll envy the fellow, with money to spare.
> No doubt he started by saving somewhere.
>
> When all has been done, and everything said,
> The money you save, is what gets you ahead.
>
> The man who salts his dough away,
> Is getting richer every day.

> The money you save, and bank today,
> Will come in handy some rainy day.
>
> To make your life a big success,
> You've got to stop your foolishness.
> You can't just hum and haw and guess,
> You've got to plan to win success.
>
> If you have money, let us use it.
> It's guaranteed, you'll not lose it.
>
> What good is money hidden away,
> When interest works both night and day?
>
> Why not bring us your hidden dough,
> And watch our interest make it grow?
>
> If you keep spending every cent,
> You'll soon depend on the government.
>
> What ever your intentions are,
> If you don't save, you don't go far.
>
> Don't keep on spending all your dough,
> Save some with us and watch it grow.
>
> Saving with us, right along,
> 1500 people, can't be wrong.

He was serious in writing his firm convictions about saving. His lighthearted verses were from the heart. Isn't that the source of true poetry?

In my childhood I thought everyone knew Uncle Ort was rich because of such spectacular things as building Eloise's super-duper Ferris wheel. Being a fire chief, having a place to eat outdoors under a large scuppernong arbor with the luscious fruit. I equated being rich with his being on the edge of such things.

Things were not always as good as they seemed, I learned. In 1989 Charlie Bodden told me about the refrigerator he sold Uncle Ort in the twenties. Charlie's account exploded my belief–at least some of it.

Uncle Ort bought his family an electric refrigerator long before our family had one. It was the General Electric "Monitor-top" (with coils on the top). It dominated the pantry and made ice.

I was sometimes privileged to be allowed to remove the ice cubes from the trays. I'd been instructed how to do it. There was a knack to allowing only a minimum of the precious frozen water to melt away. Being able to make your own ice was a real luxury in comparison to our icebox. Ice was delivered to our home in a big foot or foot-and-a-half blocks. For tea we picked off chunks. I was never any good at picking. The temperature in the box was never very cold, so we often had soured milk and spoiled food. Having an electric refrigerator long before most people put Uncle Ort in the "rich" class. But I learned the rest of the story from Charlie Bodden, an appliance salesman for Alabama Power Company.

"I had not been in Bay Minette long," Charlie said, "when the Depression hit. I sold Ort a refrigerator. There was no money circulating; no one had any. The only businesses in town were the tar plant and a couple of sawmills. Nobody could pay their bills. Alabama Power took scrip in payment for electric bills. They were really nice to people. School teachers, preachers, the probate judge, everybody paid in scrip until they had the cash to pay.

"Back to Ort. He got behind in his refrigerator payments. He couldn't sell insurance, nobody was buying land, there was no need for abstracts. It was bad. The credit manager for the power company was a tough old guy. I remember him well. He kept riding me about Ort's bill.

"Ort was behind three or four months, so he wanted me to collect or repossess. I kept telling him I didn't want to repossess Ort's refrigerator, but I couldn't collect. Well, finally he made a date with Ort. He was going to get tough. So we went to see Ort. I made it clear to the credit manager, 'You do the talking–this is your idea.'

Charlie paused a moment and thought. "I'll never forget the answer Ort gave. 'No, I can't pay for the refrigerator now; there is no way I can do that. But if you take the refrigerator away from me, what are you going to do with it? You have two options: you can keep it–and that is not going to do you any good–or sell it to someone else. Who are you going to sell it to? No one has any cash.'

"I was snickering behind the man's back. He did not have an answer for Ort. Ort kept the refrigerator. When he could, he paid off. Those Monitor-tops were good old refrigerators. I don't think his ever wore out. He just got tired of it and traded for a later model."

I remember what happened to it. It was taken to Orange Beach like a lot of other things Aunt Tillie got tired of and carted off down there.

To think that I felt envious of my uncle because he was rich enough to have an electric refrigerator years before my father bought one for our family. I never suspected he had trouble paying for it. The remnants of my uncle's experience stuck with him. Time payments were not for him.

The Ford agency, circa 1935, touted the new idea on the front page of the newspaper as something novel. "Buy now, pay later" is so common today that many do not know there is any other way.

> FORD'S OFFER ON TIME PAYMENTS. These popular cars may be had this month on a special deferred payment plan. Dewel Reese announced the scheme this week. Our main reason in making the offer is that those who have no cars will be helped to this enjoyment by our offer. We want to make this the biggest month in Ford sales.

My uncle never bought a car on deferred payments. After the unprecedented predicament with the refrigerator, Uncle Ort paid "up front" for anything he bought–anything. He refrained from having charge accounts.

A black Ford was Uncle Ort's trademark. Dewel Reese, the manager of Adams Motor Company, planned on it. Every year when the new models came out, a four-door black Ford had Uncle Ort's unwritten name on it. Henry Ford is reported to have said about the Model T, "You can have it in any color you like, as long as it's black." My Uncle Ort liked black.

Uncle Ort's respect for money impressed me. His thrift made him clever, to my way of thinking, and that helped him have what he had. He knew how to improvise and invented ways to make do, using a length of bamboo for a fishing pole, an accountant's book for his journal. He was a fisherman, but he did not buy bait. He raised his own worms in a special place in the back yard where he kept the soil porous with coffee grounds. He was not a miser, but he was not wasteful. He was resourceful.

In those days most businessmen went to the barber for a shave, but not Uncle Ort. He stood in the kitchen window and shaved himself every morning and put the money he saved in a common jar designated for his coins. The jar did not look common because it had been converted into a savings jar. Aunt Tillie had decorated it with beautiful flowers cut out of a seed catalog.

The money in the jar was for something on his wish list–a motor for his boat, or perhaps a trip to Indiana. Uncle Ort made saving seem so appealing. He insisted that the coins collected quickly. My parents were trying to teach me to save part of my allowance each week, but I squandered it on anything I found enticing at the moment. He influenced me in ways they did not.

Eloise graduated from high school in 1934, the year Uncle Ort unsuccessfully ran for Baldwin County tax assessor. He was dead set on sending her to college, which was a financial challenge. Undoubtedly, his motivation in running for office was at least in part to finance her education. His one and only campaign for office was done in his Ortish way. He declared himself qualified through experience–in real estate, land appraisal, insurance, abstracts, and titles.

At a political rally, according to the press, he was "like a breath of fresh air." He made it clear that he was running because of the money, declaring that he had never grossed in a year what he would earn as the tax assessor. He was respected for his honesty! He applied his energy to his campaign. In 1934, while campaigning hard all over the county, many times he wrote what for him was an unusual admission: "I'm tired."

Being thrifty was one thing, but "saving smart" was important, too–having money work for you by drawing interest. Uncle Ort to me was the epitome of both. There were absolutely no exceptions; everyone could save. Everyone should. When asked if it was the right time to invest, he often replied, "The right time is when you have money."

In 1989, Mrs. Alice Duck, a demure lady in her nineties, chatted with me in her den. She told me about the 1930s.

"He helped us get started investing in the stock market. One evening stands out. Mr. Ort dropped by to talk about investments.

"We were having supper. My husband and children and I were at the table when he knocked. 'Come on in and have supper with us,' I called.

"'Just let me stand here a moment and look,' he said. 'I wanted to have a big family. Ottilla almost died when Eloise was born; she won't have any more. It does me good just to stand here and look. Your healthy boys and girls are a sight for sore eyes.'"

Alice was winsome when she quoted my uncle. Her twinkling eyes and strong voice were convincing. "We were great buddies," she told me.

Many other town folks were introduced by Uncle Ort to buying stocks on the New York Stock Exchange. He actually purchased the stock for them. Never did he think of charging a brokerage fee, nor was he afraid someone would get mad and sue if his advice turned sour. He trusted people and they trusted him.

Instead of being leery, he was tickled pink to help people invest. the maxim "God helps those who help themselves" and the hymn verse "All that we have is Thine alone, a trust, O Lord, from Thee" were not contradictory philosophies to my uncle. A person's use of his money, his stewardship of it, was something sacred.

During his later, post—heart attack years, he felt content with what he'd acquired. As he put it, "Ottilla and I have enough to live on as long as we live." His investments and bank account were not the things Uncle Ort treasured most. People and their trust in him more than his portfolio gave him a sense of security.

Uncle Ort wore an ear-to-ear smile as he told me he was the wealthiest man in the world. His portfolio was only a small part of his wealth. His priceless treasures were of another vein.

9

Education Makes Sense

JOKINGLY, UNCLE ORT REFERRED TO HIS BRAIN as his "bean." God gave him his brain and expected him to use it. This meant being attentive, willing to change, and aware–an ongoing process. Uncle Ort thought of himself as self-educated. He was cognizant of not having a college education, but this did not often show. He did what he could with what he had.

Keepsakes, things worth keeping, impart a unique sense of values and impressions about the keeper! They present a potpourri of one's soul. Uncle Ort's keepsakes lay quietly for years out of sight and out of mind. My explorations into these keepsakes–brag book, diary, journal, and so on–gives form to this book. One bundle strikes me as most meaningful: his report cards. The ones from his schooling in Huntington so thoughtfully assembled are a symbol of his respect for his education and the times.

These cards, dated 1896 through 1908 and discolored with age, are resplendent with black numerals written with a fine-nibbed pen and black ink. The writing of each teacher during the twelve years is neat and precise. The elementary school format for evaluation indicates what was considered important–Character, Recitation Grades, Deportment.

Numerical rather than letter grades were given. A legend on the front of the cards for the first six years, at Huntington's Tipton School, interprets the grades:

>100 is perfect [Trying to be perfect? Imagine!]
>900 to 100 excellent
>85 to 90 very good
>80 to 85 good
>75 to 80 medium
>70 to 75 poor
>65 to 70 very poor
>below 65 is very unsatisfactory

At Tipton he studied reading, spelling, writing, drawing, numbers, and language. Both of his parents signed the report card before it was returned. In the sixth grade, he was an outstanding student in Vocal Music. His attendance throughout the twelve years was perfect, save when he was ill with typhoid fever. He had the habit of being punctual. I think he agreed with Horace Mann, who is quoted as saying: "Habit is a cable; we weave a thread for it each day, and it becomes so strong that we cannot break it."

With the report cards in hand, my attention was drawn to a row of uncanny zeroes in the section labeled Character. I blinked and looked closer, and then I saw that they were the number of times tardy–0, 0, 0, 0, 0. Beneath the zeroes was a string of 100s. 100, 100, 100, 100, 100–one for each month of the term–for punctuality.

German, geometry, English history, algebra, physics, botany, geography–heady college preparatory courses–constituted his high school curriculum. On his last report card is written in red ink, "final average 85.5, rank 6." It is inconceivable to me that a young man with his drive and brain did not aspire to a college education. The lack of money and his poor health made such aspirations impossible.

I am second-guessing, but I suspect he kept the report cards for more reasons than mere grades. They are evidence of his achievement, of having completed tough courses and twelve years of public school, of being prompt and reliable. They confirm the claim he made: "I was never tardy."

Let me digress to embellish his habit of punctuality. The *Times* reported in 1931 as follows:

> ATTENDANCE RECORD
>
> I give you Ort Ertzinger, abstractor and insurance agent of Bay Minette, who has gone to Sunday School more than 38 years without ever being late or missing a Sunday. Even when ill he always managed to attend Sunday School. For the last 18 years he had directed young people in their annual conference at Shocco Springs. We would be willing to venture that his record of following Bay Minette's football games is almost as good.
>
> Mrs. Ertzinger confesses that she does not always adhere to the family traditions for promptness and sometimes keeps him waiting.

I well remember being dressed and ready to go, sitting in the car in their porte cochére waiting for Aunt Tillie. He was ready to go before she was. The slow and deliberate way she moved was in direct contrast to his speed. With the years, some of each person rubbed off on the other and their traits blended so that each was a better person.

Uncle Ort kept two hand-written copies of a speech he had made. As I read it I drifted back to the Huntington High School auditorium in 1908. My mind went wild. I saw my handsome, brawny uncle, the firm set of his jaw and his towering height as he took long strides across the stage. He stood at the podium, and the audience became silent.

> The American Laboring Man is needed everywhere. He must be on the great ship building docks, on the railroads, in the new buildings and factories, packing houses, mills, and mines. America is moving at a wonderful pace.

Throughout his six-page handwritten speech, he paused at the appropriate places (they were marked on his script). Probably he'd practiced under the tutelage of his elocution teacher. Occasionally he wiped perspiration from his upper lip. He gestured elegantly, looked out across the audience, and then, in a voice that filled the auditorium, he concluded by saying:

> It is an honor and glory to work. On judgement day the laborer here will stand on equal footing with the laborer there.

His identification with the laborer came naturally. Focus on the worth of the individual in the workplace was an important topic. A metamorphosis was taking place in perceptions of the value of human labor, and slavery had gone, but the workplace was often inhumane. His father pioneered in the movement to eradicate inhumane conditions in the steel mills.

Uncle Ort's heartfelt appreciation for his own public education probably led him to give of his time, energy, and resourcefulness in behalf of public education. I cannot explain Uncle Ort's philosophy of education, but I do know of his dedication. It was tremendous. He believed in educating the total person—body, mind, and soul. That included Christian education and athletics for girls as well as boys.

Circa 1920 the Alabama Board of Education mandated that each county in the state would have a new high school building. Bay Minette was the chosen site in Baldwin County, with the stipulation that the town put up half the cost. Funds were procured, the school built, and Baldwin County High School, with model physical facilities, opened. Developing a curriculum and adequate program of instruction was more difficult to accomplish.

The high school opened with no bus system. Think about what that meant. Although the school was centrally located in the county, the roads were bad, and some children lived over sixty miles away. Parents who wanted their children to have a high school education really had to sacrifice. If parents could pay and were willing for their children to leave home, there was another obstacle. Where could they stay?

Reporter Ort Ertzinger, with the cooperation of the *Baldwin Times*, appealed to citizens in Bay Minette. He asked them to open their homes to the youth who eagerly sought an opportunity that had been denied many of their parents—a high school education. Bay Minetters responded. Many children boarded in the homes of town folk Monday through Friday. Only on weekends did they go home to their parents.

Uncle Ort's interest, assistance, and support in school sports is legendary. Usually a teacher with no preparation in athletics was given the responsibility of building a team and coaching. Uncle Ort pitched in and helped–to line the playing fields, see that proper equipment was on hand, keep time–you name it. For several years he coached basketball.

He was often invited to speak in the weekly assembly in the high school auditorium. Uncle Ort could communicate with young people, and he had something worth saying. The fact that he was at liberty to leave his business to participate in such things impressed me. This freedom put my uncle in an exonerated position in my mind. My father's work time as a locomotive engineer was set. It did not allow him freedom to manage time as Uncle Ort's did.

The value of a high school education was not universally accepted. Proving its worth required diligence and ingenuity. There were only three graduates in the Class of 1917, the year mother finished Baldwin County High. Unstintingly Uncle Ort gave his time and energy preaching the value of education, supporting his claim with information.

> The illiterate will earn $15,000 during his lifetime; the person with a grammar school education will earn $30,000; the high school graduate will earn $460,000. Conclusive evidence of the economic worth of an education. It made sense and cents.

During his daughter's grammar school days he was elected to head the annual Field Day. School authorities conceived the idea of a rally for teachers and *pupils* from all over the county. Uncle Ort, the originator of ideas and a motivator of people, put his mind and talents to work.

"Field Day Draws 4,000!" proclaimed the headline. "Gathering declared most successful yet." Imagine this event on a spring day in March when the azaleas and dogwood were blooming–and 4,000 people descended upon the town. The magnitude of the crowd alone seems awesome; the population of Bay Minette at that time was about one-fourth of that.

The Fairhope band furnished music all day. The L&N lowered the rates and ran special cars to accommodate the tremendous crowd. A monster parade from the Bay Minette depot to the school grounds was led by the County School Superintendent S. M. Tharpe.

Ort Ertzinger was Field Marshal in charge of the event. He arranged matters to perfection and the program went off without a hitch.

Following the events of the morning, 300 barbecue lunches were served. Business men in the community volunteered their time to help with the lunch. [Uncle Ort had recruited these volunteers, a talent in itself.]

This was the first year athletic trophies were given. Uncle Ort instigated this method of awarding achievement. Bay Minette High School boys defeated Foley in baseball, while the girls' cup was captured by Summerdale.

Professor Thorpe, the county school superintendent, pointed out:

> Students and teachers from Elberta deserve special accolades. I am delighted to tell you of the special effort they made to be here. School trucks went seven miles in the country round Elberta and collected students, eighty-three in all. They then rode another five miles together to Foley where they joined the group for their train trip to Bay Minette.

Being the grand marshal for Field Day was another of Uncle Ort's accomplishments in behalf of education for all. Throughout Baldwin County the morale of teachers and students was boosted by this gala display of public support.

His experience in money matters interfaced with the school's continual need for the green stuff. Raising money to spend properly for education was no simple matter. Around 1925 a tax on gasoline to raise revenue for the schools was a new idea. Within the Ertzinger family this topic was hotly debated and caused tension.

This was the time Uncle Ort spearheaded a new business venture for his father–selling gasoline on the courthouse square. They called the filling station Chief's Place, a holdover from the hamper factory, where Grandpa had been chief engineer.

More and more cars traveled the streets every week, increasing the demand for gasoline. At the weekly Tuesday night meetings of the Bay Minette town council, the matter of taxing gasoline a penny per gallon to pay for education was ironed out.

Uncle Ort was between a rock and a hard place. His father was struggling to make a living selling gas, and every gallon he sold made a difference. Any additional cost per gallon he sold would hurt his new business no matter what good cause benefited. Uncle Ort understood his father's position. Stations outside the city limits would sell the fuel for less, so people would drive out of town to buy cheaper gas.

As a member of the school board and a father with a daughter in school, however, Uncle Ort had a special interest in supporting the tax. He addressed the council supporting the tax. He was backed by Carthus Irwin. His fellow Presbyterian churchmen Glen Page and Malcom Hodgson led the discussion for the opponents. (Their business was in oil and gas.) A high-spirited disagreement followed. Finally the council members voted to delay the vote until the next meeting.

At the next council meeting, October 6, the members voted to continue the tax. All present were unanimous that the schools must have funds! Charlie Bodden, a living historian, threw some light on how this difficult situation affected Grandpa. He recalled a sign Grandpa posted in his station: "We pay taxes, we also sell gas." Charlie reckoned many of the people who complained about the gas tax vented their wrath on the Chief. "The sign was the old man's defense," Charlie chuckled.

Records show that Uncle Ort did not let the use of the gasoline tax go unknown. Every opportunity he had, he did his part to publicize what was going on.

> The school auditorium was filled to overflowing with pupils and parents on September 8 when the 1926—27 grade school opened. Mr. Ort Ertzinger, chairman of the city school board, presided.
>
> Following a Scripture reading and a piano selection, County Health Officer, Dr. Marlette, made an effective health talk, dwelling on the matter of proper preparation of the children for school. "Nutritious lunches are important! If parents co-operate, the results of proper lunches will be improved health and grades. Health is closely related to good school work." He was persuasive in his delivery.

The inimitable Ort Ertzinger introduced the teachers in his own style. Everyone listed as he announced that for children living outside the school district the tuition of $2.50 per pupil and $1.00 for incidentals would be charged.

He urged all present to patronize the filling stations inside the city limits when buying gasoline. "The one cent a gallon gas tax levied within the city goes directly to the schools," Ort Ertzinger said. "Through this source the School Board has been able to lay aside $1,000.00 to be applied to the building fund for a new elementary school."

Construction began in 1927 for a new grammar school. In January of 1929 the new school was ready. Wistfully Eloise recalls, "I never attended classes in the new building; it was completed the year after I finished."

"Inimitable," defined in my book as "matchless, unrivaled, in a class by itself," is an apt word to describe Uncle Ort. Although the *Times* writer does not furnish further description of Uncle Ort's remarks, readers would have been able to imagine them. Uncle Ort was well known in person as well in print, and readers knew how he conducted the opening exercises of a new school year. My guess is that he interspersed jokes with the usual flock of Ortish stories, coupled with flattering remarks about each teacher. Each person would have been treated as an individual, different from all the others. Teachers trusted him and believed he cared about their welfare and happiness.

As you might expect, Uncle Ort was active in the Parent-Teacher Association. Aunt Tillie collaborated with him in behalf of education, and they were faithful PTA supporters.

One Saturday in April, the PTA sponsored a Day of Phun and Phrolics (the name was my uncle's invention). All kinds of entertainment were planned. The advance notice explained:

> The ice cream ladies are planning an unparalleled state of cold ecstasy–an ice cream eating contest. Backers of Ort Ertzinger challenge the world.

> Ort is the champion, according to ice cream statisticians, although there is a move afoot to prepare for competition. Sam Whitley is the challenger.

Sam's favorite ice cream is almost unheard of and adds to the aura of excitement to this contest. Sam's favorite flavor is one you'd never guess, onion.

Ort relishes all flavors, but when pushed to choose declares his favorite is tupelo. [Ever hear of that flavor?] Regardless of how it works out it will be fun to watch those two men eating piles of ice cream. The churn freezers are being readied.

In April 1931, the new Bay Minette Grammar School graduated 62 sixth-graders. Students who received diplomas were eligible to attend junior high school. In addition to receiving diplomas, eleven of the students were awarded medals for having a perfect attendance record for the entire year. (Doesn't that smell like Uncle Ort?) Diplomas and awards were given out by Ort H. Ertzinger, chairman of the local board of trustees.

Uncle Ort describes the school situation in this letter to a friend:

Bay Minette, Alabama
March 13, 1933

Dear Boze,

Your comment concerning the vital role of public schools in a democratic society struck a responsive chord. After serving eight years on the Board of Education I was appointed a trustee. This responsibility put me face to face with the realities of how the depression is hurting our children.

The first trustee meeting was an eye opener. I learned there was only enough money to keep the Baldwin County High School open through April–20 days short of the 160 days required by law. We had to find money to run the schools for 20 more days, otherwise no credit would be given students for their year of schooling. Unless we held school for four more weeks, their work would not be recognized.

This is intolerable for the only high school in a county larger than the state of Rhode Island_! I knew we must do something (maybe that is why I was appointed a trustee).

The city council promised us $350,000, about a third of the money we needed. The trustees called a public meeting. A large gathering met in the high school auditorium where we explained the dire situation. The mayor and Dr. McLeod spoke eloquently about the need. Then it was my turn.

"This is a time when every penny counts," I told them. "The money you give is an investment in our children and our future." The contribution that evening was $289.00 short of the minimum amount needed to keep the schools open.

When I stood to announce the amount collected I looked at the eager expectant faces of the parents and I could not tell them the truth. I heard myself saying, "The schools will continue another month." I figured someway we'd dig up $300.00. Frankly I didn't know where but I had faith that the good citizens of Baldwin County somehow would come up with the money. And by golly they did.

Spring has sprung and it is getting warm here now. How many are graduating this year from Tipton, my ole' grammar school?

Your old pal
Ort

The money to keep the schools open for the additional 20 days was especially vital for students headed for college. Otherwise, graduates going to college, including Eloise, would not have met college requirements and would have been required to take additional entrance examinations. People all over the county were ecstatic, and their faith in Ort Ertzinger grew.

Not many spheres of the school activities evaded Uncle Ort. He was instrumental in coaching the debating club, and he also played a strong supporting role in the school plays. In 1934 he arranged for the cast of the senior play, *Attorney for the Defense*, to go to Stockton to perform. Eloise played her part well according to her doting father's diary. Taking the play "on tour" was not only extraordinary but indeed unprecedented. My rich uncle broke the code of the conventional.

When Eloise was in high school, he knew all the young boys and girls by their first name. Contact with them through sports and the church helped. I envied Eloise for that. It would have made my love life easier I thought, if Daddy had been more familiar with my friends.

"I was on the school board every year Eloise was in school," Uncle Ort claimed with satisfaction. That was 1923—1934.

Along the paper trail of keepsakes, a simple sheet of paper contains a note from the school principal in Loxley.

April 20, 1942

Dear Mr. Ertzinger:

As you will recall you were with us as guest speaker at Elementary School Graduation three years ago. Those pupils to whom you spoke are now graduating from Junior High School (nineth grade). They asked me to tell you they would like to have you return to us as guest speaker at Junior High School Graduation. I think this is a fine idea too. The graduation is to be held Wednesday night, April 29, at 8 p.m.

Sincerely,

W. C. McGowan

The Superintendent of Education, Professor S. M. Tharp, had joined the educational system in Bay Minette in 1909, the year Uncle Ort moved from Huntington. Their work together on behalf of Baldwin County schools paid off. The following editorial appeared in the *Mobile Press* on Friday afternoon, September 20, 1946.

HONOR TO BALDWIN COUNTY SCHOOLS

Congratulations to the Baldwin County school system and to S. M. Tharp, Baldwin County Superintendent of Education!

The October issue of LOOK magazine lists Baldwin County school system on the Honor Roll of American Public Schools. The listing of 100 of America's best schools appeared in an article entitled, "The Hope of American Education."

This signal honor is one in which South Alabama can take pride. It is no small distinction to be singled out as among the 100 best in the nation. We are indeed happy to see that Baldwin County has made this notable contribution and gained national recognition for Alabama.

The true impact of my uncle's efforts on behalf of education, like that of countless other educators, cannot be measured, only imagined.

10

AAA An Athletic Achiever

> The things he did for sports
> No one can recount to you.
> Were I to speak and tell them,
> They would be too many to declare.
>
> —Anonymous

NOWHERE WERE MY CHILDHOOD perceptions of Uncle Ort more exalted than in connection with athletics.

In high school he was a track runner. The *Huntington Herald* reported in 1907:

Though Ort Ertzinger was unaccustomed to running on turf [Huntington did not have a turf track], that did not prevent him from making a good showing at the Marion, Indiana, meet. He won the entrance run with ease.

My puzzlement was considerable when I heard Mother brag about her brother running track. The railroad track I walked on to school was the only track I knew. Balancing myself to *walk* on the tracks was all I could manage. To think my uncle *ran* on them? When I questioned him, Uncle Ort straightened me out.

You recall, one of the first things he did when he moved to Bay Minette was to help build a tennis court. True to the norm, he was an athlete who excelled in several sports. In December the *Mobile Press Register* declared:

> Greet the new bowling leader of the week, Mr. Ort Ertzinger of the Adams Glass & Furniture team. Mr. Ertzinger's efforts netted him a total of 587 pins and top position in Merchant's League.

Uncle Ort's record was 212-201-174. Later he rolled high single, 223, and high for three games, 586.

But the game he loved the most was baseball. Incessant and indomitable are words used when describing his baseball spirit. He played, promoted, reported, managed, umpired, and later was entertained by the game. He knew baseball inside out. He began playing when they lived on First Street in Huntington. I don't recall any talk of him as a Little Leaguer.

Around 1910, while Uncle Ort was visiting Huntington, the *Herald* carried this story. It seems that Huntington's Johnnie Strans, the baseball manager, had chided that if he could see his way to playing,

> Ort would prove quite a drawing card. His playing position is receiver. According to southern papers he has a wing which makes base runners fear him. Little thieving is done when he covers home base; he's caught too many in the act. He is not a bad actor with the stick; he runs bases like wild fire.

> What Ort would like to do is to play ball in the summer in the north and attend business in the South during the winter. Looks now as though he will soon be one of the Northern autocrats in the south in the near future.

My uncle joined the town team in Bay Minette soon after he moved there. The notations in his 1909 journal tell about the pretty ladies who came to the ballpark to watch them practice. "When practice was over the damsels brought out a box of choclate candy which they passed around. I noticed they were wearing powder on their faces."

The womenfolk were a part of the baseball scene, as they were admitted free on Wednesday afternoons. This proved a good strategy.

The ladies were credited with donating money to build a roof over the spectator stand.

In the 1914 Baldwin County Fair, he saw to it that baseball games were a part of the entertainment. Organizer Ort was active in starting the South Alabama Baseball League in the twenties, with teams from Brewton, Frisco City, Century, Atmore, and Bay Minette. He had quite a reputation as a hitter.

> For a letter writer [a reference to his business] he's a plumb good catcher. Seriously when it comes to all round filling in, we nominate the old Hoss. Ort Ertzinger's hitting was the feature and main factor in winning the game. He slammed out a single, doubled and hit a home run in three times at bat. In the 4th inning he hit the ball over the left field fence for a homer.

My little-girl baseball experience with my uncle has not been forgotten. One summer Mother had surgery for a sinus condition. (Uncle Ort kidded her about having everything taken out of her head except her tongue.) Because Mother couldn't take care of me that summer, I went to Bay Minette. Aunt Tillie and Eloise were in Indiana, so I stayed next door with Grandpa and Aunt Hattie.

The situation in my family must have been desperate for me to have to stay with them. Aunt Hattie, Grandpa's second wife, was a character. She had had two childless marriages before she became Mrs. Ertzinger. During the frequent summer thunderstorms she sat on a feather pillow and trembled. Her heart was made of gold, but her nerves were flaky. Children made her nervous. Nevertheless, I was there.

Sensitive to the explosive potential, Uncle Ort tried to help entertain us. He invited me to go with the baseball team to Frisco City. Can you imagine a man letting a ten- or eleven-year-old girl tag along amidst a flock of burly, tobacco-chewing baseball players? Later I bragged about the trip, going with all those handsome ball players.

We rode in a school bus to the town 60 miles away. The roads were dusty, and we bounced along together with bats, pads, balls, and all sorts of extra baseball gear. I remember more about the bus ride than I do about the game. I was a bit subdued and ill at ease in the situation, so I sort of clung to my uncle. As one of the few very young girls who ever went on such a baseball adventure, I considered my uncle very special indeed.

The year he made his one and only bid for elected office, 1934, he worked like a dog campaigning. But he did not give up baseball; he played regularly. In August, months after the campaign, while his wife and daughter were visiting relatives in Indiana, he wrote, "Played ball in Stockton in p.m., stayed to lead singing in revival at Presbyterian church at night."

The day after returning from a visit to Indiana the following summer, Uncle Ort wrote this terse note: "Hot baseball meeting, Bay Minette won penant, planned banquet." That was a big year for the South Alabama League (SAL). Uncle Ort was 44 years old and going strong.

In July 1935, the year Brewton left the league, the quarreling finally led to the break-up of the league.

Baseball injuries were about the same when Uncle Ort played as they are now. The summer of 1931 he noted several: a strained shoulder and neck and a collision at home plate. After catching four innings of a game with the reforestation boys from the C.C.C. camp, he broke the little finger of his right hand and was taken out of the game. In a few days, however, he was playing again. Gnarled fingers became a lifelong companion.

The topic of one keepsake was a bill introduced in the House of Representatives permitting Sunday baseball in Alabama. This legislation was significant to my uncle.

Burt Chamberlain, from Mobile, introduced the bill. "My people want it," he declared. "They go to far worse places than a baseball diamond on Sunday afternoon." Uncle Ort did not go along with Mr. Chamberlain's reasoning. To him Sunday was a special day set apart by God Almighty to worship Him and to do good deeds. The legislation passed, but Uncle Ort never played baseball on Sunday.

Judge Smith's son, Hamilton, a few years younger than Uncle Ort, was a great admirer. The day of Uncle Ort's funeral, Hamilton talked about my uncle and baseball.

Jimmy Archer of the Chicago Cubs offered Ort a contract as a catcher, the toughest and most dangerous position in baseball. Ort was a good batter, batted fourth, the cleanup position. He was a real slugger and a morale booster.

At one time he was the manager of the Bay Minette team. They had a pitcher who was good as long as he kept cool; Ort could settle him down. He'd call time out, talk with the pitcher, and get him to calm down and pitch. Nobody could do that as good as Ort. Ort had an ideal temperament for managing–he was always alert but cheerful. "Happy Warrior" they called him. He aimed to win.

In the twenties, new high schools were being built all over Alabama. High school athletic programs were in their infancy, and Uncle Ort's conviction that playing team sports was a good way to promote a healthy body and mind inspired him. The athletic field was on the other half of the block that Uncle Ort and Grandpa owned.

Uncle Ort kept up with what was going on with every high school sport. He coached basketball for both boys and girls, and he was general do-flunky. On many occasions, when some detail important to the game had been overlooked, Coach Dale called my uncle. Ofttimes an item needed to be picked up in Mobile–additional baseballs, special pads for the football tackle, a new net for the basketball court–you name it, my uncle fetched it, usually at his own expense.

Those were the days when driving to Mobile could be a bit uncertain. The only road was the U.S. 31 causeway, which was sometimes closed because of high waves and tides. Countless times he hurried to Mobile, in a race to beat the rising water, with the good of athletics foremost in his mind. He was a hero in the show-must-go-on tradition.

Umpiring high school baseball games enabled Uncle Ort to remain active after his playing days were over. Being a member of the school board and an umpire may have set precedent; both jobs were without pay. According to the April 6, 1937, Times:

> The *first* baseball game to be played on the home field was staged with Robertsdale. Umpires were Mr. Ort Ertzinger of Bay Minette

and Mr. Comstock from Robertsdale. Randall Arant and Robert Thompson were lead off batters for Bay Minette. The score, 2 to 1, Bay Minette.

One March he umpired a game and goofed.

Coach Dale's boys showed rare early season form. There was no question about the final result after the first few innings. A very unusual finish occurred when the "Old War Horse," Ort Ertzinger, who was behind the plate, missed one. A ball batted by one of the Mobile lads struck the plate and bounded to Becker who fielded it cleanly to first. The Mobile batter was called out–the third out. The game was over.

Ort, with his head gear down over his ears, failed to hear the impact of the ball on the plate. After a mild protest the Mobile players went to the showers.

Someone spoke to Ort and convinced him of his error. Ort tried to recall his decision, he ordered game play to finish. When told to go back to the playing field, the Mobile players were dumbfounded. In various stages of undress they did not want to go back to the field.

The Mobile coach, a sensable man, said "It's alright, there is no doubt about how the game would have ended anyway." The final score was 16 to 4. No blame was attached to Ort, it was an honest mistake. He is known as one of the squarest shooters that ever lived.

Football players could count on a loud and enthusiastic cheering squad when Uncle Ort was there. He led pep rallies and sometimes was a timekeeper. A multitude of Uncle Ort's activities created, for me, an image of a fabulously fantastic fellow.

Once he led the fans in new escapades in frivolity.

The Baldwin County High School eleven played a home game against Atmore last Friday. B.C.H.S. won 13-0.

The town boosters started their part of the game with a big Pep meeting on Court House Square Thursday night. They rehearsed songs and yells before a monster bonfire with fireworks and noise making devices. [Uncle Ort was big on noisemakers.]

At the game Health Officer Marlett gave the fans mimeographed copies of the song parodies he composed. The battle of the side-lines [was] waged merrily for hours with cheers and shouts.

A person unknown, but rumored to be Ort Ertzinger, President of the Bay Minette Manufacturing Company, provided a coffin, grave and headstone for the final ceremony of the afternoon. A black Ford touring car was commandeered as hearse, and immediately after the game members of the football team acted as honorary pall bearers.

Atmore refused an invitation to attend en masse, but one of their substitutes, overcome by curiosity and the cordial invitation, made his way into the crowd. He was promptly installed as chief mourner at the graveside. The audience doffed hats, a trumpeter blew taps on a cornet, and the ceremony ended. It was a mournful event for the losers.

No one was surprised by tomfoolery when my uncle was around.

When Atmore's turn to host the Baldwin Tigers came around, Uncle Ort was on hand. Twenty cars of Bay Minette people drove to Atmore to witness the football game. Twenty was many. Cars were fewer and roads narrower then. Excitement was in the air. The high pitch of the spectators reflected the rivalry.

Ort Ertzinger led the human contingent, and carried along a billy goat, the team's mascot. Ort led the Indian snake dance over the gridiron during half time to the edification of the crowd.

Can't you just imagine my fun-loving uncle "living it up" amid all the yelling, clapping fans? Chief Ort, dressed in colored feather headgear with the tail flapping as he hopped, skipped, and danced. His impressive six-foot-two-inch stature cavorted around leading the pep squad. He promised more of the same the next time, with their goat mascot attired in a finer costume. Bay Minette won 13 to 6.

A side note about football. Uncle Ort's mother never allowed him to play. He compensated by being a wholehearted spectator. Spirited competition and strong school support are a healthy mix for football fan fun.

Basketball, especially girls' basketball, had Uncle Ort's attention and time. The girls wore bloomers and traveled by train to out-of-town games. He had made and gave to the school a bronze plaque bearing the names of the girls' state basketball team of 1921. He had promised the team if they won he would do that.

Nothing about Uncle Ort's devotion to athletics is more compelling than the poem he wrote. In later years, Uncle Ort, a popular toastmaster, was often invited to do the honors at the annual Baldwin High Football Banquet, an event he relished.

The old Trammel Hotel was the place the thirty-five players attended the banquet. Following dinner the speakers complimented the team on their fine sportsmanship and hard playing. This had not been a winning year for Bay Minette. Coach Dale awarded sixteen football letters; then Ort Ertzinger read a poem he'd composed for the occasion.

> We are proud of the team of '31
> We're proud of you, one and all
> Proud of the boys who formed the line
> And those who carried the ball.
> We're proud of our team.

> We love you because you belong to us
> You stood every grueling test.
> We love you because of the grit you've shown
> Because you have done your best.
> We love our team.

> We praise you because you could take defeat
> Were modest in victory won.
> But you were always loyal and true.
> The team of the year '31.
> We praise our team.

Who wouldn't appreciate and find endearing a man who so openly expressed his appreciation for a losing team?

Uncle Ort played with the town baseball team until he was fifty years old. As his enjoyment of sports became more sedentary, there was radio sports news, then television. The first New Year's Rose Bowl game he heard on radio was special enough for mention in his diary. He was one more delighted fan when games first appeared on TV.

Baseball friendships continued long after playing days were over. One baseball chum became a Virginia state senator and lived on the James River. In 1956 Uncle Ort visited him and wrote of the pleasant afternoon they had together watching baseball on TV. On his last visit in Indiana, he drove to Chicago to see a major league baseball game.

Baldwin County High School alumni, in 1991, initiated an Athletic Hall of Fame. At the football half-time ceremony, David Lindsey, on behalf of the family, accepted a plaque that signified placing Ort Harmon Ertzinger's name in the Hall of Fame. One of the alumni gathered for the occasion remembered: "At football games Mr. Ort carried the big red umbrella when it rained. He had the measuring stick to check the yards gained or lost. He worked for all school sports–all."

Uncle Ort's award was for his enthusiasm, support, energy, and heart. His contribution was as a *supporter* of athletics. The other Hall of Famers, for the most part, are players recognized for their athletic prowess.

> The things he did for sports
> No one can recount to you.
> Were I to speak and tell them,
> They would be too many to declare.

11

Music, Music, Music

MUSIC WAS A STRONG TRANSLUCENT thread interwoven into the fabric of Uncle Ort's life. To be more explicit:

He whistled or hummed while he worked or did not work.

He yodeled.

He played the piano and organ.

He played wind instruments.

He sang solo and with others.

He pitched songs in a key everyone could sing.

There is a lot to tell about Uncle Ort's singing. His strong, clear tenor voice was the first thing many people remember about Ort Ertzinger. It was his "crown of glory." He sang with any combination of singers you can imagine–duets, trios, and both men's and mixed quartets. He sang in choirs, glee clubs, choruses, and concert groups. Perhaps more important, he sang at his work.

He led singing in Sunday School for a long, long time. Many Presbyterian gatherings automatically considered him the leader if there was any singing to be done. Music was his responsibility at the youth conferences in the summer.

I was fourteen, writing a theme for English, when I received this letter.

Bay Minette, Alabama
January 15, 1935

Dear Janice,

Singing always seemed the natural thing to do. Mama and Papa met at choir practice in a Lutheran church. Their good voices led to their courtship.

Mama sang all day long. I remember her singing lullabies to Florence. [No radios to intrude.] Papa had a deep base voice and our family sang as a quartet–Mama sang soprano, Florence alto, and I sang tenor. I grew up with a song in the air.

In response to your query, the course I took in school, called vocal music, was about the same as glee club. Mr. Brown, our director, taught me to sing tenor. A piano teacher in Huntington gave me the only private music lessons I ever had.

Singing brings joy to my heart. "I've got joy, joy, down in my heart, down in my heart, down in my heart to stay." You know the song? Hymns should be sung with spirit, not slowly or drug out like a funeral dirge. My pet peeve is with pianists who drag the music.

Soon after we moved south, a crowd of people I did not know gathered around when I played the piano in the hotel parlor. Someone explained I was a bit of a curiosity in Bay Minette–ladies were supposed to play the piano, not men.

Janice, how much do you practice the piano? I liked your teacher when I met her.

Your loving Uncle
Ort

His French horn was a part of Bay Minette's musical agenda from Day One. As the *Times* records,

> Ort Ertzinger and the Bay Minette boys made a name for themselves last week at the way their combo played. In the evening they entertained in the Rynd home with Ort at the piano, Charley Dieta the cornet, and Mr. Irwin as basso profundo. A delightful concert was rendered to an overflow audience.

Another observer during his bachelor days wrote:

Chief Ertzinger's little boy "Ought" trotted the gathering back to the old days. He sang for a special request, "Carry Me Back to Old Virginia." He met more than mediocre response, but again refused to get into the audience's web. He did not come back for an encore.

A lot of people thought only sissy boys played the piano, not athletes like Uncle Ort. Playing the piano charmed men; it was considered the ladylike thing to do. At first his playing was considered odd by people in Bay Minette, but in no time my uncle was recognized as a good pianist.

The first pipe organ in the community was installed in the Presbyterian church in 1925. Uncle Ort bought, gave, and learned to play this instrument. Good music in worship was important to him. The organ put Presbyterians on the musical leading edge. In a sinister way, 45 years later, this very organ, with the help of a mouse, was the vehicle by which the church moved forward.

That was the era when he and a young pianist, Esther Knudsen, had great fun with music in Bay Minette. She played and he directed the choral singing for special occasions such as Thanksgiving, Christmas, and Easter. They exchanged poetic thank-yous. Uncle Ort wrote:

> Miss Ester is our musician,
> She plays with greatest ease,
> Her fingers play fiercely
> Upon the ivory keys.
>
> She stomps upon the pedal,
> And makes the music ring.
> This helps our rotten leader
> To make the young folks sing.
>
> So surely we could never
> Succeed without this kid.
> She merits heavy praises,
> If any ever did.

Esther was not to be outdone. About a week later, he found a pretty pink envelope on his desk with this in it.

> Mr. Ort is our leader, and
> I mean he's quite the thing.
> If you don't believe me, brother,

Come out and hear him sing.

He stands upon the platform,
And waves his hands around,
The people, in spite of themselves,
Make the building ring with song.

Who says he's a rotten leader?
Why people, I tell you the truth
If it wasn't for our leader,
The people would indeed be mute.

Mutual admiration!

Uncle Ort was a drawing card for me at Christmastime. I happily left my school chums and festivities in my hometown to visit my Bay Minette relatives, partly because I wanted to go caroling with Uncle Ort. The *Times* announced who, where, and when:

> Mr. Ort H. Ertzinger, himself, has been made Chief Mogul of the Christmas Carol Singers.
>
> All the young people of town who want to sing carols, please meet at the Presbyterian Church, Friday night, December 24th, 1934 at 7 o'clock. Bring a flashlight with you.
>
> Those who want carols sung for them should place a lighted carol (not an electric light) in the front window. Carolers will come and sing for you. Any shut-ins wanting carols sung, please send word to Ort H. Ertzinger before Friday night.

Under my uncle's direction, caroling, an idea he brought to town, grew. All who wanted to sing blended their voices and hearts. Stay-at-home people looked forward to the happy faces and voices of the carolers led by Uncle Ort with his good-natured manner.

My jolly uncle led us from one lighted window to another. We trekked all over town on cold winter nights. Someone where we sang usually passed a plate of fruitcake, fudge, divinity, or some such holiday goodie as an expression of thanks.

The Mignon Music Club was one of the leading cultural groups in town. Ort Ertzinger was often the feature of their program. Among other Music Club activities was his role in *Carmen* circa 1952.

The Mobile Choral Society was invited to join the Mignon Music

Club of Bay Minette at the home of Mrs. J. D. Crosby. Uncle Ort was featured with other Bay Minette singers cast in the roles of Bizet's French opera. The title role was sung by Mrs. Embree Smith. Collins Cameron, the high school principal, sang Don Jos_. Uncle Ort sang the leading male role of Escamillo, the toreador. Jean Robertson and Alycia Cane were the two little gypsy girls.

When he sang the famous toreador song, he gave a musical portrait of a swaggering bullfighter. Whether or not he sang in costume, this was a great experience for my 48-year-old uncle with a self-trained voice. Some still remember his singing those powerful songs in which Escamillo, taken with Carmen the cigarette girl, quarrels with Don Jos_.

Uncle Ort was generous with his talent. From the private Palmetto Club near the train tracks where the young male quartet he organized first entertained to just about every church in Baldwin County, at some point in his life he sang or played almost everywhere. He encouraged others to use their talents and do the same.

Scrutinizing his notations about funerals made me aware of singing in celebrating the dead as much as the living. Although he and Aunt Tillie rode together to funerals, after they arrived they seldom sat together; he was always a participant in the service in one way or another. Often he sang, either a solo or a duet. Aunt Tillie, to my knowledge, never sang other than in the congregation.

On other occasions he was a pallbearer. Frequently he conducted the Masonic funeral service. Not only did he give the Masonic burial service from memory, but he was highly acclaimed for the elegant way he performed this ritual.

One day, a year or two after his heart attack, he told me that he'd given up singing solos at funerals. The reason was surprising. "The doctor advised me to avoid things that upset me. So, no more singing at funerals for me."

He was sensitive to musical talent wherever he found it. Encouraging young and old to develop their God-given ability was as natural for him as eating ice cream. Helping make available opportunities to grow was another challenge Uncle Ort faced. He was a prime mover in uniting residents who sponsored workshops and brought outstanding vocalists from Mobile. These educational affairs upgraded singers and singing.

He attended young students' musical recitals as an attentive listener. He consistently commended the children for their performance. You can imagine, for a man of Uncle Ort's nature, his delight in attending his grandchildren's recitals. (His granddaughter's dance recital was a first of its type.)

Among his keepsakes with a musical theme are programs from performances in which he participated–sacred concerts, Christmas pageants, musical teas, piano recitals, Easter cantatas–the types are varied. Scores on which he's penciled notations giving pointers on pauses, crescendos, fortissimos, etc., are precious.

Mementos of concerts he and Aunt Tillie attended are nostalgic. When Rubinoff gave a violin concert in Mobile on a Sunday afternoon in February of 1939, Uncle Ort and Aunt Tillie were there. They drove to New Orleans to hear the renowned All Girls' Orchestra. Grey Cane gave them those tickets. A Victor Borge performance in Mobile found him in the audience. They took Penelope and Jane along. Seldom did they go by themselves to an entertainment; they invited others to go along.

Hosting his grandchildren to musical entertainments was a deep-down pleasure for Uncle Ort. On December 31, 1957, the weather was freezing cold when he took his three grandchildren and their parents to see *Around the World in 80 Days*. Being together as a family on such occasions was his idea of family.

The years took their tool on the church building. The roof leaked, and the windows rattled. Mice ran freely about the place. One made its home in the pipe organ.

According to the sage Charlie Bodden, each Sunday morning after the hymns and anthem had been sung and the offertory played, it happened. Just when the minister got serious and into his sermon, a little grey mouse came out to play. Right there in front of God and the congregation, he ran out from the dark recesses of the instrument into the bright light of the church. The venturesome little creature scurried round and about.

The organ was located behind the pulpit. The preacher was in the dark about what was happening behind him. The way Charlie tells it, this four-legged animal was keen competition for the minister. Many laughs were stifled, but the parishioners' attention was with the mouse, not the minister.

Furthermore, the mouse was known to take part in the service. Those who were attuned to it could hear. The voice was not strong, but the high-pitched squeaks could be heard if not seen.

As one thing leads to another, that little grey mouse had a part in the building of a new church. the mouse, it could be said, yielded the winning vote to construct a new building. But that story comes later.

Uncle Ort's ear for music was fine-tuned. His ear was not limited to people's voices and instruments; the sounds in the woods and swamps had their own music that also attracted him.

12

A *Special Place* in His Heart

BACK IN INDIANA, Grandpa and Uncle Levi had taught a lively little boy to fish, and that let loose something in Ort Ertzinger that was never contained.

He first wet his hook in the waters of the Wabash River, his last in Winona Lake, Indiana. In between were thousands of times when he baited his hook to catch a fish. Never, never did he fish on Sunday.

During the icy wintertime and long, hot summer days, even when he was up to his neck in work or vacationing in Wisconsin, he made time to go fishing. In fact, the main reason he was in the cheese state was to fish. Fishing was a sport and more to him. Fishing had a special place in his heart. This smattering of his fishing jaunts in one year will give you an idea:

January: To Orange Beach, no luck with sheephead, got three sacks of oysters [if one thing did not work out, he had an alternative].

May: ...cat fishing with George Page and John McLeod [boys from the church group] up on the fresh water lakes_

June: Crappies and bluegills biting good, water low–no rain.

July: Up at 3:30 a.m. to Bon Secour white trout fishing with Buster, John Alfred and Roland. Nice string. To Prayer meeting at night.

August: Took Rev. Cook to Orange Beach floundering.

September: Fishing at Hollinger with Baptist Revival preacher and Rev. Cook–37 fine ones. Rev. Cook [the Presbyterian minister] here for fish supper tonight.

October: Orange Beach for speckled trout–did not get a bite.

He seldom fished alone. To Uncle Ort, fishing was a kind of mixer–a way of getting to know a person. Fishing and friendliness were twins. He could do his favorite thing and fraternize simultaneously, good stewardship of his time. For common-sense reasons, a fishing buddy, most often his wife, went with him. He assumed everyone he invited to go fishing would like to do so.

Owl Creek, the spot where Uncle Ort's fresh-water floating camp was located, was the focal point for his fresh-water fishing pleasure. The camp was built on a raft so it floated, rising and falling with the tide of that brackish water. It was a neat outdoorsy arrangement open to anyone who wanted to use it–no lock or keys. He inlaid a portion of the camp's floor with brick to provide a place for building fires and cooking.

The game warden, a trusted friend, checked on the floating camp from time to time to be sure everything was okay. Uncle Ort was glad for woodsmen to use the camp provided they took care of it. That was not always the case.

One winter's day Uncle Ort was out squirrel hunting and fishing (he often shot squirrels from his boat) when he stopped at the camp to stretch his legs. The cabin had been desecrated. Instead of lighting a fire on the bricks, the culprits had built a fire on the pilings that formed the floor, using wood they had chopped out of the thick camp floor. The mess was unbelievable and deplorable. This was sacrilegious!

The wanton disregard for his camp so infuriated Uncle Ort that he went directly to Warren Taylor, the game warden. Taylor immediate started the hunt for the perpetrators.

When the word got out that the warden was on their trail, the offenders went ape and burned down the camp. This calamity really disgusted Uncle Ort. Several weeks passed before he had the heart to go and see the damage for himself.

A few days after a festive Valentine's party in their home, Uncle Ort mustered the courage and went to see what was left of his cabin. His fishing buddy Andrew Martin went along.

The rising and falling of the clear brackish waters of the Tensaw River was unchanged as they rowed toward the burned-down camp. Uncle Ort and I agreed there was a sense of the everlasting and quieting in the swamp environment of the river.

The ambiance of the woods we loved so dearly must have helped quell his anger and reinstill in him the desire to rebuilt. Nothing of the camp was left above the waterline. They found the submerged part of the raft with black, charred places amid the surrounding woodlands in undisturbed cypress swamp. That afternoon, he and Andrew made a plan to rebuild.

The burning took place in January 1930, when money was hard to come by. The aftereffects of the market crash on Wall Street a few months earlier had shattered the economy. He and Andrew rebuilt the camp themselves. In February they worked underwater, removing charred timbers from the old raft. The first day of March they moved the raft to a new place in the creek.

Once or twice a week, Uncle Ort took off from the office and went to work on the camp. This was no ordinary construction job. He picked up Andy, loaded the building materials in the black Ford, and drove to Kilcrease landing. At the landing, all this stuff had to be unloaded and put into Uncle Ort's long, narrow boat for the five-mile trip through the root- and alligator-infested streams to the campsite.

In March the camp began to take form; by May they had finished what Uncle Ort called the sleeping porch. It was a place with two bunk beds–sleeping space for four–enclosed with screen wire. A few days later he took Aunt Tillie to see the new camp: "Tide too high to fish, but we stayed all night."

The new camp was an entertainment center. He had parties for his friends and relatives from far and wide. Church youth groups went to this extraordinary place for an Ortish-style bash. On one such outing eight girls, a boat full, went along for the day.

Uncle Ort rigged up a pole for each person and dug plenty of worms from his own bait bed in advance. The fishing tackle box, with all kinds of hooks, sinkers, floats, pliers, and first aid supplies, was first in the boat for their five-mile journey through the dark waters to the camp. Aunt Tillie stayed aboard the raft camp with the girls and fished while Uncle Ort came back to the landing to get the lunch and cooking utensils. The boat was not large enough to carry all this in one trip. Uncle Ort's special box of food supplies for his hideaway included two mystery cans.

Amid the flour, pans, and salt the box contained these two cans without labels. No one knew what they contained. The day no one caught any fish the mystery would be revealed. On that tragic day the campers would eat the contents of those simple, unmarked tins. The aura and anguish of the unknown radiated from this Ortish arrangement.

You can be sure that after he took the girls to his floating camp, the boys expected equal treatment. Young people, most of them, considered it a treat to go to the floating camp. Most thought going anywhere with Uncle Ort and Aunt Tillie was fun because they were entertaining people. A few youngsters, I know now, went along even though they were squeamish about being in a boat surrounded by wild things.

The enchantment of the wilds around the camp did not appeal to everyone as it did to Uncle Ort and me. As his true disciple I thought every sane person in the whole wide world would want to go fishing in this most beguiling place. His widowed mother-in-law, now in her seventies, happily went along. Visitors, friends and relatives from faraway places, came anticipating fishing in the Southern jungle.

The exception that proves the rule were my cousins, Carolyn and Paul. They did not feel too ecstatic about "roughing it." The whole truth came out when I began writing this story. Paul Ertzinger explained.

> I visited Ort's Owl Creek floating camp on two occasions. The first time was early in the 30's as a college student, then later when my son was about six. This was truly an experience. The first time

going fishing with Ort was strikingly different than any fishing I'd ever done.

Prior to my college days, I'd only caught sun fish in the small clean creeks which ran through my father's farm. That was the only fishing I knew anything about. I was so startled by all the wild life–snakes, alligators, bugs, lizards, etc. I didn't remember much about the fishing.

I was very glad he did not ask me to spend the night in the swamp even though the camp was screened in. There was as much wild life inside the screens as there was outside. [As usual, Uncle Ort recorded the count in his diary: twenty-three fish were caught on that 1935 fishing expedition.]

The second visit was about 1949. Ort took my son and me out to his camp. Dick, too, was dumbfounded with all the wild life and the boat ride dodging alligators. Ort invited my wife, Carolyn, to visit his floating camp. She flatly refused.

Ort told her she was the first person ever to refuse his invitation to the camp. She thought she had offended him, at the time, but he soon got over it. It never interfered with their relationship. Carolyn enjoyed her visit in his home, she prefers to remember the many beautiful Japonica flowers from their yard. He made corsages from them for her.

Paul's confession makes me wonder how others may have felt. The evangelists, for instance–how did they feel about going fishing at Owl Creek? Uncle Ort led the singing at many revival meetings conducted by visiting ministers. So it was not unusual for him to invite these preachers to fish with him–his form of hospitality. They often went. From time to time his own pastor and the Methodist and Baptist ministers in town fished with him. Did they fish with him more out of respect for him than from their desire to bait a hook? In a blind sort of way, whatever Uncle Ort liked–fishing, frogging, music, swimming–I thought everyone else liked, too.

Eloise did not go along with all her father's interests in the same way I did. She vividly remembers some hairy experiences she had. In the summer the creeks and streams where we fished in the daytime became a haven for froggers at night. She describes an occasion on a dark night in August in the swamp–"the worst night of my life."

Daddy wanted to go frogging. None of his buddies could go that night, so Mother and I went. The narrow boat was not much wider than we were. Daddy was in the back paddling, Mother in the front; I was in the middle. The edge of the boat was just a few inches above the water. We had to go very close to the bank to get to where the frogs were croaking. It was pitch-black dark; the water was full of logs and limbs.

Sometimes the boat got stuck on a log and it tipped, letting in water. I could look out in the dark and see these bright things–the eyes of an alligator–glaring at me. The spotlight aimed toward the shore spotted the frogs.

This was the night Daddy was going to teach Mother how to gig the bullfrogs herself. [Aunt Tillie baited her own hook, whether with worms, caterpillars, or shrimp. She was a real sport.]

Daddy was sitting in the back guiding the boat as he paddled through the dark debris. Up in the front end Mother was holding the spotlight in one hand and the three-pronged spear gig in the other.

The frogs were blinded by the light she pointed toward them. She was then supposed to stick the gig in. Then she had to lay the spotlight down, pick up the frog with her hands, and put the creature in the boat. Can you imagine doing all that with just two hands?

One frog almost scared me to death! When Mother reached down to pick up the lamp, the frog made a loud sound–whff, whff. My heart was in my throat. Another time, one of them got away and jumped in the boat and hopped past me and out the back of the boat. And those were big frogs–the size of both your hands, at least.

Mother couldn't handle everything the way Daddy thought she should. They had quite a round. I was in the middle of the boat and of the argument. I guess that was good–I separated them.

In listening to Eloise, I came to the conclusion that as the altercation grew in intensity, so did Eloise's fears. She thought her pounding heart was going to jump out of her body. The boat rocked, numerous eyes glared from the dark–a situation of danger and fright. I doubt that Uncle Ort was aware of his daughter's feelings, he was so intense in his own. Aunt Tillie was in the same predicament. That left Eloise to her own fears.

My aunt was a wonderful, companionable wife. She did things some men's wives simply would not think of doing. She went hunting and fishing and found interest in what he wanted to do. I doubt Uncle Ort let their frogging quarrel disrupt their relationship for long.

He cleaned the frogs, but she cooked them, which was sometimes hazardous. The legs almost jumped out of the pan; nerves in the frog's muscles contract when fried, so cooking them was no ordinary job. Eloise went on to talk about her father:

> A few times when Mother was quite sick, I would be at home alone with her. I remember a time or two when he left us to go fishing. He said it helped him to get away from the pressures of his business. Going fishing seemed to ease his restlessness, give him peace of mind or something.

In 1934, immediately after Uncle Ort's unsuccessful run for county tax assessor, he went to his floating cabin for a week. Spending a week amidst nature and with a fishing pole was the best way for him to lick his wounds.

Though fishing was like a charm to my rich uncle, I think almost as scintillating was the experience of telling stories about his adventures.

> Last summer at my floating camp I constructed a "live box" in which to keep fish alive until I wanted to have them cooked. This "live box" was surrounded with two-inch mesh chicken wire.
>
> In the morning I had taken a two-pound catfish off the trot line and after breaking off the dangerous horns placed the fish in this live box. Later on, after returning from the morning fishing, I put more fish in this box, five goggle-eye and several other bream.
>
> During the afternoon I pulled up the box to see how they were getting along and found a large moccasin. This snake made a number of attempts to crawl through the mesh and get out of the box. He drove his body through the mesh up to the hump in his body. That snake had eaten the catfish and several of the bream, which distended his body to such an extent he could not get out. That hump in his body was the two-pound catfish.
>
> With a rifle I killed the snake and threw him into the water. Hardly had he struck the water when a huge gar struck him and made off with moccasin, catfish, bream and all.

You can laugh this one off if you want to; but I invite other fishermen and hunters to tell their odd experiences. It will make good reading for the lovers of outdoors.

Clippings among his keepsakes attest to Uncle Ort's unusual hobby as a shooter of snakes. In 1938, a journalist remarked about Ort Ertzinger, the *Press Register's* demon correspondent. The occasion was the dedication of the brand-new United States Post Office.

Bay Minette has wanted this post office a long time. It is a fine looking building. Then I said, "Ort here you are, a leading citizen on hand in your best bib and tucker. Where would you be, if you weren't at this dedication?"

"I would," said Ort, and a far-away look came into his eyes, "be snake shooting. I would rather hunt snakes than eat."

"Do tell," we said. "And do you ever get any snakes?"

"I've killed 386 moccasins since the high water started."

Now, if most of you had told us this we would not believe it. We would just walk away shaking our head. But when Ort Ertzinger says he shot 386 water moccasins, we know it is so. For he is a sterling character, a faithful church goer, 29 years a truthful reporter for these newspapers, and not addicted to corn likker.

Ort explains he just gets in his rowboat and drifts down the river with his trusty rifle and a box of shells and the snakes just naturally come around to be shot. Sometimes "Chief," his father, goes along. Now and then, just for fun, he lays the gun aside and wangs a snake with an oar.

Ort's wife also seems to have a knack for snake annihilation. Ort reports, "the day she goes out with me there is a good slaying."

A year or so later my uncle was still killing snakes.

Ort Ertzinger loves to fish. He can kill snakes as well. He reports killing 492 snakes during the high water. Figure that out for yourself. If each snake ate one fish a week that means 492 more fish are alive because the snake did not eat them. Another way to think of it, if the snakes had lived there would have been 492 less fish to catch so in fifty-two weeks, a decrease of 25,584 fish. Wow!

Uncle Ort started shooting snakes to protect fish, found fun and pleasure in killing the deadly creatures, so he invited select friends to go along on these unusual snake-shooting expeditions. My young brother, Jack, felt like a man when Uncle Ort took him to shoot snakes in the swamp.

Even those who found snake hunting downright distasteful had to admit that it caused a bit of a stir amid the usual humdrum and heat of the summer. The editor of the *Times*, Jimmy Faulkner, expressed it this way.

> We still don't believe snake killing is such a hot pastime. The only person we've run across that is envious of Ort is W. O. (Billy) Lott. He has been stopping us on the street daily to ask for the latest on the Tensaw snake shoot.

Protecting fish from their predators was the focus for sportsmen who did not take to snake shooting. On June 1, 1939, Pat Moulton, sports editor of the Mobile Press, put forth an idea about the conservation of fish. He thought some means should be taken to provide a bounty on alligator gar. An alligator gar, a fish with a large snout, resembling an alligator, lives in brackish water. These strange-looking fish, like snakes, prey on bream and trout.

Thus began an attempt to protect fish. It was called the Gar War. The war raged for years in newsprint and swamp streams. An awful lot of gars were killed. Makes one wonder what fishing would be like in these parts today if man had not intervened to save the fish and destroy their predator.

Pat Moulton was encouraged by the response in the Mobile area to his idea for putting a bounty on alligator gar. Later Pat suggested that Mobile legislators sponsor a bill to add twenty-three cents to the cost of rod-and-reel fishing licenses in order to provide money for a bounty.

> The proposal was quickly picked up by the *Baldwin Times* editor:
> The Baldwin County delegation should make a copy of the bill, or draw one themselves, and put it through the summer term of legislature. Baldwin, like Mobile, attracts many of its tourists because fishing is a favorite sport. Anything we can do to improve our fishing grounds will be to our advantage.

Sportsman Ort Ertzinger proposes a gar rodeo. It should be an easy task to raise $50.00 from fishermen in the county, then offer the money in two or three cash prizes to persons who kill the most gar in a given time. (The Mobile movement is bearing fruit. Mobile fishermen are sending in money to carry on the war.)

Ort will keep the records and pay 25 cents for every gar brought to his office, perhaps sufficient money can be raised. Mr. Ertzinger starts the contribution with $5.00. The *Times* editor adds $2.00. All fishermen and sportsmen who wish to see the gar eradicated from the county fishing streams are asked to make contributions to the fund. Send them to Mr. Ertzinger or to the *Times* All persons catching gars, bring them to Mr. Ertzinger and collect your 25 cents bounty for each gar killed. All donations will be acknowledged in the *Baldwin Times*

An August editorial commended Ort Ertzinger, secretary of the Baldwin County Hunting club, for his effort in the gar war. But the response of the Baldwin County sportsmen was not as expected. The editor wrote:

About the only thing Ort Ertzinger has to show for his time and effort in trying to help kill gars in fishing streams around Bay Minette is disappointment.

Mr. Ertzinger offered his cooperation in fighting the gars. He has worked hard to get the campaign under way, but hardly anyone has donated to the fun. Why shouldn't you contribute? You are the one who will benefit. If wholehearted cooperation were given there would be better fishing this fall.

Mr. Ertzinger comes up with a plan. It is impossible for him to do it alone. How about it Mr. Angler? If every sportsman in Baldwin County would work and back Mr. Ertzinger we would soon be rid of most of the gars.

Uncle Ort did not give up. Many sportsmen rallied to support the fund. Uncle Ort kept accurate records of persons, their contributions, the number of gars caught, and the money awarded. To this day, you may read the statistical details of this war.

Of the many ways Uncle Ort fished, the most bizarre was in salt water when we went floundering. Many of us do a lot of "floundering around" in our lives but nothing like floundering with Uncle Ort. We waded in the shallow water at night with a long, sharp gig in hand and floundered by stabbing fish.

We used a light to see down into the water as we waded looking for these flat fish with eyes on only one side of their bodies. Eventually he carried a battery-powered light, before that an Aladdin kerosene torch light. Farther back, a flaming orange pine lighter knot supplied light in the darkness. The aroma of that burning wood full of rich rosin was pleasant, and we hoped it would curb the mosquitoes. The eerie sound of our voices over the water, in the composure of the night, is like a haunting refrain in my head.

To gig fish, the conditions had to be just right–clear water, waves calm enough to let us see the flat fish dug into the sand, and a little, but not too much, wind to keep the mosquitoes off. More than once Uncle Ort yelled to me, "Stop, you are about to step on that flounder." I looked where he was pointing on the sandy bottom. The ripples in the sand imitated the ripples in the water and to my eyes obscured what was underneath. Only after his warning could I make out the outline of part of the flounder dug into the sand. A jab with the spear by the strong arm of my uncle secured the fish. He gleefully picked it from the sand and put it in the bucket one member of the party carried.

Like the smile of a winner, his facial expression assured his companions that he was having fun when he caught a fish. Mainly he kept his fishing simple, but he liked fishing in various places for all kinds of fish.

Judge John Voelker, a former member of the Michigan Supreme Court, is also a nationally known author. He wrote *Anatomy of a Murder*. Everyday in trout season the now-retired judge fishes. Uncle Ort's attitude was identical to his:

> I fish because I love to. Because I love the environs where the fish are found, which are invariably beautiful. Because in a world where most men seem to spend their lives doing what they hate my fishing is at once an endless source of delight. Because only in the out-of-doors can I find solitude without loneliness. And finally I suspect that so many of the other concerns of men are important and not nearly so much fun.

13

Reaching Out

NOT IN A MILLION YEARS would anyone suspect the treasure contained in a tattered notebook with tarnished gold lettering on the cover: BAY MINETTE VENEER & HAMPER CO., INC. Opening the book, I noticed the the rusted two-ring binding that held the paper. The book Eloise handed me contained an assortment of information Uncle Ort had clipped and saved.

I pointed to the name on the cover. "That was the name of the factory he and Grandpa owned, wasn't it?" Eloise nodded.

The contents of the notebook, however, were not related to the hamper company; the disreputable-looking binder was Uncle Ort's coveted "vanity book." His reuse of the notebook for this purpose is typical of his thrift. This collection is chock-full of clippings and letters. His spirits were lifted by people's thank-yous and kind remarks, so he saved them. On the cover page he explained:

Dear Reader,

Occasionally I have a thought that seems to me worth-while and I proceed to put it in writing. I may get old some day, when these thoughts will cause me much amusement. If I don't save them, no one else will and so this book is where I am proving my vanity by compiling products of what little brain I have.

Other things that please my vanity appear from time to time and I always take great delight in applying the scissors or my pocket knife and making a clipping for this book. These, too, will be placed on the succeeding pages for my further amusement.

You are welcome, dear reader, to your own opinion as to the value of any of the contents of this book. But for goodness sake, don't take anything out of it! I can't afford to have my vanity injured by having any of its collection disappear.

Ort H. Ertzinger

One of the letters Uncle Ort had saved was mysteriously signed "The Lady," and suddenly, as I read it for the umpteenth time, it began to make sense as I recognized Mrs. Rothermel's handwriting.

Uncle Ort had few secrets. His wife knew all about his lady friends. Uncle Ort introduced me to Mrs. Rothermel, unabashedly claiming that she was his sweetheart. My visits to this unusual Donna de Casa came at an impressionable time in my life, so they left their mark on me. Those were Depression years, too.

Mrs. Rothermel and her husband lived together with grown son and daughter, but theirs was not a typical family. Mrs. Rothermel got around her house in a homemade wheelchair. Her husband, now a frail, sickly man, had at one time earned a living as a carpenter. Their son Leon, in his thirties, was retarded and could not take care of himself. Mildred, their daughter, taught in elementary school. Even as a child I knew that it was Mrs. Rothermel, a diminutive white-haired lady with a strong, resolute voice, who kept the family together.

Uncle Ort was then the advisor for the Presbyterian Youth. After the young people's meeting each Sunday night, the Ertzinger three took supper to the Rothermels' home, where the two families ate together. Sunday suppers at the Rothermels' were a regular part of the lives of Uncle Ort, Aunt Tillie, and Eloise. Occasionally I went along. It is difficult to put my finger on exactly what, but there was something extraordinary in our meals together. The Rothermel story exemplifies Uncle Ort's characteristic behavior.

One particular cold Sunday night in January stands out. I recall driving over the railroad track on the south side of Bay Minette. Eloise and I, youngsters in school, giggled as we rode over the bumpy streets.

"Mildred has the light on for us." Uncle Ort pointed with one finger of his right hand to the house where the Rothermels lived. When she saw us drive up, Mildred opened the front door and came out to welcome us.

"May I help bring anything in?" Mildred cordially offered as we opened the car doors to get out.

"We have everything, thanks," Aunt Tillie replied as each of us took a container of food and got out of the car.

"You remember Janice?" Uncle Ort asked, gesturing toward me. Mildred gave me a warm smile and held the door open as I walked past carrying Aunt Tillie's fresh-baked coconut cake. I followed Aunt Tillie, who went directly to the kitchen. The Rothermels' home was simple and cozy.

The dining room table was set with a fresh white cloth; a place was laid for each of us. Leon's place had a bib. When Aunt Tillie's stew had been warmed on the kerosene stove, we all sat down. Uncle Ort said the blessing. Then we ate. No one paid attention to the fact that Leon's food did not go in his mouth. He ate the best he could' someone cleaned him up afterward.

Table talk was lively. Uncle Ort told jokes and a story or two–just the right ones to make everyone laugh. He had a way of getting people to laugh. He was genuinely interested in hearing what the Rothermels had to say. No insincerity, no "making conversation" just to be polite; this was a real exchange of news and views between people who cared about each other. Supper was a pleasant, easy time.

After we ate, the leftover food was put away for another time. The younger women did the dishes amid newsy chit-chat while Uncle Ort rolled Mrs. Rothermel into the living room, then helped Leon get situated. Eventually we all sat down there together. Then it was time to read the Bible.

This particular night Mrs. Rothermel read Psalm 19:1: "The heavens declare the glory of God; and the firmament sheweth his handywork. Day unto day uttereth speech, and night unto night sheweth knowledge. There is no speech nor language, where their voice is not heard...." Mrs. Rothermel was supported by the wonder and hope she found in the Bible.

Uncle Ort was turned on by Mrs. Rothermel's cheeriness. Mrs. Rothermel was physically crippled and mentally alert, while Uncle Ort was energetic and tuned to see another's inner beauty and character. "She never complains about anything. She finds sunshine in life in spite of her built-in problems."

That evening God's grace shining brilliantly through the lives of those two people ricocheted and touched us all. Sharing a meal in the humble home of a shut-in was a distinctive experience.

All the Rothermels looked up to Uncle Ort. He and his family were the shining stars in their lives. Undoubtedly Uncle Ort's loving acceptance of each member of the Rothermel family was inspired by divine love. His actions triggered the way Mrs. Rothermel opened up her heart to Uncle Ort. These two people had a common optimistic quality. Both wrote poetry.

I was reminded of all these things as I reread the letter in which Mrs. Rothermel poured out her soul.

> Dear Ort,
>
> I know you have lots to worry you, but your shoulders are *so broad* and your heart is *so big*. I am going to take advantage of it and say some things I cannot say on Sunday night.
>
> I just want to be on the safe side, not that I am borrowing trouble, but I could drop off. Others might beat me to it or I might have a stroke, or my vocal cords become affected. (Wouldn't that be awful?) But I feel you are more of a son than my own boys and I want you to still have a brotherly oversight over Mildred if anything came of me.
>
> The Lady

The major problem within that small family, another keepsake revealed, was caused by Mr. Rothermel's drinking problem. My uncle's compassion for the beleaguered family took more courage then perhaps than it would now. In those days the church and society ostracized alcoholics.

It was the old man who died first. Uncle Ort visited him several times that week. Dr. McLeod did, too. Uncle Ort bought medicine for him at Stacey's Drug Store, but the old man continued to weaken. Then he quietly passed away.

Mr. Rothermel prized his tool chest, so it was with high regard that Mrs. Rothermel gave it to my uncle. Uncle Ort put the tools to work and finished Mrs. Rothermel's kitchen cabinets, a job her husband had begun.

At the request of the Rothermels, Uncle Ort arranged for Leon to go to the County Home, then took him there. But he did not forget Leon, nor did Leon forget Uncle Ort. The church young people, under Uncle Ort's leadership, visited the home regularly to talk, sing, and have devotional programs for all the residents, with a focus of attention on Leon.

During the years the two Rothermel women lived alone, the Ertzingers continued their Sunday night suppers. By now the church had a full-time minister and an evening preaching service after the young people met. The ladies were interested in his weekly update. Uncle Ort kept an attendance record, which revealed that there were often more at the young people's meeting than at the service.

After her husband died, Mrs. Rothermel (I have never known her first name) wrote this poem:

> Who is it comes to us Sunday night?
> And makes the evening so cheery and bright?
> Who helps one to learn more of God above?
> Whose hearts are filled with kindness and love?
> Who brings sunshine to the weary heart?
> Who does to others their loyalness impart?
>
> THE ERTZINGERS
>
> Oh! how one feels when they have a friend,
> On whom they know they can always depend.

One day in 1934 Uncle Ort wrote, "Mrs. Rothermel is sick." He visited her often in spite of his extra-busy schedule as a candidate for the tax assessor's office. The day she passed away Uncle Ort wrote, "Up at 3 a.m. to meet Fisher Rothermel." Her son Fisher, a newspaper reporter, had arrived on the bus from his home in Birmingham just a few hours before his mother died.

The lessons I learned, the tremendous enjoyment that came from simple kindness, set a framework for me. Uncle Ort took time to care, to look beyond outward appearances, to catch hold of the true spirit and heart of his friends. His example left me with a valuable inheritance, one more precious than gold.

* * * * * * * *

Also among the contents of Uncle Ort's vanity book is a letter, written in pencil, from a twelve-year-old boy, Willard Dahlberg. His father, a dentist, had helped build the tennis courts. Dr. Dahlberg was also a famous turkey caller and a hunting friend of Uncle Ort's. Willard almost died once when his appendix ruptured. Uncle Ort drove over the Cochrane Bridge to visit him at the old Mobile Infirmary. The three-year-old bridge was still new in the minds of many. There were fewer cars, so the drive to Mobile was not as casual as it is today.

Willard appreciated the visit. Uncle Ort let him know that he was missed by his chums back home. From the hospital Willard wrote:

Mobile, Alabama
January 20, 1930

Dear Mr. Ort,

I [am] having a better time than going fishing. I have gotten three boxes of candy, and three boxes of flowers. They have dressed my side three times. They have taken the tube out of me and put a piece of gause in my side. They let me have some meat today.

Your friend,
Willard

Claudia Dahlberg, Willard's mother, had added, "You see Willard's idea of the hospital is anything but gloomy. Good of you to come see my boy."

From another vein came a memento of Uncle Ort's kind consideration for others. Walter Shepard held an administrative office in the hierarchy of the Presbyterian Church, U.S. After his young son died, Walter wrote this letter while traveling on the Southern Alabama Division Train No. 1, June 27, 1931:

Dear Ort,

Your fine letter and the resolutions from your young people sure help us. We are grateful to you.

God has never been more beautifully revealed to us. And hard as is our loss, we bow in humility and gratitude to Him. It is wonderful to think of having such a life for nearly nineteen years and his returning to God so clean.

My last physical contact with Frank was to place over his heart the Christian Endeavor pin I have worn over mine for many years. It will rust and decay, but our fine fellowship and service "for Christ and the church" will go on forever.

Love to all
Walter S.

An unexpected pleasure was mine when I found a note written by my namesake, Mrs. Warrene Anderson. I never met this lady, but she had many qualities my parents hoped I would emulate. The letter was written from Mobile on her personal stationery and with impeccable penmanship.

June 16, 1930

My dear Ort,

I have been thinking about you a great deal this afternoon, and your beautiful goodness–putting up that board for Mrs. Jones and me.

As I lay on the bed near four o'clock going over it all in my memory, I said to myself, Ort is the only person I know in the world who would have taken that trouble for two old ladies, and I have never been grateful enough to acknowledge it.

Do you remember how indignant I was when Mike told us what Jesse called us? I have forgiven Jesse for that blunder.

I hope you have completely recovered from your trouble. If you and your wife would come down some day and take lunch with Judge

Anderson and me you would make us very happy.

With love for dear Mrs. Ertzinger, Eloise, and your father and his wife–and your dear self.

I am most affectionately yours,

W. W. Anderson

I chuckled to myself as I tried to figure out what she meant by "putting up that board for Mrs. Jones and me." Maybe Uncle Ort accommodated them by laying a board so as to prevent the ladies from getting their feet wet in the water standing in the churchyard. Whatever he did, you get the picture. He was a man who did thoughtful things for others in an unpretentious way.

The kindness phenomenon characteristic of my uncle is described by my late friend Howard Thurman: "Nothing is more searching in its exhilaration than the experience of meeting the need of another." My uncle, a person of goodness and perpetual enthusiasm, was energized and recharged by his own deeds.

Uncle Ort's approach to people was described by his grandson David like this: "He treated everybody alike–rich or poor, young or old."

Insignificant incidents influence. During my grammar school days, Aunt Tillie had a white cleaning lady. Employing a cleaning person with white skin was strange to the world I knew. Furthermore, this person ate at the table with us. I was accustomed to black maids who ate after we did, never at the table with us.

In my uncle's home, their maid sat and ate at the table with us, but she was treated like anyone else and included in the table conversation. This made an impression on me. I remember going home and sitting down with our maid, who was eating in the kitchen after the big table had been cleared. Immediately I was told, "Don't bother Zettie; go on about your business."

But I did not forget the way it was at Uncle Ort's house. I thought about it. Why should a person in one's hire be treated as though she were not quite on the same plane as the employer? This question still rolls around and perplexes me.

The same respect was given the Durgins, both Susie and her husband, Joe, the African-Americans who worked for the Ertzingers. They never felt comfortable eating with us and preferred to eat later. Susie loved and respected the Ertzingers. She told me herself that Uncle Ort provided security for her family; she could depend on him. If for some reason she needed a loan or advice about financial matters, Uncle Ort was there to help.

Susie often went to the cottage at Orange Beach in the spring to clean the place for the summer. On one such occasion, Uncle Ort found out that she wanted to go fishing in the bay, so he took her. "Susie's first time bay fishing," he recorded. The relationship of the Ertzingers and the Durgins was one of respect and loyalty. Like many other Southerners, the Ertzingers provided a safety net for their trusted servants not as a legal obligation but as a matter of the heart. In a very Southern way Susie was a part of Uncle Ort's family. This relationship is continued today through Eloise and Walter and Susie's grandson, who recently graduated from Auburn University.

As I contemplate why my attitudes about race and bigotry are so different from those of many I know, why I am considered by some a liberal white, I come back to the seed planted at Uncle Ort's table and nurtured unobtrusively.

There seems to be no end to the ways Uncle Ort was a friend to man...and to women also. He reached out and touched someone in more ways than by telephone.

14

The Automobile

UNCLE ORT WAS A SUPERMAN behind the wheel of an automobile. Through rainstorms, mud, snow, and ice he drove over roads others found impossible. He had flat tires, hot radiators, and just plain car trouble but took them in stride: all was a part of driving your own automobile.

The horseless carriage and the development of streets and roads brought something rich and wonderful into Uncle Ort's world. The automobile was perhaps the biggest change agent in his life. Henry Ford and his assembly line changed many things, with Uncle Ort in the middle of it all, having a ball.

In 1908, Senator Bankhead's platform focused on road building. Most of the highways were unpaved and uncomfortable, with few bridges. Overland stagecoaches traveled the ferries and dirt road routes that connected towns and cities.

When Grandpa and Uncle Ort first came from Huntington to Bay Minette in 1908, the silver ribbon of rails was by far the most expedient way to travel. The following year Uncle Ort established his business, J. A. Ertzinger & Son. Newspaper advertisements at that time printed schedules for the hack line that left Bay Minette every day at 1:30 p.m. heading north to connect with the Mt. Pleasant hack in Montgomery.

One of Uncle Ort's first enterprises, a dray business, was short-lived. About that time the Model T assembly-line car brought on a revolution in the transportation system. My uncle was quick to see that there was no future in horse-powered transportation.

Ten years later when Uncle Ort drove his wife and daughter to Huntington in their own car, he made a family record in travel.

I'm not certain when Uncle Ort first bought a car. Buying a car was a news-making event during the first few decades of the twentieth century. As we have seen, the delivery of a Ford Uncle Ort had ordered was reported in the "Personal and General" column of the Baldwin Times. A Ford was Uncle Ort's trademark. He and the first Henry Ford were contemporaries. Henry Ford was the son of Irish immigrants who, with his partners, formed the Ford Motor Company in 1903. The Model T appeared in 1908. By 1913, mass production permitted him to sell this revolutionary machine for $500. In that year he introduced the successful assembly line. A new model, the Model A, was introduced in 1927. Ford's business philosophy was to reduce the unit cost and increase the volume of sales.

Uncle Ort's keepsakes from the newspaper make me know he admired Henry. A clipping from February 1917 reports:

> Henry Ford was strong for peace. He spent many thousands of his money and got generally ridiculed for his efforts to stop the war, but if war is forced upon this country, he proposes to stand behind the president with his money and his services. He says, "Whatever part the government needs of what I've got, it may have–whatever it requires. And the loan will be without interest. No percentage, no profit. I don't want to take any profit from the government under any circumstances."

And here's one written about 1927:

> It is said the reason Henry Ford is successful is that while other manufacturers build automobiles in which they like to ride, Ford built one for the other fellow.

Uncle Ort and Henry Ford were both men who thought for themselves. Neither had been born with a silver spoon in his mouth.

Both were hard workers and clear thinkers. Henry, like my uncle, was a benevolent patriot.

Back in 1901, the streets of Bay Minette were laid out with a 300-foot public square at the junction of Hand Avenue and Second Street. After the town was incorporated six years later, a municipal code extended the town three-quarters of a mile in all directions from the courthouse. There was no open stock law. Efforts to make the dirt streets of Bay Minette fit for automobiles were slow in coming. Uncle Ort got into the act.

Town officials kept the streets scraped and graveled, but automobiles faced another annoyance causing real, tangible problems. Bob Vail editorialized about it. Uncle Ort wrote a poem about it. Just about everyone in Baldwin County knew about the trouble their county seat was having. The *Courier*, a Fairhope weekly, noted:

> Bob Vail is making a great fight to get an ordinance passed by the town council which will take the cattle and hogs off the streets of Bay Minette. No citizen of Baldwin County can take pride in a county seat, in which cattle and hogs are permitted to roam in the streets.

Uncle Ort's poem was written before the 1916 election. As you would expect, his attempt to encourage containing livestock was on the humorous side:

> There is an old cow in this city,
> That tries out its voice on a ditty,
> It makes such a fuss,
> That I nearly cuss,
> And say many things most unwitty.
>
> But now, you poor, old, ugly bossy,
> You've had things your way 'til you're sassy.
> The people will vote,
> And then you will note,
> That our backs are no longer mossy.
>
> So when you are gone from our highways,
> And we find you tied on the biways,
> The walks will be clean,
> No stepping between,
> Our town is then out of its dairies.

The cows did not get "tied on the byways" that year as Uncle Ort had hoped. There was strong, strong, stubborn opposition from the owners of pigs and cows.

While Uncle Ort was establishing a business, the state created the Alabama Highway Department. That was in 1911. Bay Minette was struggling to have proper streets.

That year $115,000 was appropriated to the department charged with the task of building a system of roads to connect the county seats of Alabama. Engineers supplied their own instruments and worked for five dollars a day. They used a 300-dollar pair of mules to haul wagons of earth in building the roads.

In 1916 the Forest Highway Association met to determine the route of Highway 31, the first U.S. highway to be built in these parts. When Uncle Ort headed the Fair committee in 1914, you may recall, the terrible roads made travel to the county seat an arduous feat. Only six years later, in 1920, Alabama was proud of the farm-to-market road system in all sixty-seven of its counties.

A reporter in the twenties wrote of his two-day automobile trip from Mobile to Pensacola as though he had taken a trip to a foreign country. Departing by car from Mobile on the *Bay Queen*, he spent the night in Fairhope. The next day, he traveled east to Silverhill, where he visited the tobacco farms; then he drove to Foley for a rest stop and gasoline, then on to Pensacola. The scenery was beautiful, he reported, and people everywhere friendly. Uncle Ort and his Ford were familiar with these roads; he traveled them often, as his business was county-wide.

The battle for a stock law continued in Bay Minette. The Women's Civic League did what it could to sway the city council. Over a decade after other towns in the county had such ordinances, the law against unpenned hogs and cattle in the streets finally came.

> Sunday, July 1, 1928 marks a mile post in the advancement of Bay Minette. Cows will be outlawed from running at large on the streets....Our streets will henceforth be highways for the use of human beings alone.

Soon after the ordinance came the concrete mixers, and the streets were paved. But old habits die hard. People who had nice horses and carriages did not immediately embrace the horseless carriage.

Servicing the automobiles was a whole new industry. The Baldwin Buick Company and the Nash Sales Agency were located on Courthouse Square in the center of town. Cars were not started simply by pressing the gas pedal but by turning a crank outside the vehicle. Accidents were bound to occur—and the damage was not always to the car: Abner Smith, the *Times* editor, was reported to be the victim of a Ford kick—his arm was broken while he attempted to crank a car.

A great step forward was storage batteries to supply the needed charge for a starter. When the Baldwin Motor Supply Company boasted a new battery-charging machine that would fully charge a battery in only eight hours, that represented an important advance.

The twentieth century was proving to be a century of progress—improved roads and streets, better automobile engines, tires, and batteries, and more comfortable cars. But service was still a problem. Tire, gasoline, and auto repair services were very limited, and stations along the highways offering any type of road service were few and far between. Once while traveling south near Fort Deposit on U.S. 31, the highway newly cut through the woods, Uncle Ort hit a mule. He damaged his car (likely the radiator was smashed) and had to telephone my father in Georgiana forty miles away to come and get him. Daddy did. Such uncertainties made private car travel overland much more daring than it is today.

As horses and horse-drawn vehicles became fewer and fewer, livery stables closed and filling stations took their place. Uncle Ort was on hand to put up signs advertising Chief's Filling Station, on the square. The Chief was my grandfather, and I recall some sensational road signs that Uncle Ort put up. Every road into town had signs telling about Chief's Place.

These signs, modeled after the very popular Burma-Shave jingles, dotted both sides of the country roads leading into Bay Minette. Often when my uncle drove to another town for business or pleasure he took along nails, hammer, and the tools needed to put up signs. I've been with him when he was deciding where to put the string of signs so they could be read without causing a safety hazard. I watched him pound the stakes into the ground, each small sign bearing a few words of a jingle he'd composed.

SOME THINK THESE SIGNS

ARE CUTE AND NICE

WE THINK THEY GIVE YOU SOUND ADVICE

CHIEF'S SERVICE STATION

U.S. 31 BAY MINETTE

or

OUR SIGNS ARE NOT JUST TO BE FUNNY

THEY'RE HERE TO SAVE YOU

TIME AND MONEY

CHIEF'S SERVICE STATION

U.S. 31 BAY MINETTE

Another improvement in travel was provided by bridges, though not all were in favor of them. The bay boats were good enough, some argued. Lively discussions in opposition to the bridge over the Mobile River took place, and tempers flared before the money was granted for the construction of Cochrane Bridge. Progress won out, and the bridge, completed in 1927, was an immediate success. Ten years after its opening the toll was removed, but in the meantime Uncle Ort had paid for his share of the bridge. He made many business trips to Mobile, some for the Bay Minette Manufacturing Company, others to purchase athletic supplies for the school teams.

The escapades and adventures he had with his automobile are amazing and downright exciting when one considers the unpaved roads, the scarcity of services along the way, and the dearth of directional signs.

In the winter of 1914, you may recall, Uncle Ort fished a load of oysters out of Bon Secour waters and took them to Huntington, where he shucked them in front of his uncle's meat market. All who watched were fascinated by this strange procedure, but equally impressed with this adventurous man who had made the 900-mile trip "from nowhere" in his own car, over unpaved roads, in only two days.

Traveling for Uncle Ort and his wife in those years focused chiefly on visits with the Stahls, his in-laws in Indiana. On occasion he wrote his impressions:

> Isn't it wonderful, wife of mine,
> When we've got money and the time
> To pack our duds up in our car
> And leave so early and drive so far
> To get to where your parents are
> Up to Father Stahl's.
>
> We start before the night is down
> And hasten toward the rising sun,
> Hoping that all the roads are good
> That the tires will hold up like they should
> The motor keeps purring under the hood
> Till we get to Father Stahl's.
>
> We pass Montgomery on our way
> At nearly nine o'clock that day.
> The sun is shining hot and bright
> The roads are dusty and we're a sight
> But we are happy and dirt's all right,
> We're going to Father Stahl's.
>
> Oh keep on running, all through the day
> The miles just seem to melt away
> We pass o'er many a hill and dale,
> The roads are sometimes just a trail
> But on we hasten, we must not fail,
> To get to Father Stahl's.
>
> By ten we've reached the old toll gate
> And passed into our native state.
> The car seems eager to hurry through
> And finish the task it has to do
> To safely land both me and you
> At Father Stahl's.

By noon we've sent a telegram
> We could not wait on Uncle Sam
To let the folks know where we are
> That we are pushing the good, old car
And that the distance is not far
> To Father Stahl's.

And now we find at five o'clock
> That we are in the very block
Where live the folks we've come to see
> These folks that love both you and me
With whom we long have yearned to be
> Dear Father Stahl.

Soon we are cuddled in their embrace
> And tears come trickling down each face
Our journey's o'er and we are glad
> As any newly barefoot lad
Because of pleasures to be had
> At Father Stahl's.

We find the biggest supper there
> You can imagine how we stare,
At all the lovely pies and cakes
> The cookies covered with dainty flakes
And bread that only mother bakes,
> Dear Mother Stahl.

And then as soon as supper's done,
> And our unpacking has begun
We tell of all the thrills we've had,
> And all the news both good and bad
But leave out all that would be sad
> To Father Stahl.

Then late at night we climb the stairs
> And offer up our ardent prayers,
To Him who is our guide and stay,
> Who cares for us each night and day
Who brought us safely all the way
> To Father Stahl's.

The press of Uncle Ort's business sometimes kept him in Bay Minette while Aunt Tillie and Eloise drove alone to Huntington. That was after the roads were paved all the way. Uncle Ort had great confidence in his wife's abilities, so he supported her in what she wanted to do–drive to visit her parents in Indiana.

What a Spartan thing the Ertzinger women did,. Eloise and Aunt Tillie, driving all by themselves all the way to Indiana. They stopped one night on the way. My admiration for my aunt and cousin was tinged with a bit of envy. Their trip was not only adventuresome but took them to the heavenly-sounding places I'd never seen–the land where popcorn grew and snow fell.

Uncle Ort was careful to get the car in tiptop condition before his family departed. Such things as a new coat of paint, five new hubcaps, and new windshield wipers were essential. He remained in Bay Minette to work for two or three weeks before he joined them. Then they drove home together.

One summer he arranged with a lady from down-county to drive her from Bay Minette to Indiana in her eight-cylinder Buick (in those days, that was a real' fancy car). He had an accident en route, Eloise remembers, and his 1932 diary records it:

> Left [Bay Minette] at 6 a.m. with Mrs. Taylor and Mrs. Cawthon. Car turned over in Decatur. No one hurt and car not injured. Drove on to Scottsville, Kentucky that night, a 600 mile trip. Left Scottsville at 5:45 the next morning, made Peru, Indiana by 2:40. Ottilla and Mrs. Stahl met us, drove to Huntington by 4 p.m.

When Uncle Ort arrived in Indiana, I'm sure there was a special feeling of joy in being reunited with his family. He got good mileage out of his tale of turning over in an automobile and walking away unharmed.

His car served other people as well as his immediate family. Geraldine Hall, now a grandmother, recalls:

> He picked us up and took us to the meetings on Sunday evening. Some of the young people lived out of town, really out in the country where there were no roads. He'd drive up to a meeting point and honk his horn, wait for his young passengers to come out of the woods. When we got in the car, then off he'd go to church. He always took us home, too.
>
> Other times he'd pile the car full of us kids and take us with him

wherever he was going. We'd be crowded in like sardines, but we didn't care. He'd take us to a picnic at Hawkins Grove, or to Fairhope to swim and picnic, or to Orange Beach.

But the most fun was going to Shocco Springs. We'd sing and play games; he always kidded us and told riddles or made up stories. He made up words to sing to a tune we all knew. Sometimes the trip with him was as much fun as the conference itself.

Shocco Springs, near Talladega, Alabama, was the conference center where Presbyterian youth from all over the state gathered each June for a wingding. Two conferences were held each year, one for juniors and one for senior high school youth. Uncle Ort rounded up all the young people who wanted to go from Stockton, Mobile, and the surrounding area and took them to camp. Uncle Ort's comments about one trip represent it as less enjoyable than Geraldine described:

Up at 3:15 and drove to Shocco. Had bus trouble, radiator boiled dry every 20 miles. Arrived at 7:05, good and tired. [A week later, he wrote about the return trip.] Up at 4:30 started home with bus at 6:45. Burned out universal joint 14 miles south of Montgomery at 11:30. Repairs took until 8 at night. Drove all night, got to Mobile at 5 a.m. Home from Mobile at 6:30 a.m. At office a while in a.m. Building & Loan Director's meeting in p.m.

Undoubtedly the young people with him had a good time in spite of what really happened. He handled the situation, so they did, too.

Uncle Ort was a safe driver; to my knowledge he never had any mishaps with the hundreds of boys and girls he drove around, nor with adults. Mind you, no one had thought of seatbelts, either. Eight passengers in a four-door sedan for a two-hour drive was not unusual. One person today declares there were 17 in his car on one pleasure jaunt: no one who wanted to go was left out. Going places and doing things in his car brought sheer pleasure to my uncle.

15

The Communicator

SELF-TAUGHT! THAT IS THE WAY Uncle Ort described himself. His Huntington High School education, especially the courses in English, laid the foundation for his writing and him communication skills. Ort served as sports editor for his hometown paper in Indiana before moving to Bay Minette. He continued as a reporter after he moved South. He became the *Mobile Press Register* correspondent in Baldwin County.

His work as a reporter came about so naturally that it seemed to just happen. As I write I recognize how clever and smart he was about his journalistic endeavor. I wish I knew how many news reports he filed; there were a heap. At one time he was a reporter for the *Montgomery Advertiser,* the *Birmingham News,* and the *Alabama Farm Journal* in addition to the Mobile papers and the *Baldwin Times.*

Remember the report he wrote about the murder of Marshal James Smith? Apparently it was on the edge of his consciousness; he could not forget it.

It began when he heard the gunshot. This startled the twenty-one-year-old neophyte reporter for the *Mobile Press* in 1911. Upon investigation, he learned that the sheriff had been shot dead. The town went wild. Everybody who heard about the shooting was outraged. A black man had killed a white man; someone had to pay!

Two black men were seen at the scene, but only one could be found. The news spread like wildfire. The law enforcers and plain citizens all over the state got the word and searched for Henry Presley. Out in the bushes and woods, in the cities and towns, the search was intense, but the man got away–no trace of him was found.

Uncle Ort's age more than doubled before he learned the whole truth about the killing. Keyser Brown was hanged in the jailyard months after the murder. The newspaper account in 1936, twenty-five years later, gives this account.

ORT SETS A RECORD

Bay Minette's city marshall J. L. Barrow told Ort Ertzinger, *Press Register* correspondent, about the arrest near Georgiana of Sidney Hunter, alias Henry Presley. Henry turned himself in and confessed to the murder of the marshall, James Smith. When the marshall was killed Henry Presley vanished. Ort did not hunt through the files of the killing.

Ort who is probably the *Press Register's* oldest correspondent in point of service, recalled the full details. He was sitting on his front porch, when he heard a shot. The marshall had been shot dead. Keyser Brown was arrested at the scene of the killing. Another man got away. Ort immediately telephone a report to the *Register*

Ort wrote articles about the search for Presley, and of the hanging in 1912, of the negro arrested at the scene, Kyser Brown. Keyser Brown professed innocence even from the gallows. He lifted his voice in prayer to God Almighty. Most Bay Minette people at the time didn't believe Brown guilty, even though he paid with his life.

Now after 26 years, Ort who covered Brown's arrest will report the details of the negro's trial by the circuit court and the jury's report of guilty to the murder charge by a 1911 jury.

What a story! To double-check, I did more research and was dumbfounded to discover another family connection with this horrible happening. The marshal who was killed was investigating a call from my paternal grandmother, Linda Feagin. Someone suspicious was prowling around in her yard while she was there alone, so she called the marshal. I'd never heard about this before. People do not talk about such things.

The first and only brutal hanging Uncle Ort reported on took place a few blocks from where he lived. He remembered it, I think, because deep down he knew that justice had not been served, but he was totally helpless to do anything. He could not stop the hanging of an innocent man; that bothered my uncle. I doubt that any other story in his many years of reporting involved such injustice.

My uncle's facility with words and numbers expressed itself in so much of what he did. For relaxation he worked crossword puzzles, and he enjoyed writing limericks, jokes, stories, poems, and travelogues. In a more lucrative vein, he wrote abstracts (detailed descriptions of land), letters, deeds, contracts, and news stories.

He was the secretary-treasurer of the Baldwin County Hunting Club, the Bay Minette Lodge No. 498 (Masons), several conservation groups, and I don't know what else. His colorful paper trail revealed some of what he was; his small notebooks reveal a more personal insight.

I opened the well-worn black leather notebook gingerly, believing this small item I held in my hand would reveal important stuff. It did. The contents depict his character and thought process. Typed or carefully printed outlines, the scaffolding for his speeches, fill the pages of the small loose-leaf book. I judge this served more to help him put his thoughts in order than to prompt him when he was speaking. He did not read his speeches.

The loose-leaf binding allowed for flexibility and updating. The jokes to go along with the basic part of the talk were typed or pasted in the body of the outline. In the margin he wrote clue words.

Other T-tiny clippings, just as he'd cut them, were loose. These cutout stories and jokes could be sandwiched into his talks and adapted to the circumstances–a common maneuver requiring quick wit. Between the lines of the notebook I could hear him talking enthusiastically, see him laughing.

"The Future of the Church, Concerning Young People"

Pray for them
Play with them–Don't grow old
Give them something to do
Don't ask them to do things you would not do yourself.

In the margin he wrote, "wild oats and broadening period." Other points were "the age when crucial decisions about life are made," "won't take 'no' for an answer." The following is a story he told to make a point.

The Devil's Kind

Once upon a time the devil held an anniversary meeting and called upon his princes to report what they had done on earth to hinder the Kingdom of God.

One emissary said he had turned loose some wild beasts who destroyed missionaries. The chief of devils said, "That's nothing, you can't hurt a Christian by killing him."

Another reported that he had wrecked a ship and many Christians were drowned. The devil said, "You have done nothing. You may kill a Christian, but his influence still lives."

The third emissary reported that he had set fires to a large church which became a total wreck. "They will rebuild and be stronger than ever," said the chief.

The fourth one, with great pride, said he got two different denominations into a quarrel. The devil clapped his hands for joy. "You have done more than the others combined. This is the best way to hinder the progress of the Kingdom of God on earth."

The outlines are like a window to his thinking. They contain the wisdom and wisecracks as he delivered them. Many of his thoughts instill in me the relatedness of past and present, of human behavior. Uncle Ort knew that in some mysterious way laughter–telling jokes and stories–helped an idea stick.

He was forty-two or forty-three when the church young people gave him his first five-year diary. This gift exemplified in another way how much he was liked and respected and held in high esteem. Though times were hard, his young friends saved their nickels and dimes and purchased for him a line-a-day diary with a lock and key. They surprised him at a Sunday evening meeting. The card accompanying the gift read: "Your Gang feebly expresses their love. May the five year diary record five years of happiness and success."

Thirty-three youngsters wrote their names inside the cover. That gift put him on a pedestal from where I sat. My uncle treasured the diary, wrote in it every day, and commenced a diary-writing practice that he continued the rest of his life.

Without exception, for every day of the years from 1932 to 1936 there is an entry. Equally consistently, every seven days there is mention of his attending Sunday School. His special Sunday activities set the day apart, clearly dividing time into weeks.

No erasures appear in Uncle Ort's pencil-written diary. He marked through but did not erase. He wrote about the weather, ball games, the names of people who died or were sick, and, of course, fires and fishing. He had a mania for numbers and counting. He noted the number of snakes, deer, and other animals he killed, the people in attendance at meetings, the miles traveled, the steps to a shrine, and the scores of ball games. Once, after visiting his aunts who lived in Lutz, Florida, he packed the car with fruit and noted that he'd brought home 313 pieces of fruit–oranges, kumquats, grapefruit, and lemons.

Rev. Cook came right out and said, "I bank on Ort to count the number in church each Sunday." Uncle Ort's seat in the choir gave him a clear view during services to do just that. Presbyterians keep attendance records for Sunday School–that was an official part of his job–but "counting the house" during the church service was just a private habit.

The number in attendance at Young People's meetings on Sunday night was entered in his diary. Numbers were vital in the attendance contests. Such competitive fun provided an exhilarating zest that was missing from the Epworth League I attended. The party at the end, when the losers entertained the winners, was a doozie. On special invitation I traveled from Georgiana to attend a few of those affairs–favors, streamers, games, good food, and lots of laughter.

I am digressing, I suppose from developing my thesis that Uncle Ort was a great communicator. But communication is a broad theme.

His writings and movies took people to places they would never visit and gave them a glimpse of the world they might never have known. Remember, this was before television brought pictures from all over the world into our homes.

Uncle Ort delighted in showing his pictures to others. He was never shy about that. I was with him one day when he took his projector and a reel of film to a Courthouse Square office. Four or five people there wanted to see pictures of his first trip by air. he set the projector on a counter and proceeded to show the movies on the wall. Curious people wandered in from the hall, and soon the room was filled. They watched in wide-eyed amazement as the hula dancers and other pictures paraded before them. One man walked over and touched the "screen" in awe. Who can count the value of the enlightenment?

Uncle Ort was so effervescent about his travel experiences that he made you feel you had gone right along on his travels. Many a school child in Baldwin County saw people in other countries for the first time on Uncle Ort's screen. Home movies were a novelty, which, tied in with his flair for show and tell, gave him top billing. Another up-front thing Uncle Ort did!

He was invited by an unbelievable number of people to show his movies–women's clubs and missionary societies, men's groups (Kiwanis, Rotary, Lions), church folks, school children, friends and relatives. He carried his own screen, projector, extension cord, and slides, with a flashlight to read his notes and script. The theaters where his movies were shown included homes, offices, restaurants, and clubhouses. He was prepared. In fact, he often took his movie equipment with him when he visited his out-of-town friends.

While writing this book I reviewed the movies he took. Most are not up to today's standards, but hearing him tell stories about the travel adventures they recorded made a whale of a difference. he had charmed me as he did everyone else. Without him and his exuberance and talk, the movies are dismal.

Uncle Ort, a great communicator, could rival Ronald Reagan. In scrutinizing my uncle's life, I find his poems surfacing time and again.

They are his own self-portrait. His poems show a facet of his character otherwise unknown.

Uncle Ort was an admirer of the communication skills of Edgar A. Guest. When he was an aspiring young man, he paraphrased one of Guest's poems:

> If I can do some good today
> If I can serve along life's way
> If I can something useful say,
>   Lord, show me how.
>
> If I can right a human wrong
> If I can help to make one strong
> If I can cheer with smile or song
>   Lord, show me how.
>
> If I can aid one in distress
> If I can make a burden less
> If I can spread more happiness
>   Lord, show me how.
>
> If I can do a kindly deed
> If I can help a soul in need,
> If I can sow a fruitful seed,
>   Lord, show me how.
>
> If I can feed a hungry heart,
> If I can give a better start
> If I can fill a nobler art
>   Lord, show me how.

The power of the written word! Such poignant feelings are often communicated only to God.

Composing and writing a poem for a person has its own uniqueness. Eloise was in college when she was the target of this letter.

> If you don't receive a letter,
>   That's long overdue,
> You must make up your mind and say,
>   It ain't been mailed to you.
>
> But please, dear lady, won't you try
>   To find the needed time
> To write a letter to the folks,
>   Down in the southern clime.

Uncle Ort was a communicator like none other!

16

Fun and Frolic

TAIL TWISTER, AN OFFICE IN THE LION'S CLUB, was a job cut out for my uncle. A jokester, a storyteller, a prankster who loved people and wholesome fun, he had a quick wit and a good sense of timing.

His Ertzinger flair for fun came to the surface when his Uncle Albert married. They both gained notoriety in the process. The *News Democrat's* front-page story in November 1906 was headlined, "Ertzinger and wife have much misery."

Uncle Ort, a teenager was with well-wishers who gathered at the abode of Uncle Albert Ertzinger and his bride in Huntington. She was the former Eva Hanson.

> Mr. Albert Ertzinger, a traveling salesman for Swift and Company's packing house, married Miss. Eva Hanson of Chicago. Before her marriage Eva held a high position with the Armour Packing Company.
>
> Their home on Tipton Street had been furnished in elegant style by Mr. Ertzinger before their friends took over. They added every imaginable variety of packing house signs. There is hardly a space as big as a pin head in the large residence which has not been filled with pictures advertising Swift and Armour meats and extracts.

These posters constituted the wall paper, draperies, bed spreads, curtains, table cloths, mantle pieces, etc. giving a unique effect.

In plain view to attract much attention, the tormentors hung a sign in the large bay window of the house–SWIFT AND ARMOUR HAVE COMBINED THEIR FORCES AND WILL OCCUPY THIS HOUSE AFTER NOVEMBER 29. LEAVE ORDERS AT THE OFFICE.

The spoilers of Mr. and Mrs. Ertzinger's comfort, having completed the sign decorations, found a new field for jokes. They sewed up nearly every piece of the groom's wearing apparel so it would be impossible to put on.

Their prankster friends planned to have them arrested at the train station. The newly weds outsmarted them by disembarking from the rear while the gang of arresting officers stood dumbfounded at the train car door. Not to be outdone, the tormentors proceeded to the newly weds home on Tipton Street where they found Albert and Eva admiring the packing house signs.

Then the real fun began. The uninvited guests had no intention of letting the newly weds spend their first night alone. Only after much pleading by the bride and groom did the tormentors leave, on condition that they be treated to cigars. Poor Albert opened his cigar box only to find sugar cubes. The trickster had fixed things.

Mr. and Mrs. Ertzinger were aroused early the next morning by a dreadful noise in the culinary department where two cooks prepared breakfast. After the meal the guests left the couple had a few hours of solitude before noon when they were expected for Thanksgiving dinner with Albert's parents.

The newlyweds did not arrive at the stroke of twelve so the men of the family went after them with a two wheeled cart. As they entered the honeymoon heaven, Uncle Albert got suspicious and tried to escape. Ort Ertzinger, one of his nephews, followed the flight of his uncle with the swiftness of the wind. Ort captured Albert to loud applause. He and Eva were forceably placed in the ancient looking cart and carried to the Thanksgiving feast.

From Iowa, Maryland, Ohio, and Indiana, Ertzinger cousins wrote. In recalling their youth, each expressed eager anticipation of Uncle Ort's visits to their home, delight in his company, and genuine admiration for him.

Uncle Albert and his wife Eva Ertzinger were not alone for long.

George, Paul, and Ruth were born, in that order. The oldest, George, is retired from a successful dental practice in Fort Wayne. He now lives near his daughter in Iowa, where he wrote this letter.

> My first memories of Ort are [from] when I was about six years old. His visits to our Indiana farm had a thrilling flavor and were punctuated with interesting stories of his journey in the car from Bay Minette and happenings at the hamper factory.
>
> At that time I was interested in bee keeping and had six hives. Ort sparked my interest in that endeavor. To further encourage me, he bought and sent me the number one book on the subject—*The ABC and XYZ of Bee Keeping* by A. I. Root. He was the grandfather on the subject. Ort also subscribed for me [to] a beekeeping magazine. I studied it all and was in the bee business until I was through high school.

George's story jogged my memory about the bees my uncle kept. One day Uncle Ort spotted a group of men standing around a wagon parked in front of the courthouse. He walked over to see what was going on. A farmer pointed out a queen bee trying to settle on a wagon. This was a good opportunity for someone to get himself a beehive, they remarked. That was all Uncle Ort needed.

Somehow he captured the queen and got the swarm to his yard. He was in business. He kept a separate bee account in the bank. "I make money with honey," he used to say. As a young girl I was enchanted because he dared to go among the swarms of stinging bees and did not get stung. The marvelous way the bees made the sweet, smooth syrup from nectar baffled me. George had more to say.

> Our visits to Bay Minette and Orange Beach will never be forgotten! Us kids had so much fun at the cottage sleeping on the porch, swimming, and fishing. Once Ort took us out on the gulf in a big boat; the motor stopped. Immediately, he shot-off a disaster signal, and another boat came and towed us back to the Marina. Such excitement! But Ort was always in control of the situation.
>
> At the beach we fished. At night we would wade around the edge of the bay to spear fish. With the help of a strong light we could see the fish just lying on the bottom waiting for us to spear them. Getting oysters and gigging fish with a barbed spear was a super sport. In Bay Minette Ort was always anxious to take us fishing in Owl creek.

In later years when my wife and daughter accompanied me to see Ort, one thing I always marveled at was how every morning Ort would be the first one up. By the time the rest were up, he had gone somewhere, or done something to prepare ahead for things needed to show his visitors a good time that day. Everything was well organized. He was a perfect host.

George's sister, Ruth, a public school teacher, remembered, "Ort was always involved in tomfoolery." Ruth gave me the newspaper accounts of her parents' arrival in Huntington as a bride and groom. Ruth now lives in Fort Wayne. Her two children have almost grown children. About Uncle Ort she wrote:

> My first and clearest memory is that Ort was a very jovial person. He was a tall cousin who came tearing into our drive with the horn blowing and a lot of dust flying from the wheels of his Ford. The long driveway and surrounding land kept us from associating closely with our neighbors. He made a great impression on me as a small girl who lived a very seclusive life on a farm.
>
> He jumped out of the car and grabbed me, gave me a big bear hug and kisses. [I have not forgotten those bear hugs. The very crush of our bodies, a measure of his gladness to see me, made a special impact on my psyche.] Then he'd dig in his pockets and pull out a treat for us all. He brought us pleasure so we looked forward to his visits with great expectation.
>
> After he retired they took yearly trips to foreign places and we looked forward to their visits eager to hear of their travel adventures. We expected a *National Geographic* type picture show and were not disappointed. They left us a printed copy about their travels which we and later our children enjoyed.

Paul, their brother, who found Owl Creek fishing too wild to be enjoyable, had a distinguished career with the Federal Bureau of Investigation before he retired the first time. Next he was on the administrative staff of the *National Geographic* magazine, then a specialized income tax accountant. He and his wife Carolyn have one son, Richard. From his home in Rockville, Maryland, Paul wrote:

> Ort my cousin, by relationship, was more like an uncle since he was much older than I. My earliest memories of Ort (1915—1925) were not as a daily, weekly or monthly relative. I saw him only once or possibly twice a year when he visited my family on our farm in

Huntington. Usually these visits were around the 4th of July. He always brought fireworks to shoot and spent the evening with us.

I enjoyed listening to him talk with my father and mother. He told us happenings during his drive from the south and about the hamper factory he built and operated in Alabama.

Ort always impressed me as a successful business man. He gave me my first insight into the business world. During my college years I visited him in Bay Minette, then after my marriage my family and I visited.

In 1935, as a vacationing college student, Paul came to visit. Uncle Ort wrote in his diary the day after his arrival, "Up at 3:30 in the morning. To Owl Creek with Paul- caught 23 bluegills, crappies and bream and an eel."

Uncle Ort was so enthusiastic about his wilderness shack that he didn't give Paul, or any guest, a choice. He told them the plans he'd made, and off to his floating camp they went. That was that. Everyone should enjoy the fishing camp, the beautiful delta, the swamp-the outdoor extravaganza. Several days later, according to the diary, Uncle Ort and Paul went frogging. In the pitch-black frogland wilderness, Paul held the light as the frogs croaked and Uncle Ort gigged.

To continue with Paul's remembrances:

My visits to his home were filled with fun, great food and meeting many of his nice friends. He introduced me to business associates in Bay Minette. Several of the men were able to give me employment, if I so desired. [Attempting to help a college student find a job and perhaps a career rings true to Uncle Ort's character.]

Later when my son, Ricky, was about 5 years old, we visited Ort. He took us to his fishing camp in the swamps filled with alligators. Ort was just as active in his recreation activities as in his work. He never failed to show us a good time or to make us feel comfortable.

Ort always had a repertoire of funny stories. One he told us when we lived on the farm, I have remembered and retold many times.

A circus manager heard of a man 105 years old and went to ask him to join his circus. He asked the centurian to tell how he lived to be 105. After the offer was thoroughly discussed, the old man said, "I can't do it without first checking with my father."

The circus man inquired, "How old is your father? Where is he?"

The old man replied, "Oh, he's upstairs putting grandpa to bed."

I have always remembered Ort as a very happy and contented man who took great pride in his family, his business, his church and his community. He was a hard worker who often took himself to his office at day break. Even though my association with Ort was limited I always considered him to be one of the most impressive individuals I have ever known. one great man!

Strong family ties existed among Grandpa Ertzinger's brothers, Albert, Levi, and John Adams. The co-owner of the Brill and Ertzinger Meat Market, Uncle Levi, was the recipient of Uncle Ort's oysters in the shell. Uncle Levi's adopted daughter, Dorothy Ertzinger, married Dr. Howard Dill and spent her career teaching in Fort Wayne's public schools. Now a widow, Dorothy resides in the town her daughter Jane calls home, Columbus, Ohio. Dorothy wrote:

> Ort was one of my favorites. He was a truly wonderful person, honest, trustworthy–a man of rare humor and a true Christian. I always looked forward to his visits. He recounted funny incidents, like the time in his office at the Bay Minette Manufacturing Company. He was dressed in his baseball uniform, cap back on his head [proper gentlemen did not wear the caps indoors then]. His feet were up on the desk, he was totally relaxed, when a man came in and asked to see the boss. Ort said he removed his feet from the desk, took off his cap, straightened his uniform and replied, "I'm the man you want to see."
>
> When my parents and I went to Orange Beach he gave us such a wonderful time. Remember his reading nook there? [The nook was in the bathroom, where he built a magazine rack conveniently close to the commode.] And I'll never forget our trips to get oysters or the big pile of oyster shells in the yard. He was very well liked by the men who worked for him.
>
> One New Year's Eve when we were there we all went to the fireworks display. He was the one who put it on. I remember the boys and girls begging him to let them shoot the rockets. "Mr. Ort, let me. Mr. Ort, please." He was very popular.
>
> In later years after he retired they visited us upon their return from Hawaii. He put on his hula skirt made of the native ti leaves and danced for us. My husband and daughter enjoyed his stories and

visits. He got so much out of life just having him here was fun.

Wasn't it on a trip to Alaska that he had two birthday parties? [You can bet Uncle Ort made the most of having two birthdays. That story comes later.]

I recall how much Ort liked to fish. He and Dad used to fish for hours at Winona Lake. I too remember the happy times we had when they came here to Fort Wayne and to Winona Lake where we had a cottage. He was the kind of person not easily forgotten. He used to send us the fruit of the month too, from Harry & David's in Oregon. The fruit was always so delicious and appreciated.

Dorothy's mention of Harry & David's jogs my memory. They were less well known in the 1950s. Uncle Ort talked about marvelous Oregon fruit-growing area after he witnessed apples and pears being gathered. He described the fruit-handling techniques whereby beautiful large fruit was placed in temperature-controlled storage to mature. This technique impressed him. The late summer harvest was thus kept for the Christmas market.

Those juicy, tasty, luscious pears were an impressive taste treat which he sent year after year. Aunt Tillie continued with the annual feast after he died.

Telling a good story and making people laugh brought to Uncle Ort the kind of enjoyment some men get in smoking their pipes. People laughed even on hearing him tell the same story a second or third time. He was a whiz at adapting a story to fit the situation, so many of his tales were based on something that really happened. Uncle Ort's wonderful sense in knowing when to tell what story or joke or to read a poem was a part of his charm. The right words seemed to roll off his lips and from his heart like magic. Relevancy, appropriateness, the pat-on-the-back words came because he worked at it. His reputation as a story teller, humorist, and speaker was achieved the old-fashioned way: he earned it.

Uncle Ort worked as hard as he played, or he played as hard as he worked–take your pick. He was full of fun and frolic.

17

Relationships

THE IMPORTANCE UNCLE ORT ASCRIBED to his family and the delight and pleasure he derived from it are not easy to measure. His family and home were a large part of my uncle's world. He was a caring son, a faithful husband and father, a thoughtful brother, a sensitive father-in-law. You already know what I think of him as an uncle.

From his youth Uncle Ort entertained friends in his home. A few months after he moved to Bay Minette, when his family lived on Hand Avenue in a rented house, Uncle Ort gave a party and made news.

> Thursday evening Ort hosted a party in honor of his guest, Herbert Bartmus from Huntington, Indiana. Guests enjoyed a marvelous evening of entertainment. A Peanut Hunt and other games were followed by delicious refreshments.

A peanut hunt?

As a bride, Aunt Tillie quickly made the house he built into a home. At a time when the popular notion was that "it takes a heap of living in a house to make it home," Uncle Ort had no difficulty in making their place a home. Early in their marriage they established a reputation for being the ideal host and hostess.

Entertaining hundreds of guests in their home was a part of the fabric of their lives. Some were guests for a few minutes, others for a few weeks. On holidays–Valentine's, Halloween, Christmas, you name it–or in-between times, guests came. Parties, luncheons, teas, and dinners, singing groups galore, Sunday School class meetings, clubs of all kinds found a hearty welcome under their roof. Naturally their home was open to Eloise's friends.

Uncle Ort entertained. Yes, I mean that. Of course, so did his wife, a very charming and gracious hostess. But Uncle Ort's individual way with guests was such that those who spent time in their home knew they had been in his home. His jovial manner was inextricably mixed up with his ability to put their guests at ease. He made each guest feel important and welcomed. He gave each a memory to keep.

As a bloodhound sniffs the scent and follows a trail, Uncle Ort had a knack for detecting the interests of a guest. With a genuine interest in people, he gave an individual twist to his hospitality. For example, if you were a guest in their home for dinner, he'd likely invite you into the dining room to watch him ring the dinner chimes. If you showed interest, he would tell you more about them and perhaps entice you into a conversation about chimes.

Or, if you expressed an interest in fishing, he might take you outside to show you where he grew worms for fish bait and, in passing, point out the monkey puzzle tree that grew in the yard. He managed a clever interaction of listening to what you had to say and making you feel like a special guest. He never completely left you to be entertained by his wife or daughter.

During an animated conversation with a guest he could also play solitaire. His devotion to that card game was unequaled in my experience. Solitaire helped him follow his doctor's orders to rest and slow down. He designed, cut out, and finished a Masonite lap board for playing while he sat in his easy chair. He loved winning and confessed to the temptation to cheat, but usually resisted.

When we were girls, Eloise had taffy pulls. The kind of taffy my uncle made used white sugar, flavored with peppermint and wintergreen. I think taffy pulls were a "sorta Northeren" idea. Cane syrup from nearby cane fields was the ingredient used for most candy pulls my friends had. My father did not make candy, nor did the fathers of anyone else I knew. The fact that my uncle did was another special feather in his cap.

In his time stereotypes and clichés about the head of the household had to be modified to fit Uncle Ort. Traditionally the wife did the shopping for the family table. Aunt Tillie, however, merely drew up the list of things to buy, and Uncle Ort did most of the shopping and always bought the meat. He knew the proper cuts for stewing, broiling, roasting, and so on, as well as the fair price. He was a genius at picking ripe melons. In some ways he was a forerunner of the husband of the 1990s.

He literally brought home the bacon, too. On his trips to Huntington he discovered a place on Route 31 in Tennessee that sold smoked hams and made bacon. The bacon struck his family's fancy so much that he became a regular customer of the Tennessee smokehouse. This delicacy was a regular Christmas breakfast treat.

Picking berries was for Uncle Ort a rite of spring. He knew exactly where they grew along the roadside. Lush, juicy blackberries and dewberries spread themselves over the red clay banks. Going down a dusty road in the off season, he'd be likely to point and say, "I picked a quart of dewberries on the left side of the road, in that curve. The snake I saw didn't bother the berries." If he passed by ripe berries and didn't have a pail, he'd pick them and put them in his hat.

Unlike most husbands of his day, my uncle assisted his wife in canning summer vegetables. The year Eloise graduated from high school and he ran for tax assessor, he helped Aunt Tillie can sweet corn, tomatoes, and peaches.

A woman's place was not limited to her home, in my uncle's view. "President" and "chairwoman" were familiar titles for his wife. This would not have happened without his encouragement. Her ability to organize, her good judgment and clear thinking matched his. He encouraged her to use her talents, and she found real satisfaction in doing so. He was proud of her.

The Ertzinger family, circa 1905, in Huntingdon, Indiana. Bottom row, left to right: Jessie France, Florence Leota, and Ort Harmon Ertzinger.

Bay Minette City Band, circa 1910.

Baldwin County Courthouse, Bay Minette, 1910

| ORT H. ERTZINGER | J. A. ERTZINGER | HERBERT R. WESTON |
| PRESIDENT MANAGER | V.-PRES.-TREAS. | SECRETARY |

BAY MINETTE MANUFACTURING COMPANY
INCORPORATED
MANUFACTURERS OF

| MILL | THE NEW "BALDWIN" HAMPER, CABBAGE CRATES, ORANGE BOXES, | OFFICE |
| HURRICANE, ALA. | VARIOUS KINDS OF VEGETABLE SHIPPING CONTAINERS, BOX SHOOKS AND EGG CASES | BAY MINETTE, ALA. |

BAY MINETTE, ALA.,

You said you wanted oysters,
We'll have them by the peck,
Just be on hand next Friday,
And fill up to your neck.

This is your invitation,
To join us in our feast,
We want all members present,
The greatest and the least.

So don't forget the evening
And don't you dare be late,
Six Thirty is the hour,
The twelfth day is the date.

COME.

Author--Ort H. Ertzinger.

Uncle Ort composed this invitation, which he typed on company stationery. He organized the Bay Minette Manufacturing Company in 1919.

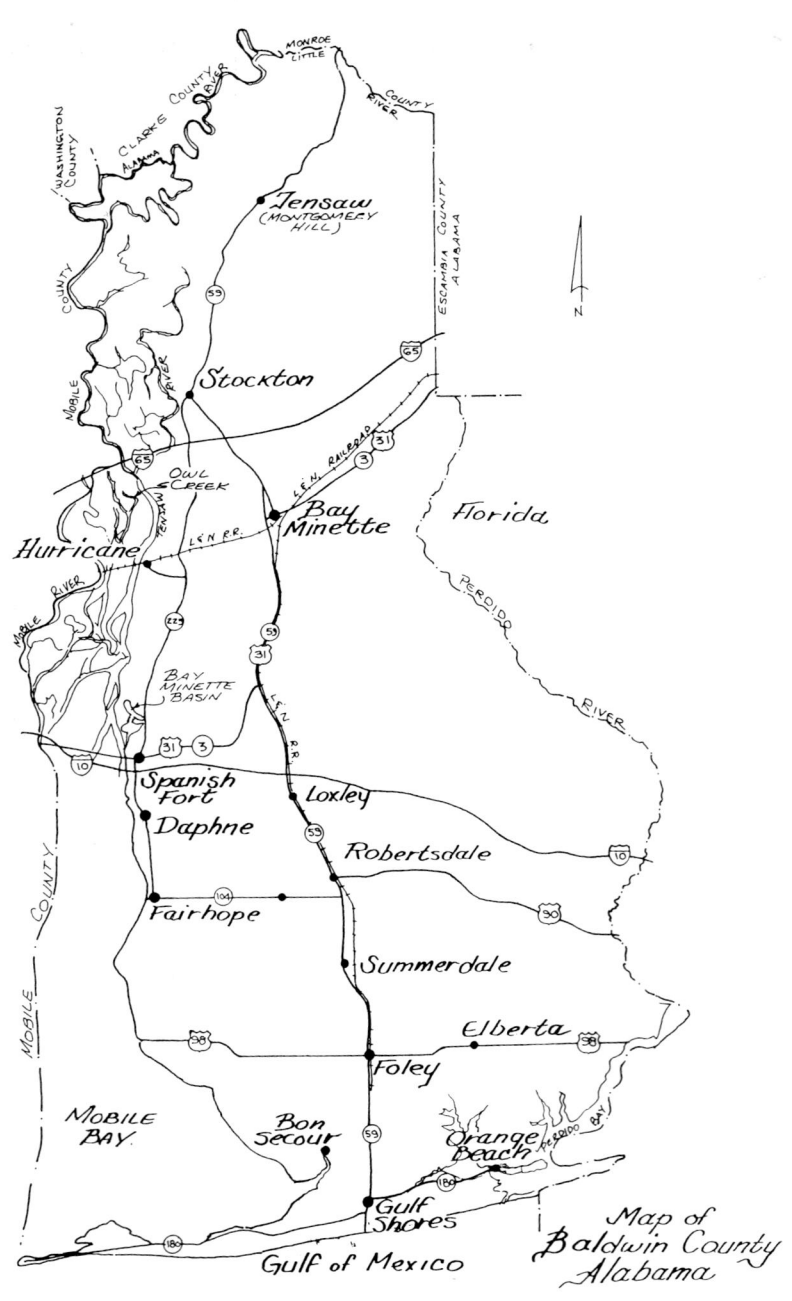

Map of the Baldwin County Uncle Ort knew.

Bay Minette in 1915.

The unique water tower under construction.

Baldwin County Bank at left, the Presbyterian church, and, above, the two-storied grammar school.

The floating camp at Orange Beach circa 1958.

Uncle Ort in his river boat.

A favorite Orange Beach pose for Uncle Ort.

The caption for this 1951 newspaper photo read: "Mr and Mrs Ort H. Ertzinger of Bay Minette flew to Hawaii via United Air Lines last week for a 15-day vacation at the Royal Hawaiian Hotel. It is the first visit to the islands for the retired realtor and his wife."

At Waikiki, near Diamond Head (left to right): Ottilla Stahl Ertzinger, Janice Feagin Britton, Ort Harmon Ertzinger.

Her zest in working with women's groups was unmatched. She gave me the impression that she felt it a distinct honor to have been chosen to serve in numerous leadership positions. Never, to my recollection, did either my aunt or uncle complain or act put upon when doing church and community work. They gave of their time and energy willingly and on countless occasions worked together.

Aunt Tillie's leadership role in club and church work demanded that she be away for days at a time. One Sunday night at 10:00 my uncle put her on the train to go to Birmingham to attend a synodical training conference. The following Wednesday afternoon he met her at the depot. Uncle Ort was amenable to whatever adjustments he had to make; he cooked and took care of the house. When out-of-town guests unexpectedly arrived while Aunt Tillie was away, he was not caught short.

Financial matters were different. When Aunt Tillie needed money, she asked for it and explained what she intended to buy. He gave her cash. (He did not have charge accounts, and credit cards had not come along. He distrusted credit, anyway–remember the refrigerator?) She explained to me once that he gave her more than she would have asked for. After he died, she needed coaching in writing checks. He was the provider and business manager for his family.

His mother-in-law, Rose Stahl, at 1631 Jefferson Street in Huntington, was probably not surprised when the Western Union boy delivered this telegram to her home on Mother's Day in 1935:

> Good morning Mother, how are you
> On this new Mother's Day?
> We send our love by telegraph,
> For you're so far away.
>
> Our fondest hope, dear, is that you
> May have all wants supplied,
> And that your smallest heart's desire
> May never be denied.
>
> Our prayers are for your happiness
> Our love is ocean wide.

May each succeeding day bring peace
And happiness your way.

Love

Ort and Ottilla

My uncle and his father lived next door to each other for an awfully long time and saw and talked to each other at least daily. Both Ertzinger families were companionable in every way. The men hunted and fished together, sang in the choir, and shared a multitude of interests. Naturally, however, they sometimes had different points of view.

Their most important undertaking together was the Bay Minette Manufacturing Company. Putting their heads together, Grandpa and Uncle Ort did a masterful thing. They turned a sawmill into a factory for making shipping containers and money.

Their accomplishment seems especially laudable when one considers that neither man had any formal education in business administration or engineering. Their ideas worked, but the manager absconded with the entire bank account, so it was necessary to close down the mill. Sharing that tragedy forged a bond of indestructible strength between the two men.

****

As you've discovered, relatives looked forward to being with Uncle Ort whether he was the host or the guest. Without question, visiting in each other's homes was a coveted way their families learned to know each other. This close and intimate association was the crucible in which family values were formed. Keeping up with relatives was part of being a family.

When I graduated from Graceville High School in 1939, Uncle Ort honored me by being there. My graduation was important to him; it merited his time. He brought a carload of relatives—Grandpa and his wife, Aunt Hattie, Mrs. Stahl, and of course Aunt Tillie. I do not remember where we all slept, but our house was full.

I felt very important to have an entire row in the high school auditorium occupied by people who cared about me–guests who had traveled over 250 miles from another state for the occasion. This stroked my ego. I needed that, as growing discord and conflict between my parents had created uncertainty about my home.

My situation did turn topsy-turvy. My parents separate, and a nasty divorce ensued. My parents moved from Graceville, my home town, and I went off to college feeling homeless. My brother and I felt deserted and torn between my parents, although both offered us a place in their homes. My fun-loving uncle suddenly became much more to me. Quickly I learned that he was on my side no matter what. He became a guardian angel!

Mother returned to Bay Minette in shock. She lived with her father, next door to Uncle Ort. Immediately upon her return, Mother began to help in the care of her father, who died before the year was out. Then she had to begin her life as a single.

After twenty years of marriage, having her own home and raising two children, Mother had to make a terrific adjustment. Never having worked outside the home a day in her life, she was not equipped to go it alone.

My loyalty to my mother was strong, but I had my own problems. In college I was just managing to keep my head above water, about to flunk out of the School of Nursing at Vanderbilt. I needed counsel.

My brother, still in high school, was equally bewildered. Jack, in the blush of his youth, was a very confused young man. After our parents separated, Brother lived with our father, played football, and graduated from Hope High School in town neither of us had ever heard of before he moved there. He and Daddy disagreed about what he would study in college, so he did not go. With his parents caught up in an ugly divorce, Jack was really down on the world.

Each of us was adjusting to the demise of our comfortable, often happy home. We were a family in crisis, in a world in crisis as World War II raged. Uncle Ort was a stabilizing force in our devastated existence. He helped each of us set sail.

Brother was downright bitter over his parents' divorce. Because his parents couldn't get along, he felt shame. Deep down, to Jack, his parents' divorce was a disgrace and humiliation. Not yet eighteen, Jack came to Bay Minette to visit, and he was almost more than Mother could handle. He was peeved with her for letting the split-up of their marriage happen.

Uncle Ort spent a great deal of time with him during his visits. My wise, congenial uncle helped my brother pull himself together. Jack chose to be one of the "few good men" and signed up for the Marines. He was not yet of age, but Mother signed the necessary papers. He asked for and was granted sea duty and was soon on his way to the South Pacific, not caring whether he lived or died.

Ironically, about that time the beginning of the end, in Uncle Ort's parlance, came for Grandpa at Orange Beach when he stepped on a stingray in the sand. The poison in the old man's foot led to the loss of that foot and leg. At eighty, Grandpa had one leg amputated, but with the help of a prosthesis he walked no differently than any man his age.

Poor circulation soon necessitated the amputation of his other leg. Grandpa's life wound toward the end of the spool; Uncle Ort continued a faithful and loving son through thick and thin. On the first day of April in 1942, Uncle Ort wrote, "At 3:45 in the afternoon, a brave good man has gone to his reward." Further in his diary he wrote:

> April 1, 1942 Papa's death came peacefully at 3:45 p.m. He had been sinking noticeably for about seven days. Grew worse Sunday. Monday and Tuesday he sank rapidly and the folks were notified by mail. Telegrams sent 4 p.m. Wednesday. The whole town grieved at his passing. Many flowers.
>
> April 3, Papa buried at 2 p.m. *A very sad day in my life.*

The day following Grandpa's death Uncle Ort was busy meeting people who arrived by bus and train for the funeral. The relatives from Lutz traveled on a through train that did not stop in Bay Minette, so he met it in Mobile at 1:30 a.m. I came from Vanderbilt, and Jack, who had just entered sea duty with the Marines, also came. The day after the funeral, Uncle Ort took Jack to the creek fishing. The opportunity for the two distressed men to be together was healing for both.

When World War II was over, Jack was a veteran of two overseas assignments in the Pacific Theater. Near the end of the war he was engaged in hand-to-hand combat on Okinawa with the Second Marine Division. Miraculously, he survived without injury. The night before he was to be discharged from the Marines, November 5, 1946, Jack was injured by a hit-and-run driver on the corner of a downtown Jacksonville, Florida, street. As soon as the news reached Bay Minette, Uncle Ort took Mother in his car, and they drove down to the Naval Station hospital.

Jack's right leg and ankle were seriously crushed, resulting in twelve months of hospitalization. By Christmas-time he had recovered enough to be granted leave. Uncle Ort drove to Jacksonville, picked Jack up, and brought him to Bay Minette for Christmas. That was a great family Christmas by all accounts. I was in Japan serving as a flight nurse with the Fifth Air Force at the time, so I knew about this only through letters.

To Jack, his uncle loomed tall. He was invaluable in helping him cope. A hospital patient for a year, Jack went through repeated surgery, healing, and rehabilitation, with plenty of time to think. During that long, torturous hospital stay, Jack decided to reenlist in the Marines. His correspondence with a high school sweetheart had grown into a serious romance so that within weeks after his hospital discharge he got married and headed for Bay Minette to see Mother and Uncle Ort.

If one made a nice soft ball of all the loving relationships Uncle Ort cultivated, it would be a large one. He wrapped his love around our hearts and loved us in a way that met our needs whatever they were. Uncle Ort loved and communicated with people of all ages, colors, and beliefs, but family relationships were the dearest to him. They were his crown of glory.

18

The Family

ABOUT A WEEK AFTER ELOISE ENROLLED in the University of Alabama in Tuscaloosa, something happened that changed the history of the Ertzinger clan. The year was 1936.

Her roommate from Monroeville, Alabama, introduced Eloise to Walter Lindsey, a high school chum. Their chemistry was right–Eloise and Walter were attracted to each other. A few months later, at the Christmas break, Walter accepted my cousin's invitation to come to Bay Minette to meet her family.

Uncle Ort had complete confidence in his daughter's choice in boyfriends. Eloise's pick for a mate was his pick. Eloise and Walter made plans to be married after completing their baccalaureate degrees.

I well remember the talk about where to have the wedding. The Presbyterian church was too run down to be suitable for such an auspicious occasion. Aunt Tillie and Uncle Ort decided on a home wedding–actually a lawn wedding–in August. As Eloise explained, "We limited the guests so if it rained the ceremony could be in the house. The living room space wasn't too big for a wedding."

Now August is hot and can be a rainy month. That year it was.

Bridal showers in Eloise's honor were appropriately held amid torrents of rain. The haunting question in the minds of many was, would it rain on the afternoon of the wedding?

Before noon on the wedding day, while the women were arranging smilax inside, rearranging furniture, and thinking about a service in the large living room, others were working outside. As he was arranging chairs in the garden, Uncle Ort, in a confident, convincing voice, pronounced, "I'm counting on sunshine."

On August 22, 1939, the garden wedding in front of the circle of azaleas near blossoming crepe myrtle trees went off without a hitch. Mr. and Mrs. Walter Meeks Lindsey left home amid a shower of rice.

From the first meeting of the two men, there was a camaraderie between Uncle Ort and his son-in-law; their cordial feeling soon grew into genuine love. Walter quickly proved himself as the head of Ort's daughter's household. Uncle Ort and Aunt Tillie were proud of their new son—the "in-law" part was inappropriate, in their judgment.

By November, the newlyweds had found a house they wanted to buy in Birmingham, where Walter had a job with Tennessee Iron and Coal (T.I.C.). They invited Uncle Ort and Aunt Tillie for a weekend visit to see the house and give their opinion on it before a final decision was made. In her invitation Eloise included several enticements geared to her father's tastes: the Alabama-Georgia Tech football game and an evening of roller skating.

Uncle Ort was very pleased and bragged about Walter's good judgment in wanting to buy rather than rent. Renting a home was wasting money on someone else's property. Uncle Ort's real estate never included rental property.

Before long, with a loan from Uncle Ort, Eloise and Walter bought their home and moved in. (From where I sat, Uncle Ort was a model father-in-law, staying on the fringes while encouraging the young couple's ambitions.)

Several months later, Uncle Ort encouraged his visitors, Uncle Levi and his wife, Aunt Roki, to drop by to see Eloise in her new home. The Indiana relatives were pleased with the opportunity. Ort's family were a part of Levi's own clan. So on their return to Indiana they stopped with Eloise. They saw and shared her happiness in her big toy–a brand-new house never lived in before.

With fresh news to share about the bride and groom's love nest, Uncle Albert and Aunt Roka looked forward to spreading the word among their Indiana friends and relatives. What better way to communicate a kind of caring, the glue that holds families together!

****

Uncle Ort fished through the ice on Kilcrease lake the fall before his first grandchild was born–the coldest winter in forty years (according to his diary). In March Grandpa had his foot amputated, and Uncle Ort was by his side. On May 8, 1940, a few months before my uncle was 51 years old, he wrote in his diary (and to his friends), "Eloise gave birth to a baby boy. Am grandpa now." His grandson, David Erle Lindsey, was born in Birmingham, Alabama. The grandparents were ecstatic.

His second grandson, Jon, lived only three years. Gaye's birth five years after David's was an especially joyous occasion. Uncle Ort's first and only granddaughter, Gaye Paulette Lindsey, was born into a turbulent world. On April 12 of that year, Franklin D. Roosevelt, a four-term president of the United States, died in office. Harry Truman, the new president, ordered an American B-29 to drop the atomic bomb on Hiroshima on August 6, bringing about the end of World War II. Then in October Gaye arrived in Birmingham.

As a university student Walter had been in the Reserve Officer Training Corps, and he had accepted a reserve commission upon graduation. His military career in the Ordnance Corps in Birmingham was unbelievable. He lived in his own home while on active duty, traveled when necessary, and was discharged where he entered, having been promoted through the ranks from Second Lieutenant to Lieutenant Colonel without ever living on a military base.

Uncle Ort's diary is again the source of this piece of family history concerning his daughter's return to the town of her birth to live and the sale of J. A. Ertzinger & Son.

November 3, 1945, reached Birmingham on train in the rain. At Eloise's by 8 a.m. Held conference with Eloise and Walter. [Gaye was five months old.]

December 21, 1945, office at 6 a.m. Bought Trawick place today [located toward town from his home].

February 28, 1946, Ottilla went to Birmingham to help with the children and their move.

March 1, Office at 3 a.m. Eloise, Ottilla, David and Gaye came on No. 1. Walter arrived at night with the furniture.

March 2, office at 4 a.m. Walter and Eloise moved into new home. [As he had hoped, the Trawick house suited the Lindseys, and they bought it from him.] Lodge tonight.

April 1, Walter began at the office today. Office at 4 a.m. and all day. [Uncle Ort had sized Walter up as a promising businessman and agreed to sell him J. A. Ertzinger & Son with the thought that he would gradually retire.]

April 3, office until 3 p.m. Walter and I to camp, no fish, water too high. Slept 12 hours.

April 17, Everett and Betty House [guests from Indiana], Ottilla, David and I to Orange Beach for three days. [Uncle Ort wasted no time in laying claim to part of his grandson's time.]

The work at J. A. Ertzinger & Son was expanding. One day Uncle Ort mentioned the need for one more person to work in the office. Walter suggested his younger brother, Jimmy. So it was that Jimmy and Betty Lindsey moved to Bay Minette, where Jimmy became a part of the business and the family circle.

As the business expanded, so did these Lindsey families. Donald Raymond Lindsey appeared at the Mobile Infirmary on Saturday, March 5, 1949. The next day, after church, Uncle Ort and Aunt Tillie peered through the window of the hospital nursery at their newest family member. Eloise and son doing fine. Three days later the boom fell: Uncle Ort had his first heart attack.

The episode occurred after a day when Uncle Ort went to the creek to tend his trot lines, but found no fish. He was around town a while, but in the afternoon a sudden crushing chest pain took his breath away momentarily; he was faint and weak. Dr. McLeod made the diagnosis—a heart attack, angina. It was a shocker.

Uncle Ort recovered as Donald grew and thrived, but the heart attack gave him cause to take stock and count his blessings. The first time I saw him after he'd gotten back on his feet, he was all smiles. "My cup runneth over!" he exclaimed, much to my surprise.

He was happy to be alive. Life itself had a new meaning. The Lindseys, down the street, were a treasure of inestimable value to him. His sister next door was not so fortunate. Mother's grandchildren lived 500 difficult miles away, in Jacksonville, Florida.

He was not blind to the inherent dangers grandparents find in close relationships with their grandchildren. He knew full well that Eloise and Walter had the primary responsibility and complete authority as to what their children did or did not do. Usurping their prerogatives as parents was improper. But there was some haziness in his mind between parental and grandparental responsibility. He wanted so desperately to be an influence for good, a meaningful part of their growing up, to bring a wholesome, well-rounded dimension to their lives.

Like many a doting grandparent, he encouraged all of his grandchildren to develop every bit of talent they had. Their music lessons, their scouting and school activities were of more than passing interest to him. He was one grandparent who attended recitals not because it was expected of him but because he wanted to. He enjoyed every note. He always sat up front so as not to miss a trick.

More than once, almost as though speaking to himself, Uncle Ort vocalized that his cup was running over. He was thankful for his grandchildren's healthy bodies. He talked about the window of opportunity that was his—the chance to watch each child grow and learn and their personalities develop, to appreciate each grandchild's temperament and individuality.

Uncle Ort had more insight than most grandfathers into child behavior because he remained active with young people in the scouts, at school, and at church. He and I both enjoyed having an inside track on what Eloise's children said and did.

On Donald's seventh birthday, Uncle Ort made a diary note: "Donnie wants to go to Mardi Gras parades in Mobile, for his birthday." A year later, Uncle Ort mentioned taking him on their first fishing trip; the two of them went alone to Kilcrease Lake. Donald told me about that trip, too.

Donald Lindsey is now an architect. His voice is soft and his manner mild. Leaning back, with a special gleam in his eye, he reminisced:

> I wasn't considered old enough to go fishing alone with Gramp until I was about nine. He died when I was ten. We got in his old fishing car, a black Ford, and rode up into north Baldwin County to where he kept his boat. It was a custom-made flat-bottomed wooden boat, long and narrow with about four seats, and he had a little five-horsepower Mercury outboard motor. Gramp sat in the back and guided the boat, and I sat up in the front. He always fished with bamboo poles and worms–nothing fancy.
>
> We got out to the fishing spot, and he gave me a pole. He sat in the back and had about six poles out. He'd prop a pole over the rail and underneath the seat, with three going out of each side. While he was working six poles I was only working one. Naturally, he caught six times or more fish than I caught, although as I recall I did catch about nine fish that day myself.
>
> As he was fishing he constantly worked several poles. One time he was pulling up the line because he figured he'd lost the bait. Doggone it if he didn't have a fish on there after all. The hook wasn't in the fish's mouth but had hooked into the side of the fish as he pulled it through the water. Fish must have been plentiful for that to happen.

* * * * * * * * *

Back when my grandfather was alive, the two Ertzinger families, John Adams and Ort Harmon, often dined together after church on Sundays. When Mother returned to Bay Minette after she and my father split up, she joined the family for Sunday dinner. Eloise, Walter, and the children expanded that familiar custom. Then Betty and Jimmy joined the family dinner circle when they came to town; soon their children, Carol and Walt, came along. The Sunday table was set for a dozen people.

Uncle Ort was the head of the whole shebang as these dinners became a family tradition. These events were much more than a mere meal that fed the needs of the body: these get-togethers had a lasting meaning.

The congeniality of sitting facing each other over good food enhances conversation as it bounces from one topic to another, and an inevitable graciousness pervades the group. As I recall, the youngsters–David, Gaye, Donald, Carol, and Walt–were center stage. Often they were excused to play while the adults talked about the day's sermon, ball scores, local happenings, and the like. Topics varied.

The once-a-week event brought a pattern, a rhythm to life, especially for Mother, who did not have a mate and felt a stigma at being a divorcee. The young ones called my mother "Auntie," a term of endearment that pleased her and made her feel she belonged. More importantly, the meal allowed her to express her love through her culinary talents. Uncle Ort's enjoyment in eating was another incentive.

Chicken curry with all the condiments, squash pickles, homemade rolls, pork loin with sauerkraut and dumplings–these are examples of foods Mother lovingly prepared and served when the dinner was at her home. She doted on the compliments her meals got and loved setting the large dining table with her best china and silver.

The planning and preparation of the dinners rotated among four homes–Uncle Ort's, Mother's, and those of the two Lindsey brothers. Although I was on the fringe of these Sunday happenings, they were meaningful to me. Even while I was on the other side of the world, the thought of these Sunday gatherings gave me satisfaction, knowing that Mother was there. Uncle Ort, the unofficial head of the family, made me feel a part of the family circle; I had a sense of belonging.

The plan of rotation of the Sunday dinners from household to household built family wholeness and values. In the protocol of the rotating open-door policy, a sort of unwritten rule welcomed friends of the family. When I lived nearby, I felt free to invite my friends to

Sunday dinner anytime.

Often on holidays such as Easter, Christmas, and Thanksgiving, the Sunday dinner crowd swelled, and leaves were added to the table. When the crowd was large, the women pooled silver and dishes. Actually, they brought matching patterns of some eating utensils so that the food would be served tastefully–another way of building unity and connectedness.

Betty and Jimmy reminisced with me. Betty Lindsey, a soft-spoken, genteel lady from Virginia, has naturally curly hair. Her pleasant, smiling countenance is an Ort-pleasing model of a happy face. She spoke first.

"We used to enjoy the Sunday dinners together so much...and playing jokes on each other. I remember when Jim had a birthday, Mr. Ort bought a loaf of pumpernickel, and Mrs. Ertzinger iced it like a cake."

Jimmy, a man with silver-white hair and a witty manner, chimed in: "Mr. Ort passed the cake to me to cut. I put the knife in it. It went thump; I knew something was wrong. It sounded like–" Jimmy rapped with his knuckles on the table to imitate the sound. "All eyes were on me; everyone sat expectantly as I tried to figure out what to do. That beautifully iced loaf of bread was a birthday cake I'll not forget. I enjoyed every minute of the birthday trick.

"I had to get even with Mr. Ort!" The glint in his eye showed that Jimmy was still enjoying Uncle Ort's trick. "You know how we both drank a lot of water?" Jimmy looked at me with a questioning glance. "When I figured out what I wanted to do, I did not know that there would be company, someone other than the family, for dinner that day. When I saw there was, I decided to go ahead with my joke anyway.

"I was not seated right next to Mr. Ort; one of the guests sat between us. I managed to be next to the water pitcher, so when anyone wanted more water I could pour it. Before I went to the table I filled a glass with lukewarm water and put two goldfish in it. I covered the glass with a napkin and set it nearby. When Ort wanted some more water, I was ready.

"Mr. Ort passed his glass down to me, and I poured it full of water.

Then I switched glasses. I passed the glass with the fish to him, hoping of course that he would take a big gulp before he saw the contents.

"Unfortunately, the guest sitting between us saw the fish. She didn't know what was going on. Her bewilderment attracted Ort's attention." Jimmy was grinning from ear to ear as he related this to me. *"Mr. Ort knew what was going on."*

Jimmy reflected, "Mr. Ort didn't pass his glass for more water until he was ready to drink it. What I'd hoped was that he would take a big gulp of water before he saw the fish."

Obviously Jimmy and Uncle Ort had fun together. Their personalities were akin: both had the gift of gab, loved hunting and fishing. When I spoke of their likenesses, Jimmy agreed.

"I liked so many of the things Ort liked," Jimmy pointed out, "and we both sang and were jokesters. Ort was a big eater. I remember him eating raw oysters. He loved them. Mr. Ort was a real good friend, and we had many good times."

I looked at Jimmy. "I can see Uncle Ort eating oysters on the half shell. The way he gulped the large ones down without cutting them was breathtaking." We all laughed. The essence of Uncle Ort was with us that day as Jimmy and Betty talked of days gone by.

Not one family member who attended those Sunday dinners has forgotten them. Most visitors remember, too. The chicken and noodles, peach pickle, and Mother's chicken pie baked in individual Mexican pottery dishes–delicious as they were–are not the reason nobody forgets. Family and relationships were the really memorable ingredient.

Uncle Ort added a spark, a lively presence to those meals that has never been replaced. This comfortable time together enabled young and old to find a common denominator and a safe harbor.

There was something else. The heart and mind were refreshed; something of intrinsic value happened. In the relaxed setting of intergenerational give and take there was a domino effect. Everyone was in true community; the value of *the family* was experienced. The whole was larger than its parts–the tie that binds.

19

Orange Beach

THE ORANGE BEACH COTTAGE and its surroundings were like no other place in the whole wide world. Uncle Ort's stamp was upon them. Everyone who has ever been to the Orange Beach cottage remembers that place. Even people who spent only a few hours recall their visit there.

The cottage sprawls out at the end of the road, facing the bay. Entering the house from the back porch into the large kitchen, a magical forward momentum propels one forward through the wide hallway to the front of the house onto the front porch with a full view of Bay La Launch. The lapping of the waves becomes audible. As you walk straight ahead down the steps and gentle slope, the pine and oak and magnolia trees surround you. The ambiance of the coast penetrates one's psyche.

Geographically the Ertzinger cottage, now the Lindsey cottage, is south of the intercoastal canal, east of Highway 59. It is located on a strip of land between Bay La Launch and Terry Cove. By road it is a short three miles from the cottage to Cotton Bayou and the gulf. Many early mornings after daybreak and breakfast we would drive to Cotton Bayou and climb on Calloway's boat to begin our adventures in the gulf fishing. The clearness of the sea-green water and the roll of the waves took over as we left land and the calm, murky waters of the bay.

Arrangements had to be made to rent the boat for gulf fishing. In the blue waters of the Gulf of Mexico, Amel Calloway knew where to find the schools of fish, whether or not they were biting, when the waters were too rough for comfort. Amel made his living in the gulf. My uncle respected Amel's predictions, so when his friend Amel said fishing was good, that was the time to go.

After the boat was untied from the pier, the motors roared and the boat headed for the fishing grounds. The air of expectation among the anglers was almost visible. Uncle Ort was the emcee of these fishing trips, which meant things never got dull. He started getting the lines ready as soon as the boat left the pier. When we were in the gulf, we began trolling for Spanish mackerel as we headed for the red snapper banks.

Uncle Ort's attention was focused on pointing out sea creatures along the way- mullet jumping, porpoises (dolphins) with their smiling faces swimming alongside the boat joyfully leaping out of the water and plunging back in. We saw jellyfish with their boneless bodies spreading themselves in all directions in the clear aquamarine gulf water. Sometimes, as we neared the snapper banks, huge sea turtles swam among all kinds of fish.

Seeing fish, however, did not necessarily mean catching fish, for there were times when we watched the fish swim around and ignore our baited hooks. Why the fish refused was a matter of supposition–the fish were not hungry or the sun wasn't right. Even Uncle Ort could not make a fish bite. More frequently, however, we did catch fish, sometimes one right after the other.

The going-home fun came as the boat returned to shore. To look at and examine what others had caught was a high point of the adventure. Who had caught the most? Carefully Uncle Ort counted the catch and kind; he was ready to give an accounting to people waiting on the pier. The scales for weighing and ice and supplies for keeping the catch awaited us.

Aunt Ella liked to tell about the time she went fishing with Uncle Ort in the Gulf of Mexico and lost her dentures.

In olden days, Aunt Ella and her husband, Uncle Warren, drove up from Lutz, Florida, to Orange Beach each spring. Fishing with Uncle Ort in the briny deep was the pinnacle of those visits. The water was rough the day of Aunt Ella's infamous fishing trip. As fast as the hook hit the water, the fish bit it. The choppy, turbulent water rocked and tossed the boat as they pulled in red snapper and grouper.

Aunt Ella was pulling in a snapper when, lo and behold, up came her breakfast. She learned over the side of the boat in the process and lost her dentures. Once the teeth hit the water, they were gone; there was nothing anyone could do but look in amazement at where they had been. Aunt Ella put her hand over her mouth helplessly as the tragedy of what had occurred flashed across her face.

She was not one to dwell on her misery. After a short time down in the more stable cabin, she felt better and resurfaced on deck and caught more fish. Aunt Ella and Uncle Ort laughed together over the fate of her teeth. Fifteen years later Aunt Ella told me:

Ort got a big haw-haw over the episode. He was sympathetic about my being sick, but what made us laugh was imagining that a big fish ate my dentures. Ort gleefully speculated over what a fisherman thought who caught a fish with the dentures in its stomach. Would he think the fish ate the teeth's owner?

Fun on the beach and in the Gulf of Mexico, in my view, was superior to the bay. The gulf sand was whiter, the sea creatures were more numerous and varied than on Bay La Launch. Hunting turtle eggs when the moon was right on the warm gulf sands was exotic. The gulf waves were taller, saltier, noisier, and more sporty.

Digging coquinas, tiny shelled creatures about the size of a thumbnail, from the white sugary sands was fun. Uncle Ort showed Eloise and me how to dig in the gulf sand and catch these bug-like shellfish that disappear before your very eyes. Miraculously, each wave washed away the sand, exposing again those little critters. If we gathered enough, Aunt Tillie made broth from them. M'm! M'm! Good!

We often floated in the gulf in black rubber inner tubes. My uncle used his own hand pump to inflate them for us. Regular car-size inner tubes were okay, but the big truck tubes were a special thrill on the gulf waves. Uncle Ort could make his long, lithe body stretch so his feet would be over one side of a large truck tube and head resting on the opposite side and float like a leaf on the water. Many of us tried to do the same, but our legs wouldn't reach.

Uncle Ort had a sort of know-your-enemy approach to the undertow. He was emphatic on one point–at certain times and places the surf is not safe and can be deadly dangerous, especially when the tide is going out. These are times to stay on the beach: trying to outsmart the tide is hazardous. More than once he carefully explained how the tides move and the dangers of the undertow. I learned to respect and not fear those natural phenomena, and I still enjoy a gulf swim and feel indebted to him for what he taught me.

The moon, gravity, the tides, and undertow, Uncle Ort explained, are forces in our universe now the same as they were thousands of years ago. They bridge the span of time and put people today in direct contact with the past. The sound of the waves, from a loud roar to a gentle whisper, their power, the way they roll one after the other on and on is awesome. Watching the waves affects me at the core. The phosphorescence of the gulf water at night is a delight to behold and experience. The foam and water filled with bubbles are pretty to see but even better to feel.

The Orange Beach house was a part of Uncle Ort before I was born. He and a member of the Hall family bought the property on Bay La Launch in 1917. The purchase was a practical way for Uncle Ort to make an investment in his own recreation, a place to relax, swim, fish, and have fun, not a second home.

The first co-owner sold his part of the cottage to Hubert Hall, a bachelor lawyer who became a judge. Under their joint ownership agreement, Uncle Ort had the use of the cottage during the week, and Hubert used it on the weekend. This was an ideal arrangement for my church-going uncle, who wanted to stay in Bay Minette on Sundays.

But the time came when Uncle Ort purchased Hubert's part and was sole owner. He began to improve it, starting with the installation of indoor toilets, screening in the porch around the house, and other creature comforts.

A trip to Orange Beach in earlier days required careful planning. There were no places near the cottage to buy anything. Supplies and food came by boat. What you took was what you had. My uncle planned by making lists, an extension of his habit of making notes. Whenever he thought of something, he scribbled it down on whatever was handy– the backs of envelopes, scratch pads, anything available. To go to Orange Beach, he made more than one list–a list of household items to buy and take, another for groceries, another of things to do before he left.

Getting ready was a lesson in organization and so was fun in and of itself. Uncle Ort was responsible for the fishing equipment and games as well as medical supplies, with pine oil as one of the basic components. (That aromatic oil was magic: it was supposed to repel insects, but if they bit anyway we rubbed more in to relieve the sting. If a crab pinched a person, someone grabbed the pine oil to help it heal.)

Aunt Tillie was in charge of the household necessities such as linens and meal planning. They worked together to ensure that we would have the proper groceries. Food was extra-important. Aunt Tillie always came up with a flock of homemade goodies– jam, jelly, cookies, usually a freshly baked ham. Uncle Ort had a hand in getting the staple provisions–oil, sugar, meal, potatoes, butter, flour, and the like. The salt-water environment doubled everyone's appetite, but we always had an abundance.

It took the better part of a day to drive the sixty miles over unpaved roads. The car was loaded to the gills, but we still stopped and bought fresh vegetables in season–corn, squash, cucumbers, onions, tomatoes–knowing there would be space somewhere. The bakery near the railroad track in Foley was a regular stop, as was the ice plant.

Travel south of Foley took an adventurous turn, as the unpaved roads were sandy. We often got stuck in the sand. When this happened, everyone piled out, pitched in, and helped unpile things from the trunk of the car to lighten the load. Sometimes this was enough to get the wheels moving; other times we put palmetto leaves or newspapers on the sand for the tires to roll on. Uncle Ort knew what to do, and he made it seem like fun while the big block of ice we bought sat melting and dripping as we worked in the hot sun.

I do not recall a single time Uncle Ort got upset over getting stuck. There were times when we had barely gotten resettled in the car when we were stuck again and had to go through the same procedure. We sort of got used to it.

Once we reached the cottage, fishing was high on the agenda. We fished in the bay most often because it was more easily accessible and less expensive. But wherever we fished, it was the morning occasions that entranced me most. "Before daybust" was the way my childhood friend Rixine Moorer labeled the early-morning darkness at Orange Beach. With Uncle Ort at the helm of the boat, I was enthralled when day was breaking. Olé, Uncle Ort! Olé!

The oldest grandchild, David, has his grandfather's build–a large man with a fair complexion. He is the father of Heather, a recent graduate from Rhodes College, and Meg, a 1992 graduate of St. Paul's Episcopal School, currently a student at Presbyterian College. If Uncle Ort had been a fly on the wall and heard our conversation, he would have been as proud as a peacock. As he brought up his recollections of his Gramp, David's talk came as even as molasses.

"I remember going to the beach with him. It seemed like every Monday morning when he and Grandma got ready, I was at their house with my suitcase, ready to go. I'd have a couple of changes of clothes and my bathing suit, and I was *ready*.

"We'd get down to the cottage and blow up the air mattresses. Gramp and Grandma each had a bunk on the west side of the porch where they could look out on the water. We'd set up the beds soon after we arrived. I'd blow up my little mattress and put it on the porch; I'd sleep right between them. I did that for many years." David's face showed he enjoyed remembering. Thoughts of the fresh salt air wafting across the big, wide cottage porch danced in my head.

"We'd get up in the morning and usually head for Swirn's pier out front. We took poles, but no fish bait. First, we'd take some crab lines, tie hunks of smelly old meat on them, and toss them in the water at the end of the pier. Then we'd fish. Gramp fished with a stiff cane pole and a treble hook. He'd jiggle the hook to try to snag any fish that just happened to swim by. It worked. Pinfish were the most common catch."

To confirm what I'd heard, I asked, "The hook had three prongs, right?" David nodded yes.

"A treble hook," he repeated. Gramp called it Scotch fishing. We'd check the crab lines periodically. You could feel the lines getting tight or moving out, and then we'd work the line very cautiously and slowly pull it in. When the crab was near the top of the water, we'd scoop them up with a net. We'd spend several hours out there on the pier each morning.

"Then we'd walk to a place right in front of the cottage to clean them. A tree that had been cut off so that the trunk remained, with its roots in the edge of the water. This made a natural platform for cleaning crabs.

"Sometimes we rowed across the bay in front of the cottage to crab and fish. We rowed everywhere we went in the boat until he got the motor."

"Did you *like* going fishing?" I queried. "Did you ever go floundering with him?"

"I enjoyed it down there. I was never what you call a serious fisherman. Oh, goodness, yes, we went floundering together in the evenings. That was a big event–all the preparations that needed to be made for a floundering trip! Getting the gigs ready and the lanterns–the mantle put on the lanterns if they needed one, checking the gas. We lit them and got the mantle just right; then we turned them out until we got across the bay. The channel marker, a blinking light across from the cottage, was our guide. We rowed toward the light past the marker. The water had to be calm and clear to go floundering.

"Even after he had a motor we rowed across because he didn't want to make any noise that would arouse the fish. Gramp would row as silently as I can imagine anyone rowing–no squeaks of the oars or locks or splashing of water. We would not say a word as he rowed; it was often pitch-dark. We could see the Milky Way; the sky was absolutely gorgeous."

In Uncle Ort's presence and boat, those nights were alluring to David as they had been to me. What pleasant, peaceful thoughts come to mind when we recall the good Orange Beach things we enjoyed–the gentle lapping of the waves, the fragrance of the tall pines, the soft touch of the gentle breeze.

"Mosquitoes were awful. We used mosquito repellent, 6-12. I don't think the formula worked–we merely put a coat of oil on our body the mosquitoes couldn't get through.

"We'd get out and pull the boat along the shore while we gigged flounders and caught crabs. One time [I was] walking along, pulling the boat behind me, when all of a sudden a spear went sailing right by me into the water.

"I turned around, thinking, 'What are you trying to do?' I looked at Gramp. 'Don't move,' he demanded, as he walked right in front of me and scooped up a stingray as big as both my hands. Gramp's spear went directly in. Ugh! He threw the spear to keep me from stepping on it.

"Fishing for white trout was another thing we did on Oranoka Bay off Bear Point, now called Terry Cove. It was quicker to drive the car than go by boat. At Pirate's Cove, Gramp rented a boat for a dollar a day–a big ol' heavy rowboat made out of cypress. He'd put his five-horsepower motor on the back and away we'd go. We didn't go very far out in the bay, but we dropped anchor and caught fish. With cut bait and some frozen shrimp, we caught white trout by the tubs full. We tried to give them away; we'd catch a ton of them.

"Gramp knew the places, an area accessible only by boat, where there were oysters about knee deep in the water. Gramp would take a garden rake and pull up clusters of them, put them in the boat, and we'd ride back. He'd be shucking oysters and throw the shells in the water all the way back to the cottage." In my mind's eye I could see Uncle Ort doing just that.

"Once every few times down at the cottage, we'd go deep-sea fishing with Amel Calloway in the wooden boat he'd built himself. Calloway would take us out five or ten miles in the gulf, and we'd fish off the deck. Every summer Gramp took the church young folks out [in the] gulf.

"I remember one summer it was so rough in the gulf that the church organist and choir director, Mrs. Crosby, fell out of her chair when a big wave hit the boat. She was scared! Gee, she was scared. In fact, we all were, except Gramp. I don't remember about fishing that day, whether we caught anything or not; I just remember the water was rough. Deep-sea fishing was always exciting.

"Gramp and Grandma were willing for me to take my friends to the beach. They wanted me to have the companionship of people my age down there. I appreciated that. It was just a marvelous experience to be with Gramp and Grandma at Orange Beach.

"Gramp had an old fishing car, one of his black Fords–I forget the model, perhaps 1940 or '41. When he drove it to the beach I would ride in the front seat and Grandma and Susie in the back. The fishing poles were a bit tricky. He had permanent fixtures to hold the poles on the side of that old car. After the poles were in place, we had to figure out how to get in.

"There was an electric refrigerator at the beach with coils on top. The cases of soft drinks we took down there were kept cool in an old Coca-Cola box on the back porch. Gramp would buy a big block of ice in Foley to put in the drink box. Probably seven or eight of the twenty-five pounds we'd bought was left–so much melted on the way. One of the jobs Gramp gave me was to clean up that box. I had to drain it and dry it out before we left.

"I always had some tasks to do. When we got to the beach, we didn't do anything until we had the whole place ready to enjoy. I had to get the air mattresses blown up, the furniture from inside the house set up on the porch; everything had to be in its place.

"Gramp would say, 'Have you done this or that? We understand it's not much fun, but it's gotta be done. Go on and do it right away, and it will be done.' It took thirty or forty-five minutes to do the necessary things, which wasn't a major amount of time, but it seemed like an eternity to me. I'd see my friends out there swimming, and I wanted to go out immediately to see what was going on. The same thing on the clean-up: everybody had their job–sweep the porch, close the windows, clean out the ice box (that was the main thing for me).

"If there was anything close to Beulah Land for Gramp, it was Orange Beach." David smiled from ear to ear. "He looked on it as a camp: it didn't have to be painted and fancy, just clean and sturdy. He loved it."

As David talked I recalled Uncle Ort's joy in having grandchildren. There was something irreplaceable about his first grandparenting experience. He prevented himself from being the mawkish, gooey grandfather by being stern, just as he had handled his daughter. Stern discipline was proper discipline for children of his generation.

He slept on the screened porch, and usually his guests did, too. Each side of the house, divided by the corner, was like a room. When he set his mind to it, he did not need an alarm clock to awaken. To awaken others he used a very simple technique. He threw a plank on the floor not once but twice, one time for good measure. The bloodcurdling sound would have awakened the dead. Strangers to his wake-up call had to recover a bit to pull themselves together before they could dress. We got up with a bang, no doubt about it!

The reason for going fishing at such an early hour, Uncle Ort told us in a most convincing tone, was to get to the fishing grounds before the fish woke up. Uncle Ort's assertion went uncontested.

We ate the abundant breakfast Aunt Tillie prepared in the predawn hours, usually without much talk. We just followed along and did what Uncle Ort told us to do. We got in the boat and sat where he pointed, the same as when we went fresh-water fishing. Each person had a responsibility–one the oars, another the bait, another life preserver cushions, and so on.

The night before going fishing, Uncle Ort collected the poles and fishing paraphernalia. While we were doing the dishes after breakfast, he got the bait and checked the boat tied to a cypress stump right in front of the cottage, about a hundred yards from the shore. When we were ready, he untied the boat and pulled it onto the beach so we could get in.

My uncle's fair skin sunburned easily, but the sun's rays never had a chance. He did not intend to get sun-kissed, and if he had his way no one in his party would, either. He wore long-sleeved shirts buttoned at the neck, long pants, and high-topped shoes. I do not recall his using suntan oil, but when he was not in the shade, he put his handkerchief folded about three inches wide so it protected his nose–his proboscis, he called it. So we went fishing protected from the sun, with our shoulders covered even though it was still dark. We wore sun hats on a cloudy day.

Against the usual gentle lapping of the waves on the beach, the quietness in the dark was broken by our chatter as we walked about a hundred feet down the slight slope to the boats. Uncle Ort pushed the boat off, then jumped in. The oar made a crunching sound as he put it in the sand to push us out into deeper water before he began the mile or two paddle across the bay. With a natural rhythm he pushed the oars through the water, but not out of it. Raising the oars out of the water was wasted motion, Uncle Ort explained.

The hushed morning air was still. In sweet anticipation we awaited the sun. Then it broke through the darkness and progressively lighted the horizon, then the sky above, until finally our entire surroundings were aglow. The sense of quiet elation as we glided through the water was real.

Uncle Ort and I had a running dialogue about the lack of attention the beauty of the sunrise receives–this gorgeous spectacle that opens a fresh new day. The sunset extolled by writers, photographers, and poets gets much more attention than the sunrise. Sunrise loveliness tends to be a well-kept secret. We decided people sleep through this marvelous part of the day, else more credit would be given to the majesty of day breaking, the beginning. The sun rising, the dawn of a new, unblemished day is magic! Uncle Ort and I thought alike about the early morning times, a rich, out-of-this-world experience.

Bay trout did not bite in the middle of the day, so we stopped fishing and Uncle Ort rowed us home before the sun's rays became scorching hot. Back at the cottage, several hours before noon, Uncle Ort cleaned the fish, then stretched out for a nap in his swing.

He'd built the swing to fit his long, tall body–the longest swing I've ever seen. He hung it in an ideal location that permitted a person in the swing to see the beach or look out the back at what or who was coming down the road. We all swung or took naps in this swing, though no one questioned his priority.

To protect the swing during high winds, it was removed and set against the house. He devised a nifty way to detach the swing. Hooks well placed on the ceiling were detachable so the swing would come down without a lot of sweat–another of his efficiencies.

When his nap was over, he was up and at 'em again. His insatiable desire to fish usually took him down on the pier to "Scotch-fish"–the jiggle-the-hook fishing David talked about.

This method of putting the hook in the water (any depth is okay), then waiting for a fish to swim by and get snagged, continues at Orange Beach. Uncle Ort's great-granddaughter, Laura, finds it as fascinating today as did the people Uncle Ort taught to Scotch fish. Laura's grandfather, Walter, is now the teacher.

Come to think of it, other fishermen with Uncle Ort's expertise and means are not likely to have engaged in such a simple type of fishing as he did. Uncle Ort Scotch-fished with the same gusto and pleasure that marked deep-sea fishing in the gulf.

The cottage was a place of rest and relaxation for Uncle Ort, but not in the usual sense. Rest for him was not sitting down and doing nothing, but respite from his regular schedule, a change of pace, a doing-something-different kind of rest. Orange Beach is a place Uncle Ort stayed busy while resting.

20

More about Orange Beach

FAMILY MEMBERS WITH THEIR FRIENDS traditionally occupied the Orange Beach cottage. I can count on one hand the number of people who used the cottage when Uncle Ort, Aunt Tillie, or Eloise was not there. Judge F. W. Hare was one exception. The judge of the 21st Judicial Circuit in Monroeville was a V.I.P.I.–a Very Important Person Indeed. This handwritten keepsake tells of an August visit.

7/30/42

Dear Ort,

Did not get to see you when we came through Bay Minette on our way home from the Orange Beach cottage to thank you for your generous kindness. I know that you know that I am most appreciative but you just can't know how much this great favor meant.

All of us enjoyed our stay at the cottage, and this is especially true of Mrs. Hare and her sister. They asked that I express their appreciation.

Your friend,

F. W. Hare

Mrs. Hare added a note: "I want to express my thanks too, for one of the happiest vacations I've ever spent. Your cottage is comfortable and cool and the water is grand. Thank you for the loan of your lovely place."

All round the cottage graceful water oaks and waxy green magnolia leaves drip with moss; the landscaping includes palmetto and marsh grass, all part of the Orange Beach essence. As was the lackadaisical lifestyle: mowed lawns and trimmed hedges were nonexistent. Uncle Ort's kingdom by the bay was alive with laughter and talk. In the afternoon, vacationers played mah-jongg or Rook on the back side of the house where the afternoon breeze stirred. In the morning and evening, the front porch was ideal.

Because of the relative isolation, Mother Nature reigned. A stroll along the shore revealed all kinds of oddities–shells of crabs, cleanly sunned vertebrae of fish, maybe the head of a fish skeleton, the curious-looking sand patterns where fiddler crabs crawled and the tiny holes marking where they had burrowed into the sand. Barnacles on old pieces of piling or driftwood added to the variety of marine life.

Fetching crabs and cleaning them, I always thought, was a specialty with my uncle. The danger of sunburn precluded crabbing in the hot sun; otherwise we crabbed 'most anytime. Uncle Ort had three ways of catching these creepy-crawly crustaceans with two claws and three pairs of legs.

One was to walk along the shore in shallow water, find a crab, capture the creature in a net with one swoop, and put him in the bucket. Crabs blend in with their habitat, so seeing them is not easy, but Uncle Ort had an eye for the lively creatures.

Another way was to tie smelly old meat to strings as bait, then throw them out into the water and attach the other end to the pier or in the sand. Crabs that nibble the bait are slowly pulled up, then scooped in with a net.

An easier and more recent way to crab was with a chicken-wire box trap. Uncle Ort placed smelly old meat in the inner compartment of the trap to draw the prey, then dropped the trap into the water off the pier. Less tending was necessary this way. My uncle's friend Howard, who lived behind the cottage, made these cages approximately three feet square.

Howard walked on his knees. He lived alone in a makeshift house he had put together, and, despite his handicap, he kept busy with his hands. He made all kinds of objects from cypress knees–the roots that grow on top of the ground. Gathering this wood from the moccasin-infested swamps was dangerous, especially for a man walking on his knees. Uncle Ort greatly admired Howard's independent spirit; he did not act handicapped. David described Howard this way:

Howard was a kind of remarkable man. He made a home for himself. He poured the concrete sidewalk. I remember watching him lay the blocks and build those concrete block benches that are still there. It was impressive.

Of course, Gramp liked everybody. I never saw anybody he really had anything against. And it didn't matter where you came from or whether you were rich or poor.

He would hire people like Howard to help him with something they could do. He thoroughly enjoyed helping other people. He encouraged Howard in working with cypress knees, such as the ways he could use a certain crooked knee or odd-shaped piece of wood to make a lamp.

Howard had a creative spirit, and he worked ingeniously making wall and table lamps and other attractive cypress ornaments to sell.

Back to the crabs. No matter which way one caught a crab, care was always taken to tear off the crab's pincer claws as soon as possible, else the lively creature would climb out of the bucket. Many people did not want to have anything to do with the crabs because of the pincers. A pincer could easily grab onto some part of you and cause great pain. Crabs looked dangerous, but by following Uncle Ort's specific directions they were easily managed. He *showed* us how.

The toe of Uncle Ort's black high-topped shoe held the crab fast while from the back he took a pincer claw in each hand and broke it off. Uncle Ort explained that crabs regrow their claws. He'd point out crabs with one claw larger than the other or a crustacean with several claws missing. Another thing he taught me was the difference between a male and a female crab. he threw away the bright-orange eggs that protruded from the pregnant mother. The claws went into one container and the cleaned bodies into another.

Even without the pincer claws the crabs clambered around in the bucket. There was a time when we cooked them by putting the whole crab directly into a boiling pot. On occasion they crawled out on the stove and onto the floor. This called for a drastic change. We found that a better way was to tear them apart and clean them alive, then cook them.

David spoke of the special stump where we cleaned crabs. Uncle Ort's strong hands and deft fingers were quick to remove the innards using the water from the bay. The spongy, lung-like tissue called "dead man's fingers" was thrown away. I never merely watched Uncle Ort clean crabs. Little by little he got me involved.

At first Uncle Ort would hand me a clawless crab, saying, "That's a female. Be sure to clean out all those yellow eggs." It would have been embarrassing to my ego to be squeamish. Uncle Ort thought I could do it, so I did. Dissecting a crab was sort of enticing. With my uncle's careful attention and patience, it was a snap. Uncle Ort would teach anything he knew to anyone who wanted to learn.

Catching and cleaning crabs was an opportunity that came only at the beach. It never dawned on me that anyone would ever consider this work or distasteful. It was something I was proud to have mastered. Having a part in preparing the crab, in an odd way, enhances the pleasure in eating them—makes crabs a special delicacy.

There was satisfaction in having a part in the delicious fried or stuffed crabs or crab gumbo that we ate at the large kitchen table. The same was true with coquinas and fresh-caught fish. In community with others I contributed to the exceptionally tasty meals we enjoyed at Orange Beach. This is akin to the chef's enjoyment in using just the right ingredients to prepare a gourmet's delight.

Orange Beach was a delight because of the things to do there. Unique opportunities to learn about coastal flora and fauna were on our doorstep. With Uncle Ort as our teacher, learning was done in a novel and entertaining way. Gathering food from the surrounding waters made the cottage an arena for special entertainment.

Next to the Ertzinger property, right on the beach, a trickle of fresh cold water ran into the bay from a nearby creek. Uncle Ort spotted an alligator there, not too far from the cottage. I do not recall actually seeing the critter. We didn't bother the alligator, and the alligator didn't bother us. It was daring just to talk about that ugly thing living so close.

* * * * * * * * *

In later years, while Uncle Ort was adjusting to a life circumscribed by a medically dictated regime, Orange Beach had a special place. Upon my return from my first tour of duty in the Philippines, Japan, and Korea, I was stationed at Eglin Air Force Base east of Pensacola, about a three-hour drive from the cottage. I saw him every couple of weeks.

I counted on being with Aunt Tillie and Uncle Ort as much as Mother when I visited Bay Minette. Their keen interest in tales of my experiences in the Pacific Theater turned me on. They added spark and laughter.

The sudden angina attack had caught Uncle Ort off guard. It heightened his appreciation for life and his depth of pleasure in everyday things. Enjoyment in living was nothing new to him, but Uncle Ort's changed perspective on life made him aware of its goodness as never before. Perhaps he became more boastful.

He was proud of his reputation for integrity and his financial security. He spoke with contentment about his friends, his family. Slower steps and the abandonment of hurry were hallmarks of his post-attack stride although he had continued business dealings. Those who thought Uncle Ort was the personification of perpetual motion and an inexhaustible supply of ideas did not notice much change. Many people advised him about his health, but he never broached the subject on his own.

My aunt and uncle became substitute parents. Without knowing it, they eased the void in my life that came from not having parents who lived together and the absence of what I perceived as a real home. The compensation and satisfaction that came as my friends became their friends brought a kind of family wholeness.

After each visit in Bay Minette or at Orange Beach, I returned to my barracks bubbling with talk about my fabulous uncle. Ellen Adams from North Dakota, Esther Earnest from Ohio, and Tommie Thompson from Tennessee visited me in Bay Minette and at Orange Beach. Strangers to the Gulf Coast, they had a keen interest in local natives, so they wanted to see and learn about their Southern environment.

That was a come-on to my Uncle Ort and Aunt Tillie. Uncle Ort delighted my fellow Air Force officers with facts, guided tours, and stories about hunting deer, turkey, squirrels, quail, and bears. He told them about the cultivation of crops—gladioli, potatoes, cucumbers, corn, and other vegetables—and how they were shipped by train from Baldwin County.

He exposed them to the life in these parts, which included the timberland, sawmills, and a veneer plant in the northern part of the county. Crabbing, fishing, swimming at Orange Beach and drives through the countryside together were a part of the menu. Sunday dinners helped mold friendships with these ladies from various parts of the United States.

Wherever he was, Uncle Ort managed his time efficiently. He could sandwich in many things in a short time. Like the military strategists, if Plan A did not work, he moved automatically to Plan B. I do not remember him ever being at loss for something to do.

Once their Orange Beach stay was interrupted. This is what he wrote: "An increasingly uncomfortable and cold East wind blew between the cracks of the cottage. Packed up and went home."

They returned to Bay Minette, not with a disappointed spirit because a storm had chased them off, but with a light heart and stomach's full of Meme's cooking. You see, they drove home via Bon Secour.

Now Meme's on Bon Secour River was a place Uncle Ort loved. Charley and Meme Wakefield, the proprietors, were his friends, so stopping there to dine was a double pleasure. He loved listening to Charley tell tales about old times in Bon Secour.

> You just can't hurry good food, Charley says. Meme has a spoon which is proof of that. The spoon is almost square across the bottom because it has been used so long to stir the slow, simmering gumbo.

Food, Fun and Fable from Meme's is a collection of Bon Secour tales of the river country and recipes. The introduction states:

> Here and there across the world are places whose names are magic, their very sounds convey security and comfort, adventure and romance. Such is Bon Secour. It is not a place, it is a tradition.
>
> To the founders of the village, the French, the Spanish, the English and the Baltic German, it meant exactly what it said, "the good security." These founding mothers and fathers wanted freedom, and a lee shore, and a little boat, and a farm, but they were sea-faring people who loved blue water as an inebriate loves liquor. Bon Secour became the golden charm which gave people their deepest desires. They preserved its stories of heroism and humor and gentleness.

Recipes for gumbo roux, summertime crab gumbo, chicken and oyster gumbo fill the pages. Without exception, gumbo at Meme's was superb, but so were foods such as sweet potato cake, green corn pudding, grits baked with cheese, persimmon bread, and buttermilk pie. Meme's cooking methods were also important to her outstanding food. Uncle Ort loved to recite this poem-recipe, "How to Make Gumbo":

> Cook it easy–let it grow.
>   If you don't, away will go
> All the flavor–all the savor.
>
> Stir it well–with Mamma's spoon.
>   It has served for many a moon,
> Served it well–many a spell.
>
> Take the oysters, shrimp, and fish.
>   Fashion many a tasty dish.
> Make the gumbo–cook it slow.

Even Uncle Ort, a restless soul, agreed that waiting while the food was prepared was a part of the experience of dining at Meme's. The splendor, the tranquillity, and the ambiance of the place amid the wonderful spreading arms of the water oaks dripping with Spanish moss made waiting an enjoyment and whetted your appetite. Meme's never took a reservation and was featured in *Ford Times*.

Uncle Ort introduced me to this legendary place. Before my first visit, he described the food in such glowing terms that my expectations were pretty high. Although the restaurant was unpretentious, I wasn't disappointed, as the food lived up to its advance billing. The setting of the restaurant, under great oaks near the wharf where the boats tied up, was picturesque, too. When Uncle Ort got a proper boat, travel on the intracoastal canal from Orange Beach to Meme's made going there even more memorable.

Uncle Ort was an unsolicited publicity agent for Meme's. He told many others about this wonderful out-of-the-way place where one could enjoy the fresh fruits of the locale prepared and served in true Southern style. Promoting something he enjoyed was Uncle Ort's way.

Across the road from Meme's restaurant he bought raw oysters right out of the bay. Somewhere in that vicinity he had bought the oysters he took to Huntington back in 1914. Bon Secour was well known for its oyster reefs, which produced very large oysters–seventeen to the quart.

I do not believe in ghosts, but I must declare that since his death in 1959, especially at the Orange Beach cottage, Uncle Ort's presence and spirit has been preserved. Gaye, Donald, and David remember their grandmother, years after her husband's death, sitting on the Orange Beach front porch telling this story:

> One day when Gramp and I were fishing in the bay, Gramp had tied a piece of meat to a rope and thrown it off the back of the boat just to see what he might catch. Suddenly the boat started moving backwards! Something had grabbed the meat and was towing us. He couldn't pull it in; it was too strong. Gramp wasn't about to cut the rope!

Fortunately it swam close to shore, and they were able to call for help. Some other fishermen rowed out and were able to kill the sea monster that had hold of their rope. It was a stingray measuring six feet tall and wide, excluding the stingers. They hung it between the gateposts in front of the cottage to take pictures. After the picture taking, they had problems disposing of it. They buried it, but the pigs running loose in the area dug it up. They buried it three times before the pigs gave up.

Once when I was at a very low ebb I went to the cottage alone. No relatives or friends were invited. I took a pile of books and food. Sometime and somehow during my week's stay Uncle Ort's optimism and stick-to-it-iveness penetrated the thick clouds of my despair. I regained my perspective on life and went home a happier person. The spirit of his presence was almost as reassuring as it would have been had he been there in person.

As another example, ten years later I was up to my ears in my work as Administrator of Nursing at Bishop State Junior College. The deadline for writing a proposal for a federal grant was nearing. The pace of activities in my office did not allow me time to think and write creatively. Fortunately, I was granted time to withdraw from my routine duties so I could concentrate on proposal writing. I went to Orange Beach.

This time the rains came, and thunder and lightning were my companions at the cottage. And so was Uncle Ort. We had sat together on that porch as the wind blew and the waves danced. We watched rain and fancy patterns of lightning across the bay. I remembered this and felt a sense of harmony with the past. You guessed it. Uncle Ort's you-can-do-it spirit transcended my confusion. I got my thoughts together and completed the proposal, which subsequently was approved.

The fishing poles Uncle Ort had arranged neatly on the porch hung there for years after his death, never used. Finally they were given away. The small sapling pines have grown to be a foot or more in diameter, and the house continues to nestle among live and water oaks, mimosa, and magnolias, which have to be cut and pruned regularly. The cypress stump at the water's edge where we cleaned crabs in almost gone, but a water oak has grown nearby and provides welcome shade for those who want to play in the sand.

The basic structure of the square house with high ceilings and attic space has not been altered. The porch has gone through several floors, screens, and coats of paint. Secure behind more bolts and locks than ever before, the cottage continues to have a unique appeal, sitting on a rolling slope approximately sixty yards from the water.

Orange Beach proper is now an incorporated town with an aggressive city government. Planners talk of a new road to connect it directly with Interstate 10. A bridge over the bay would probably be visible from the cottage. So far, the growth all around has only slightly disrupted the tranquillity and naturalness of the cottage. A new generation of the family is at the helm of the cottage now—Donald, Gaye, and David Lindsey.

Even in the present era, the Orange Beach cottage is unique to some in the way my uncle intended. Almost as if a hereditary gene had transmitted specific qualities, it has an Uncle Ort quality that is different. A hard-to-put-your-finger-on specialness still exists about the place. Uncle Ort's oldest great-grandchild, Heather Lindsey, and her college friends have been affected by the Orange Beach virus. Their comments in the guest book make me think it is the same virus I have.

> Where else does the air smell so sweet and the water glow? Thanks for another summer kick-off. There is magic here. Hope to be back again and again and again and again.
>
> My fifth year here—hard to believe. Thanks for another set of memories—grand chaotic fun. We're all headed in different directions once again. Caroline to the Peace Corps in Africa, Jay to Paris. Robert starts grad school, Michael further into politics in D.C. Andrea continues to study art history.

Uncle Ort did a good thing when he bought a place for leisure time on Bay La Launch.

21

Gramp

UNCLE ORT'S FIRST GRANDCHILD naturally remembers more about his Gramp than his brother and sister. As we talked together, David encouraged me in writing about my uncle.

> Church worship was awfully important to Gramp. He and Grandma took their trips, but every Sunday he'd go to Sunday School somewhere. He just did not miss. They'd be at the beach Monday through Friday, drive home for Sunday School and church, and go back to the beach on Monday.
>
> He sang tenor in the choir and for many years was the only man. From time to time there would be one other man, but often only Gramp.
>
> When a new minister came, Gramp was like a kid. He would get so excited he could hardly wait to get acquainted and show the new minister around. He was happy doing church work–that was a joy, never a drag.
>
> Gramp was usually at the church when anything was going on–from the time the doors opened until they closed. Sunday nights he went to Young People's meeting, then church afterwards. All through my high school days that's what I remember him doing. I'd go home with them Sunday evening and spend the night; on Monday morning I'd go to school, right next door.

Members of the congregation decided they needed a new church building. I think this was in the early '50s. Bob Seidentopf was the minister. Some of the elders didn't think we needed a new church, and there was a split because of it, but Gramp was dedicated to a new building. My father was chairman of the building committee. Church members thought of all kinds of ideas to raise money. The building costs were $100,000, a lot of money back then to that small church.

Gramp came up with the idea of selling Coca-Cola bottles to make money. There was a two-cent deposit and refund on each empty bottle. During the week when he was on business around the county, he would notice Coca-Cola bottles along the road. He could see a bottle in three feet of grass–I've never seen anything like it.

He remembered where he saw each bottle, so on the weekends he and I would go out and pick them up. He'd pull off the road; I'd hop out and pick up the bottles. Later, in his back yard, we put them in cases. When he had a load, he took them to Beasley's Grocery. He sold them, and he turned the money over to the church building fund. He was unbelievably committed to this project.

The Young People made an incredible $1200 for the new building. That's a lot of two cents and a big heap of Coca-Cola bottles. Fifty bottles to make a dollar. In the cornerstone of the church, one of the many artifacts is a Coca-Cola bottle.

Jimmy Lindsey, as well as David, recalls bottle pickup times.

He got to be almost fiendish about bottle collecting. He and I were in his car; going around a curve he saw a bottle on the side of the road, stopped his car right there, got out, and picked it up. Another car coming down the road almost hit us. He could spot a bottle out of the corner of his eye. That was when Coca-Cola came in bottles that were cleaned and used over and over, some so worn from use that the bottom edge was rounded.

Uncle Ort's idea stirred up tremendous interest in Coca-Cola bottles. To some church members, selling old bottles was a trivial way to a lofty goal. A few even scoffed at the idea that a significant amount of money could be made from discarded bottles. They did not know Uncle Ort: their skepticism did not bother him at all. There were plenty of other people who admired his effort and joined his bottle brigade.

His reputation as a God-fearing man working to build a new church was enough to gain their cooperation. Admirers of his Coke bottle idea were not simply church folk; all sorts of people brought bottles, which he accepted with grace. Pride was reflected in his voice when he told me about some of the people who'd brought bottles–unchurched people, some from other denominations, several who were complete strangers to him.

Many people who brought bottles found dignity in having a part in the building of a place of worship. People with no money to give, in the simple act of bringing him a discarded Coke bottle, could contribute to building a church. This was their stamp of approval on a good idea.

The cases and cases of bottles they brought him stacked on his back porch were a clear sign to me that Uncle Ort was making it possible for just about everyone to help build the church. Collecting Coke bottles for the church was an Ortish thing to do.

David commented: "Gramp selected and donated the organ for the new church. I never will forget sitting by him in the choir the Sunday when the announcement was made. The session voted to name the fellowship hall the Ertzinger Fellowship Hall. He broke down. He really did–he got choked up and was overcome with emotion. That impressed me. The new church buildings were terribly important to Gramp.

"I don't know whether you remember or not"–here David looked at me questioningly–"but every Sunday night we had onion sandwiches. Sometimes we ate just mayonnaise on bread with great big slices of Bermuda onions. Other times we had thick slices of roast beef and Bermuda slices. That was a kinda funny habit–Grandma and Gramp and their onion sandwiches on Sunday night.

"Everyone at church was invited to come home with them for this treat. No one ever took them up on the offer, but they were invited, week after week." I did remember their Sunday-night routine. Those big, juicy Bermuda onions were white and sweet.

"After sandwiches, he and I would take a pint of chocolate ice cream from the refrigerator. We would literally take a rule to measure, then cut the frozen brick of ice cream in half. He would eat half, and I would eat half–a little ritual between us."

"Uncle Ort was a great one for measuring and counting," I recalled.

"He sure was. Coming back from Orange Beach and going down he had certain distances in the journey that he counted. I think he called them laps. One usually thinks of a lap in connection with track. Anyhow, the first lap coming home was from the cottage to the canal bridge. The second lap was from the bridge to Foley, the third was to Robertsdale, and the next to Loxley. And there were a couple of other landmarks he had along the route. The mileage between the marks was about 15 miles. He liked to count and measure things.

"Some Monday mornings at his house, I'd wake up with a start–Ba—a—m—m. The squirrels ate his valuable pecans and got into the attic; they were quite a nuisance. They bothered him so much that he got his shotgun and shot them. That was kinda unusual, right there in the middle of town." David chuckled, looking puzzled. "After he shot at one, the squirrels would not bother them for a while.

"One other thing I remember vividly," David confided. "I must have been five years old; I couldn't swim. It was Christmastime, and we were at Orange Beach. Uncle Jack, with his leg in a cast, was with us." This was the Christmas after Jack's accident, when Uncle Ort brought Brother from the Jacksonville Naval Hospital to Bay Minette.

"We were out on the pier fishing. I was sitting on the edge of the pier with my feet on a supporting beam. When I turned around to say something, I leaned forward; all of a sudden I fell in, completely dressed. I was going down a third time when Gramp jumped in and grabbed me. Uncle Jack said he was about to go in, cast and all, when his uncle intervened. Gramp saved me!"

Before continuing, David glanced at the list of memories he wanted to share with me. "The first traveling out of the United States he and Grandma did was to Alaska. I have his copy of *The Alaskan Challenge*, the book which inspired Gramp to want to see this faraway country where hunting and fishing were supreme. They planned all their trips carefully; upon return, he wrote an epistle about his trip.

"Gramp's typing was spectacular, so you remember the way he typed using the three-finger method on an old manual typewriter? He sat down and made that machine go–I mean fast–with three fingers. He used two fingers on the right hand, the index and the middle, and his left index finger. B—o—y, he could pound away on that thing.

"He typed up the story of everything they had done and seen, including the names of friends he made along the way. He noted the dates and times of various activities. Daddy had a duplicating machine at the office, so Gramp made copies of this treatise, which he shared with interested readers.

"He also took movies. I saw the movies of his trips so many times if he had stopped narrating I could have continued and never missed a word. He really enjoyed talking about his travel experiences."

I had an unanswered question. "David, do you remember your Gramp being proud of you?"

That caught David by surprise. He hesitated. I'm not sure he had ever given much thought to that question. Uncle Ort's praise, I suppose, was not given in his grandson's hearing.

"Not exactly. He was an authority figure to me. I never felt that he did not want me to be with him." David spoke slowly, choosing his words. "So I guess he did feel proud. It was almost standard that I would be there trekking along behind him at the beach." David searched his feelings as he spoke. "Gramp was always very patient. He never hurried me. He let me drive the car when I was just fourteen and I could hardly see over the dashboard.

"Once when I was behind the wheel on the way to the beach, a highway patrolman passed us. I was scared. Gramp told me to just keep going. The patrolman never stopped us, but I was afraid he was going to. Gramp was great to me; he soothed my upset feelings, and I was grateful. I think he drove Mother and Daddy crazy with the things he let me do.

"Gramp was a very important part of my earliest memories. We'd come down from Birmingham, where I was born, to visit him. I was sick when we moved. Of course I remember my teenage years with Gramp although the word teenage was not in common use then.

"Gramp went fishing from Kilcrease landing. He had a boat made just the way he wanted it–long and narrow so it would go in between the roots, vines, and snares of the creek and river. He kept it tied up to a tree at the landing on the Kilcrease property along with seven or eight other people's boats. Stopping for ten or fifteen minutes to visit with the Kilcrease sisters was a part of going to Owl Creek. Miss Sue and her sister, Sadie, two old maids, lived there on the old family place. They gave him the key to the gate we had to go through to get to the boat.

"I'd sit there and listen to them talk. They had an old Model T Ford they kept in a garage. I don't know who drove it, but I remember sitting in that thing before I could drive. I was dreaming of driving and playing with the gears. I thought it was one of the neatest cars in the whole world. I wonder what ever happened to it." David's eyes had a faraway look as he recalled those pleasant moments.

"They had a blacksmith's shop up there in a building near the house." David's wistful expression and tone of voice matched the nostalgia I was feeling. I thought of the Kilcrease house sitting in the middle of a clean-swept country yard without a blade of grass. "Miss Sadie and Miss Sue," David repeated. "Miss Sue was the one who did the most talking. They were both so nice to me. After our visit, we would head on back a mile or two to the creek and unlock the gate chain lock and drive through their field to the stream to Gramp's boat.

"Remember that old trail, the path we had to go over to get to the landing? You really couldn't call it a road. That's what the old fishing car was for–driving over that rough trail. The same car we sometimes took to the beach. Those times are good to look back on."

Then he confirmed Don's story. "Gramp would sit in the back of the boat and scull with one paddle. When he slowed down, he would sit on one end of the poles with the baited hook in the water. He was called 'Spider'–he could work five or six poles and catch fish faster than anyone I've ever seen.

"I didn't go to Kilcrease with him as often as I could have because he was too hard a fisherman for me. He wanted me to do exactly like he said; I couldn't take a lot of it. I look back now and wish I had. He was very serious about fishing.

"The camp where we went was built on a whole bunch of logs tied together to form a raft. He built a deck on top for cooking and also a screened-in room with bunks for sleeping. We used worms for bait most of the time and took along gunny sacks to put the fish in. Sometimes we fished from the camp; most often we'd go into either Dennis or Kilcrease Lake that flowed into the Tensaw River. Gramp knew the bottom of those streams better than some people know the palm of their hands.

"He gathered wood from the banks nearby, then built a fire in an old metal cooker. After he'd gotten the coals ready, he'd throw on some potatoes wrapped in aluminum foil. While they cooked we rowed down the creek a little way and fished. He knew where the fish were! We'd come back, clean the fish right there on the raft, and immediately fry them on that cooker. Another way he'd do was to chop up onions, put them on top of potatoes in a pan to cook, then fry the fish. M'm! M'm! Good! eating!

"It was fun being with Gramp out in the open. He taught me to shoot. We took shotguns and shot two or three boxes of shells when we went snake shooting. We'd ride along in the boat, and all of a sudden he'd see a snake and point it out to me. If I saw it, I'd shoot; if I didn't, he'd shoot. Every now and then, he'd shoot just for the fun of it. I'd shoot probably thirty or forty snakes, and he'd shoot seven or eight. He always let me shoot first. We had nicknames. Gramp was 'Eagle-Eye Ort,' and I was 'Dead-Aim David.'

The family was so important to him and to my parents. Gramp certainly was interested in me and spent a lot of time with me. Our closeness and the things we shared has meant a lot. I feel terrible today that my children do not know their grandparents as well as I knew Gramp and Grandmother. It's unfortunate that today we do not have that closeness."

As my enlightening conversation with David came to an end, I reflected that *family* is in some respects a catchall word. One dictionary definition considers it a genetic fact, something we are born into. To me it is more. I think of Uncle Ort as a model for my notion of family and family values.

Too often, the term *family* is a facade, merely a word, with a sterile connotation and no essential meaning. But to countless Americans, being a family is more than simply having a common bloodline. Being a family encompasses something that does not happen automatically.

Members have to *know* something about each other–to share ideas, attitudes, likes, and dislikes–to be a family. Whether through letters and telephone calls or in face-to-face communication, something has to take place *between* people for the word *family* to have substance, to have true value. Shared circumstances, jokes, stories, and experiences are the building blocks for a family. Only these can create a common spirit.

Uncle Ort would agree with former president George Bush, who is quoted as saying:

> What makes family family? It is more than blood, it's discovering in the other what you like about them, ignoring, accepting and understanding differences, maybe even laughing at them. Every family has its own life, a soul of its own, unlike any other.

22

A Nonconformist

UNCLE ORT WAS SOMETIMES ECCENTRIC in his dress–hand-made nightshirts, high-topped shoes, and detachable shirt collars long after they were out of style. This was a part of the mystique that was my uncle. As a churchman he was no different; some of his ideas were also nonconforming.

I remember times when, as a ten-year-old, I saw my uncle stand up front at the Baptist revival and lead the singing. I was proud of him. My uncle knew the church leaders of all faiths; music was the common bond. People from three or four denominations sang together at union services on Sunday summer evenings. In all sorts of ways–quartets, duets, and choirs–they joined happy voices in special music. The interdenominational togetherness in those days was heartwarming. I read in his diary.

New Baptist minister preached opening sermon tonight. Our church over to hear him. Sunday School, then to Methodist church–Caravan here today.

He and members of the youth group attended every service of the Methodist Caravan the following week.

The countless things Uncle Ort did in the church and the community, year after year. led me to wonder when he had time to make a living. He spent a great deal of time as a volunteer fire chief, a Mason, a worthy patron of the Eastern Star, an avid hunter, and an environmentalist. He attended meetings on time as regular as clockwork.

By now I suspect you have picked up on the fact that my uncle was the instigator of many things. The *Times* described the commemoration of Dr. McLeod's twenty-five years as superintendent of the Sunday School.

> Assistant Superintendent, Ort H. Ertzinger, prepared a program which came as a complete surprise to Dr. McLeod. When the Sunday Schoolers assembled for the final prayer, Dr. McLeod's favorite hymn was sung. The superintendent stood on the pulpit platform puzzled and surprised. Unannounced, twenty-five teachers, or former teachers came forward, one at a time presented to Dr. McLeod a red carnation and each quoted a verse of scripture expressing God's unfailing love and promises.
>
> "Dr. McLeod's devotion to his church has truly been proven by faithfulness and service," Mr. Ertzinger declared. "Spending the major portion of the night visiting the sick did not prevent the doctor's presence at Sunday School the following morning."

Uncle Ort's friend Howard Williams was an evangelist. Uncle learned to know him when he was preaching in one of the many tent meetings held along the Gulf Coast. Uncle Ort said of Howard:

> Having no training as a minister, Mr. Williams' preaching is not the usual type. He knows people's needs and his message is from the heart. He is full of initiative and energy. There is not a dull moment in his services.

Howard's affection for my uncle, whose name he misspelled, was expressed in a typewritten postcard postmarked Brookhaven, Mississippi, August 31, 1936.

> Dear Art,
> Thanks for the poems. They are fine. I have read them in meetings and given you the credit. Great crowds here. Hope your fine father

is well, give him my best.

yours in Him

Howard

"From pauper to prince" describes my uncles' friends. The Reverend Sam B. Hay, pastor of the church one block from the Alabama Polytechnic Institute in Auburn, Alabama, was also Uncle Ort's friend. This 1933 letter from the well-known Presbyterian minister explains:

> Dear Friend Ort,
>
> Thank you so much for your letter. It was a whole lot like you and for that reason I valued it highly. You are a trump, if you will excuse the language. And what you don't mean to the young people of Alabama!? And that "young people" means a good many of us older ones too.
>
> I believe you contribute as much as anyone to the success of our conferences. I am sure that I could get along without the services of anyone else better than yours.
>
> Glad to hear that you are doing such fine work with the boys at the C C C Camp. A neighbor of mine is there. I would like for you to look him up, his name is Blackmon.
>
> All of the Haystack send their love to you and Mrs. Ort and the daughter too.
>
> Cordially,
>
> Sam B. Hay

David spoke earlier of his grandfather's enthusiasm when showing a new minister the ropes. Bob Seidentopf was the minister his Gramp welcomed when David was nine. Bob's health was failing, and he was retired, living in Knoxville, Tennessee, when he wrote his recollections.

My first meeting with Mr. Ort was in October 1949. The train pulled into the station and this young preacher and his wife stepped off. Mr. Ort greeted us. A larger than usual man with a larger than usual smile stretched out his hand in welcome.

Very soon we were more than business associates. My wife Alma and I, then later our children, came to rely on Mr. Ort for all kinds of things. He was a personal friend with whom I could discuss anything and upon whose judgment I relied. He was seldom wrong; if that sounds unreal it was just another characteristic of the amazing Mr. Ort.

Bob's comment about the "larger than usual smile" struck a responsive chord. Uncle Ort admired a happy countenance. Among his Lion's Club keepsakes from when he was a Tailtwister is this anonymous poem:

> A smile is quite a funny thing,
> It wrinkles up your face,
> And when it's gone I've never found
> Its secret hiding place.
> But far more wonderful it is
> To see what smiles can do.
> You smile at one, she smiles at you,
> And so one smile makes two.
>
> He smiles at someone since you smile,
> Then that one smiles right back,
> And that one smiles until in truth
> You fail in keeping rack,
> And since a smile can do great good
> By freeing hearts of care,
> Let's smile and smile, and not forget
> That smiles go everywhere.

It was an effort for Bob to pen his memories. This was the last significant writing he did.

> In the days before the new church was built, Mr. Ort and I had many interesting discussions on a wide variety of subjects. I clearly recall us sitting in the back room while the rats and mice chased each other over the organ pipes. Mrs. Crosby played away, oblivious to all that was going on.
>
> Mr. Ort was never ostentatious about his money or anything else. That would have been out of character for him. He never forced his opinion on anyone, but in a discussion he was usually able to bring others around to his point of view. He was loved and respected by the whole community.
>
> I recall the time Mr. Ort asked if I would like to take a trip to Central Florida with him in his black Ford. I had never been in that area so I eagerly accepted. We drove to Jacksonville, Orlando and then Lake

Wales. The height of the trip was seeing an outdoor enactment of the Passion Play. Taking an impoverished preacher to tour Central Florida, was the kind of thing Mr. Ort did so often. Thirty-nine years later that trip is still vivid in my mind.

One of the finest things Mr. Ort ever did was to work for the construction of the new church. He contributed heavily, too.

One morning Mr. Ort came to church with a pocketful of silver dollars. He handed out shiny new silver coins and challenged us to go make money for the church. We were to invest the money in our talents in a way which would bring a return to the church. A high spirit of resolve was generated at that time.

His idea got a lot of people involved in making money for the church. For our part, Alma and I started a rabbit hutch, raised rabbits and sold them. I do not recall the exact amount we earned for the new building.

A great deal of planning was done before the new church was built, and there was a big chunk of Ort Ertzinger in its building. Not just in contributing funds, but a big chunk of the man himself. You cannot be as involved as he was and not leave yourself behind.

The reasons for a new church building were many. Cracks in the building made it impossible to keep out the summertime heat or winter cold. More than anyone, Uncle Ort knew the difficulty of heating the old church. For years he'd been the one to light the fires in the stoves early on Sunday morning. The old building could not be patched up any more. In the summer the preacher had difficulty speaking above the drone of the fans. The Men's Bible Class met in the Sanctuary, and early churchgoers disrupted Dr. McLeod's Sunday School lesson. The list went on and on.

Members of the congregation were not united in wanting a new building, so the decision to build was not easily made. I do not know the complete story, but there was a genuine disagreement, many fervent prayers, and lots of soul searching before the vote. Several big contributors, vehemently opposed to the idea, left the church, along with their entire families. This split made financing the church even more difficult. The setback kindled in Uncle Ort a fresh supply of ideas, it seemed. Uncle Ort put what happened into a song.

"We're going to build a church," said one,
    Another; "You can't do it."
"I'm sure we can," the first one said,
    "And God will see us through it."
Another laughed a skeptic's laugh,
    "Ha ha, I think you're funny;
Just tell me how, 'mid our poor folks,
    You'll ever raise the money."
"Oh, I don't know just how it's done,
    We must have faith and show it;
And God will help us raise the cash,
    Almost before we know it."
So put aside your doubts and fears,
    For surely God has willed it;
Let's trust His power and His might,
    Come on and help us build it.

From the first planning meeting in 1949, four days after he and Aunt Tillie got home from Alaska, until the dedication of the new building in 1956, Uncle Ort was totally dedicated to getting the church built properly. Once the firm decision to build had been made, his son-in-law, Walter, was appointed chairman of the building committee. Donald was a baby when planning began; he was seven years old when the church was dedicated.

Uncle Ort was a practical man. Once the church was in use, paying the contraction debt and the future of the church's finances were on his mind. This "Ortish" idea was described in the *Mobile Press* by journalist Ford Cook in 1958.

> BAY MINETTE–Churches, though they are primarily interested in the religious side of a man's life, require a certain amount of finances to keep their noses above water in daily operations. There is a church here that is doing something somewhat out of the ordinary to assure future financing.
>
> Though it may be considered rare, almost unheard of for churches to enter into the field of timber production, the congregation of this Presbyterian church supported the idea. A member of the church offered a 40-acre tract without charge provided the church members take upon themselves to see that proper reforestation and management were practiced.

The Burkett Memorial Church, long one of the leading churches in town, is the owner and operator of timberlands nearby. The timber land is sufficient acreage to give the church a substantial return if properly managed. This experimental operation should provide income for the church for many years to come.

Nearly a year has past since the idea began formulating in the mind of the man who owned the land. Seventeen thousand (17,000) slash pine seedlings have been planted. [A number of churchmen now remember planting those seedlings when they were boys.] An estimated 23,000 long-leaf native pines already stand in sizes ranging from seedlings to five-inch stock, making a pine stand of approximately 1,000 per acre. Some of the pines will be suitable for marketing within five years, and thereafter periodic selective cuttings will bring in revenue to the church.

Ort H. Ertzinger, not a native of Bay Minette, but a staunch civic and church worker here for the last half a century, was the donor of the property.

This clipping, including a photograph of Uncle Ort squatting to examine a new pine seedling, was among his keepsakes.

****

Without hesitation, the attendant awakened Leon Leak when I entered the room. "Mr. Leak likes to talk with people and does not want to miss a single visitor." Mr. Leak did not know I was coming; we had never met. I knew about him, but he did not know me. He was a Bay Minette native, a husband and grandfather, who'd had an outstanding career as a pioneer in national radio broadcasting.

Leon was slowly dying from Lou Gehrig's disease. His muscles were wasting away, but his mind was clear. When I told him I'd come to ask about Ort Ertzinger, my uncle, his eyes brightened, and immediately he started talking.

> I met Ort on the street and we chatted; he was always friendly to everyone. I'd been away from Bay Minette about four years and was home. He told me about the building at his church, then took me over to see it. He was upbeat about what the young people were doing to raise money. They were going all over town picking up

discarded Coke bottles, which they sold to make money for the church building fund.

People who were opposed to building the church pulled out of the church. That hurt Mr. Ort.

Leon remembered that Uncle Ort had been proud of an experience he'd had with a broker from New York. The man telephoned Uncle Ort from Mobile, made arrangements, then rented a car and drove to Bay Minette. He wanted to talk about Uncle Ort's investments. After examining his portfolio, the broker gave my uncle a pat on the back: "Mr. Ertzinger," he said, "you don't need to change a thing. You've done okay. How do you do it?" Uncle Ort explained his rationale for selecting each stock, what indicators or other factors influenced him. Then he said, "I simply used my bean."

Uncle Ort taught himself all he knew about the stock market. He liked to eat and knew the demand for food was constant, so the food vending stocks were a favorite.

Gee! Leon amazed me! He had not forgotten my uncle. From his hospital bed forty years later he talked easily. Leon, like Bob Seidentopf, in his final days remembered my uncle with pleasure. They remembered how important building a new church was to him.

Something truly mystical and spiritual takes place when the memory of a man who has been dead for thirty years bring joy to the dying.

23

Leader Extraordinaire

ARE YOU FROM BAY MINETTE?

Yes, I replied.

Then you must know Ort Ertzinger.

That's the way it is all over Alabama among young people, and some not so young because Ort Ertzinger was the best known Presbyterian in the "here we rest state."

Each summer at the annual conclave of Presbyterian young people at Shocco Springs near Talladega, Mr. Ort directs athletics and puts out a daily camp paper. He leads the singing in a manner that has everyone singing.

Undoubtedly Uncle Ort was most famous for the work he did in behalf of youth. It began when Dr. Hunter Norwood came to town. He was active in Presbyterian youth work on a state level when he became the minister circa 1921. As the two men worked together, Hunter saw my uncle's interest and potential as a leader. He encouraged this thirty-five-year-old father with an eight-year-old daughter to attend the training conference for youth. In 1924, Uncle Ort first went to the Presbyterian Conference Center in Shocco Springs. That started something.

Eloise was becoming active in a youth group. He wanted only the best for her. Aunt Tillie went along with it.

The church history found in the archives of the Presbyterian Historical Society in Montreat, North Carolina, the official historical repository of the Presbyterian Church, U.S., goes back further.

> The first attempt to organize a separate society for young people was in 1909 [the year Uncle Ort arrived, and he was one of the organizers]. Seventeen joined the society. Using Christian Endeavor topics the group met on Sunday afternoons._Dr. Norwood came to town in 1921 and began pushing young people's work. A few years later the Presbyterian Progressive Program came into existence. After a general re-organization of Sunday School and the Young People's department the group grew.
>
> Soon forty members were enrolled in 1934. The meetings were divided into three parts, the first fifteen minutes were devoted to song, prayer and bible reading; the next thirty minutes to study and instruction and the last fifteen minutes to a suitable game._We graded ourselves each Sunday night on five points: attendance, on time, church attendance, daily bible reading and systematic giving. This was helpful to all.

Not surprisingly, this record in the Montreat archive is typed on Uncle Ort's typewriter.

Time after time, after a nap on the living room floor, he worked for hours. He wrote stories and created youth programs with substance and appeal. The focus of the Sunday evening programs was the program content. This was written for a special occasion:

> One evening just at dusk, when the golden sun was setting and the shades of night were softly falling o'er the land; all the birds and animals were preparing for the rest of the night, the world lay in peace and calm. Margaret walked wearily into the living room for a bit of rest. She carried in her hand her favorite book, the bible. She curled up in a rocking chair and opened the bible to read.
>
> Margaret reads Psalm 19, meditates a bit, yawns, rubs her eyes and finally falls asleep. Soon she begins to dream. Odd shapes form vaguely in her mind. She stirs in her sleep as if trying to make out what these forms might be.
>
> Memories is played softly on the piano.

> We see that she is dreaming of days gone by, first of her childhood days when she sat upon her mother's knee and learned her first prayer.
> Child and mother recite, "Now I Lay Me Down to Sleep."
> Children sing "Jesus Loves Me."

Occasionally he suggested a person for a certain part in one of the programs he'd written, but usually that choice was left to the youth in charge. He developed leaders.

It something unexpected happened at the last minute, he stood by to help. Once when the leader couldn't make it, he wrote, "Felt funny running the program." When the young people dramatized the Good Samaritan story, he wrote, "I was the mule."

His programs and the enthusiasm of the youth attracted boys and girls who did not have a church home and some who did. I am reminded of a story Uncle Ort told about a little girl he met in the hall at school.

> She had never been to the coast, and she wanted to. So we took her on a beach party. She liked the bay, the picnic and the attention. She started coming to the Young People's Meeting on Sunday evenings and soon took part. Before long she attended Sunday School, became a committed Christian and joined the church. It all began with a trip to the coast.

The warm, fellowship, and substance of the youth programs, plus the special attention Uncle Ort gave each member made a hit. The youth were a vital part of the congregation.

He recognized and nurtured each person's unique individual potential. He also kept the local young folks abreast of what was going on with other Presbyterian youth in the region and state. He saw to it that Bay Minette youth attended meetings in other towns. His young people became officers in the Presbytery of Mobile.

"Our youth put on the program in Mobile today," he wrote, "then we went to Bellingrath Gardens." The pleasure of seeing these stately gardens filled with masses of lovely azaleas was a totally unexpected reward for these young boys and girls. He footed the bill. Such treats were a part of my uncle's unpredictable behavior and his charisma.

The annual June youth conferences at Shocco Springs seemed glamorous to me. The water in the swimming pool was icy cold and the blueberries in the woods juicy and sweet. The bonfire and closing service were sacred. But there was more to it than that.

Two separate conferences, one for juniors and another for seniors, were held each June. For quite a few summers Uncle Ort drove the youngsters from southwest Alabama towns to Talladega. This meant two trips, more often than not with car or bus trouble on the way. There was no relief driver. These excursions were not all nonsense and relaxation–unless you were a passenger:

> Going to Shocco with Mr. Ort was fun. Five flat tires was the good luck on the trip. T'was interesting to see how quickly Mr. Ort patched those Tin Lizzie tires. It was worth the whole trip just to see Mr. Ort eat. The main thing was, we young people studied hard at Shocco and learned things we carry throughout our lives.

Often Uncle Ort saw a job he thought needed to be done and did it. The conference poop sheet is an example. He instigated a newsletter that became a keepsake for many conferees. The first issue of *Sometimes* is dated June 12, 1931.

> This, the first issue of *Sometimes*, makes its bow to the conference with fear and trembling. It has been named sometimes because:
>
> 1. Sometimes it will be worth reading
>
> 1-1/2. Sometimes it will not
>
> 2. Sometimes it will be published
>
> 2 1/2. Sometimes it will not
>
> 3. Sometimes it will be purchase
>
> 3-1/2. Sometimes it will not.
>
> Cost is incurred for paper, ink, staples, pins, stencil sheets, pencils, editors' salary. Hence the huge subscription price of 1 cent per issue. Buy early and avoid the rush.
>
> No paper will be sold on credit. The trust department is on the roof; take the elevator! [There were none.]

The editors of this publication are not responsible for errors in dates, spelling or any information contained herein. We are human, please excuse our mistakes. Thanx.

Sometimes was a natural forum for the lyrics he wrote about Shocco. Sung to the tune of "Jesus Loves Me," this one was a hit.

If you'd be a beacon light
For the Master, shining bright,
Take a trip to Shocco Springs,
Reap the blessings that it brings.

Shocco will help you
Shocco will help you
Shocco will help you
To walk the King's Highway.

If your faith you would renew
It's the very thing to do
Take a trip to Shocco Springs,
Reap the blessings that it brings.

Shocco will help you
Shocco will help you
Shocco will help you
To walk the King's Highway.

What a great recruiting tool! In 1933 this was published in *The Highway*, a statewide newsletter for Presbyterian youth.

All this about Shocco Springs reveals the good times. In retrospect, even the flat tires seem novel. There was more to it. In June, year after year, Uncle Ort's diaries reveal his preparation before going to the conference. He planned the games and music, took all the special equipment and supplies he thought he would need with him. Talladega is not a large town, so he couldn't go into town for a replacement if something broke or was lost.

The responsibility and business-work side of the Shocco experience–learning new names, assessing individuals, selecting hymns, conducting all the singing–is obvious to me now. Building a choir and practicing to sing at occasions such as the Sunday afternoons when they visited the Presbyterian Home for Children took thought and know-how.

Music was only half of his responsibilities. I suspect the athletics were more demanding. It was essential that the competitive and noncompetitive games be fun and fair. Selecting team leaders for all kinds of sports from horseshoes and badminton to water polo required tact. Uncle Ort had plenty to do.

The day's travel from Bay Minette to Talladega was from early to late. The minute he put his foot on the ground at the conference, he was totally consumed by the conference goings-on. Seldom did he write more in his diary than "busy at conference." Being in charge of the music and recreational activities and shepherding youngsters to Shocco was more than fun and frolic. And he always came home to a pile of work waiting for him when he returned to his office. Remember, he was in business for himself.

In case you wondered, his sidekick was more than a silent partner. On occasion, Aunt Tillie was a counselor at Shocco. She was there collaborating, sharing her ideas, observations, and heart. She was with him all the way.

The conference grew in number and sophistication. In 1939, the year the conferees celebrated his birthday, the official registration was 275. "YEA! ORT!" was the headline on an article that read:

> Mr. Ort Ertzinger, who has been helping with Presbyterian Conferences at Shocco for eighteen years, was presented a gold key by the Young People of Alabama in June.
>
> The gift is a visible token of love, admiration, and appreciation of our beloved "Mr. Ort." The key bears the seal of the Presbyterian Church.
>
> Mr. Ort is known by Shocco goers as an excellent song leader and athletic director. He is a champion cucumber eater, and the man who put Bay Minette on the map.

This comment appeared in the *Times* when he was 43 years old, a ripe old age to be playing baseball:

> Ole Hoss Ertzinger is at Shocco Springs, missing what he'd rather do than eat–play baseball. He'll be back soon and listen, there's lots of baseball in that old hide yet.

This brought to mind a dilemma I'd never thought about before.

Anyone who has had to choose among several attractive options knows it is never easy no matter how many times the choice is made. Each spring Uncle Ort must have had a tug-of-war within himself between baseball and the youth conference.

He could have been the team manager had it not been for this spring excursion to Shocco each year. He had the temperament and popularity for the manager's job. The way it was, he was only a fill-in manager. Taking himself out of team play for two weeks each summer to go to the youth conference made his priorities clear.

He stayed on the cutting edge! A "know-it-all" he wasn't; rather, he was constantly on the lookout for a better way to do something. He repeated the adage about making a fortune by building a better mousetrap. His quest for knowledge that would help him be a better youth leader was insatiable. A certificate awarded him in 1940 by the Executive Committee of Religious Education, Department of Education (Presbyterians have their hierarchy, too), reads: "Credit is hereby awarded Mr. Ort H. Ertzinger for the successful completion of the course, 'Understanding Youth.' This was after Bay Minette won the Cooper Plaque. Training does pay off.

A lady in another part of Alabama, Mrs. B. H. Cooper, had done a marvelous thing to encourage Presbyterian youth throughout the state. She instigated an awards program for youth in honor of her two sons. Each year the youth organization in the Synod of Alabama with the highest rating was awarded the Cooper Plaque. The award was based on a five-fold program of worship, study, recreation, service, and enlistment.

In 1934, the Bay Minette young people earned this outstanding service award, and the coveted plaque was presented to them. It was a mountaintop experience for Uncle Ort. Many individuals were on the sidelines giving their prayers and support to the young people's work.

These backers of the youth work were not always young. Titled "A Tribute," this poem written with pen and ink is signed "your mother Dahlberg, squib."

"Honor to him where honor is due"

Is a fine old saying when applied to you
The winning of the plaque by your local bunch
Is a warning to others—I'll give them a hunch
Just secure an "Ort" who works with a vim,
His courage and valor will surely win.
For where study and intellect go hand in hand
The grace of God will produce a man.
The love of his co-workers played a part,
The work they did came from their heart.

So, "honor to him where honor is due"
Is a fine old saying when applied to you.

His zest for the work was surely invigorated by such support.

One June Uncle Ort did not feel well. He kept his troubles to himself and did not let his health get in the way of doing what he thought he should do. His diary entries during the second Shocco conference tell it like it was:

—Busy at conference. I AM SICK.

—Feel punk, went to see doctor, conference all day.

—Still sick, hardly able to do my stuff.

—Conference closes with communion service.

—Off at 7 a.m. for Ft. Deposit. Met Raymond, John Dougal, Randall, Anne and James. [He met and exchanged passengers in Ft. Deposit, halfway between Bay Minette and Talladega.] Back to Shocco at 3:30. Senior conference opened.

—Busy day at conference, not feeling good.

—Busy at conference, visited Presbyterian Home for Children today.

—Feel punk, busy at conference work.

—Sick all day, could not lead conference music.

—Sick all day, finals [sports events] rained out.

—Busy at conference, rained all day, ruined athletics.

—Left Shocco at 8:00; home at 3:45. Doctor gave me lots of medicine and orders to rest.

What a man! Dr. McLeod treated Uncle Ort for a goiter for two weeks before he was able to go to the office even for a few hours. The *Baldwin Times* carried the quip, "Things just aren't right when Mr. Ort is not around."

By August the invincible man was back on track.

Thirty-five young people of the Presbyterian church went by bus and enjoyed a delightful picnic Wednesday afternoon and evening in Fairhope on the beach.

Ort H. Ertzinger the director and Mrs. Ertzinger chaperoned the crowd. This organization for many years has been one of the leading ones in Alabama.

Committing himself to a cause for twenty-six years was uncommon. How did he do it? What made him stand out from other youth leaders? A group of ladies who knew him sat in the church parlor and reminisced about my uncle. When I posed my question, Inez Zehner answered immediately. A retired teacher with grown grandchildren, she spoke convincingly with a calm expression but emphatic voice:

> He knew what he was going to do. He believed in what he was doing. He gave you a task, and he expected you to be there and carry out the task he'd assigned you.
>
> He gave you individual assistance if you asked or showed signs of needing it. He was sensitive to that; he did not let anyone stew in fear or anxiety.
>
> Young folks respected him and wanted to please him, so they did what he asked. He never talked down to anyone, never.

Uncle Ort was well liked, popular; he put his faith into action. He didn't fit any one box–he was too big for that.

24

A Boy and a Man

TWO MEN I KNOW KNEW UNCLE ORT. Their thoughts about him are from a different perspective. Dr. John Crowell was a young minister in Mobile when the new Presbyterian church was being built in Bay Minette. Mort McMillan was a little boy in Monroeville, the hometown of Harper Lee and Truman Capote. In both cases, my uncle's reputation preceded him.

> I'd heard about Mr. Ort from the older kids long before I met him. He was a tease. I've never forgotten our first meeting. He said, "I'm Ort Ertzinger. Or Ert Ortzinger. Or Zing Ort Ert." He made jokes about his name. It's the funniest name you ever heard. You will never forget it because it's so funny. He made an impression telling me all these switches on his name.

Thus spoke Morton McMillan, Doctor of Divinity, a man whose pastorate has included positions on the Presbyterian General Assembly staff as well as in the pulpit. He is a Scottish buff, piddles with an electric train, and lives in Stockton, Alabama, where he is the senior pastor. We talked together in my Westminster Village apartment after lunch. Mort's memories of Uncle Ort date back to when was a junior high school kid.

Mr. Ort just had a way about him that appealed to young kids. He got you laughing, for example, by exaggerating the uniqueness of his name. His appearance was a bit odd. He wore those funny shoes [always black and high-topped]. His shirt-tail was out a lot of the time. There was a way he rubbed his hand on his nose and looked at you special.

As Mort talked, my mind pictures Uncle Ort's long torso. It seems to me that when he was older and could afford it, he ordered shirts cut especially long so they would stay tucked in. He perspired heavily winter and summer: as he put it, "I can wet a postage stamp on my upper lip any day of the year." I pulled in my rambling thoughts as Mort continued.

> The first time I recall being with Mr. Ort was a trip we made to Mentone with the young people of the Presbytery of Mobile. The synod rented an old hotel for the occasion in the beautiful Appalachian Mountains of northern Alabama. It was a ramshackle old two-storied firetrap of a building.
>
> Mr. Ort had secured a school bus, and all the young folks from Mobile—Bay Minette area rode with him. My daddy took the ones of us from Monroeville over to Brewton on Highway 31, and we joined the group there.
>
> Mr. Ort drove–no air conditioning, two-lane road all the way, no bypasses. It took all day to get to Mentone. We drove through every town. He had us singing funny nonsensical songs. He told jokes and kept us all laughing over the 375 miles to Mentone.
>
> I think about times when he treated others with tenderness. If there was a girl who was overweight and not particularly attractive, that would be the one he would concentrate on to make her feel accepted. He'd get her to come up and sit with him, or he'd flirt with her. It seemed he had antennae that were sensitive to another's needs– whatever might have caused that person to feel alienated or sorry for herself or himself.

Mort, now a grandfather, was relaxed and sure as we talked. It would have been impolite to interrupt him more than I did, but I wanted to. Sometimes I just wanted to hug him: he remembered details I'd forgotten.

> If some camper at Shocco was homesick, he'd find out about it and give that person special attention. It was done in a way that was

never very noticeable. Of course, everything he did was done openly, [but] it wasn't like "you poor thing, I'm going to concentrate on you." He used tact and great finesse, giving the impression that what he was doing was great fun, that he was tickled to do something for a person.

On occasion, he'd engage one of us in his strategy. [To demonstrate, Mort put his hand to his mouth to shield the sound and sort of whispered in a clear voice, "Joe looks down this morning. I bet he is missing his mama. Why don't you go play tennis with him?"] He would often get some of us to do something with the kid who was sad.

He told stories to make a point. When someone didn't want to do something, this was a time to illustrate with a story. "There was an old fellow when I was growing up who had a fine young mule. That mule was so stubborn he caused trouble for everybody." He would never say to a person, "You stubborn idiot, do what I tell you to do." Instead, he would tell a story about an animal or someone he used to know. The kid got the point. He never jumped on anyone; he was always kind. Always.

Mort was describing my uncle to a tee. He made me ponder. I always felt that Uncle Ort understood the real me better than anyone.

If someone was unhappy and complaining, he would talk to them pretty straight. He'd say, "You know, I really think God wants us to be kind to one another. He doesn't want us to be picking at each other." He would relate our behavior to biblical teachings, but he did it in a natural way; he did not quote scripture per se. When I reflect on it, I realize Mr. Ort did a lot of Bible teaching in an informal way.

In a contemplative manner, Mort spoke softly as he emphasized this fact. The words of my uncle's favorite hymn, "Living for Jesus," walked into my consciousness. I could not contain myself; I butted in:

Living for Jesus a life that is true,
Trying to please him in all that I do,
Yielding allegiance, glad-hearted and free,
This is the pathway of blessing for me.

O Jesus, Lord and Savior,
I give myself to Thee.

I own no other Master,
My heart shall be Thy throne.

My life I give, henceforth to live,
O Christ, for Thee alone.

Living for Jesus wherever I am,
Doing each duty in His Holy name,
Willing to suffer affliction or loss,
Deeming each trial a part of the cross.

Mort and I looked at each other. Those words characterize Uncle Ort.

He did love to *sing*. He had good pitch and no trouble singing on key without accompaniment. We were at the age when our voices were changing, especially the boys. It took good leadership to get us all to sing.

If we did not sing well, he would egg us on: "I heard you out there in the ballpark, or was it the basketball court? You were yelling louder than that. I know you can sing better. Everyone can sing." On bus trips we entertained ourselves as he led us in singing.

To him, being a Christian was wonderful! Living as a Christian was a fun-filled life of excitement and joy. He, and the others with whom he worked, successfully communicated [that] to us. There may have been problems to worry about, there may have been heavy stuff to deal with in the church, but none of that got through to us. Being a Christian was fun.

Tears came to my eyes. The person whose shadow is ingrained in my soul had rubbed off on Dr. McMillan as a child exactly as he had on me. Uncle Ort was admired and understood by a little boy, now a learned minister, who still remembers. The thrill and excitement of being a Christian, as portrayed by Uncle Ort, made a lasting imprint on both of us.

"Why do you think he did not burn out as a leader of youth the way so many leaders do nowadays," I asked. "Is there a key to his long years of service? Did he influence you?

Mort replied immediately. "I do not have an answer to the first question," he admitted. "When I think about the influence he had on me, I guess it can be summed up in two things. One, the joy with which he served. Two, the sensitivity he had for other people." Dr. Morton McMillan hit the nail on the head. So did the recollections of another minister with whom I talked, Dr. John Crowell.

The circumstances of John's meeting Uncle Ort were totally different. Recently discharged from the Navy, where he had served as a chaplain during World War II, John first met and knew my uncle as a young minister in Mobile. Although John did not meet my uncle as a freckle-nosed schoolboy like Mort, he had heard about my uncle seven years before they actually met. The war intervened.

John is now retired from both the Navy and the pastorate. He and I are casual acquaintances through the church–that is, if John has an "casual" acquaintances. His great warmth and feeling for others knits a strong bond with many admirers. A husband, grandfather, and sometimes fisherman, John unabashedly admits that his plans now pivot around his wife's schedule. She is the Director of Academics for the Athletic Department of the University of South Alabama.

Dr. Crowell was not at a loss for words as he remembered.

The young people in Andalusia in 1942, before I served in the Navy, were talking about going to youth conference. As a new, inexperienced pastor trying to learn what was going on, I listened to them talk. One name kept popping up–"Mr. Ort this" or "Mr. Ort that." At first I thought he was one of their young friends. When they kept talking about him, I finally asked, "Who in the world is Mr. Ort?"

"Don't you know Mr. Ort? Everybody knows Mr. Ort." They seemed disturbed at my ignorance.

"No, I do not know Mr. Ort."

"Well," they continued, "we just couldn't have a conference without Mr. Ort and his singing and games." Then they started to describe him. "He is tall and has sort of sandy hair. He wears rimmed glasses, and he laughs a lot. And, oh, he can sing. [John's voice sounded lyrical as emphasized the word, just as Mort had.]

I heard about Mr. Ort in Andalusia, but it was while I was serving at Central Presbyterian Church in Mobile that I actually met him. At our first meeting, his warm welcome was as though he'd known me always. he came with an outstretched hand, having heard I was the new preacher. Here he was, a highly esteemed elder–and in those days an elder in the Presbyterian church was_ [John hesitated in search of the right word.] An elder was the epitome of something lordly-like. But not Mr. Ort, who came with the manner of just another young person. I felt at ease with him immediately. I didn't have to prove myself. Mr. Ort accepted me just as I was.

Throughout the region, young people knew and loved him. I can remember him si-ing-ing [again the lilt in his voice].

In those days we didn't have trained counselors, but nobody ever hesitated to go talk about anything with Mr. Ort. He was right there ready to listen. I can see him now, walking across the green grass underneath the big trees with his arm around a young person, his head bowed, nodding as he talked with an individual. He was a born counselor.

I interrupted. "Lots of people sought his advice. After he retired, Uncle Ort came to his office one day a week so folks who wanted to could talk with him. They came to talk about all kinds of things–personal, financial, fishing, etc. I wonder what made others respect his opinion and seek out his counsel?"

John's answer came as quick as a cat can wink its eye.

It's a gift. If you have it, you should develop it, as Mr. Ort did. It is one of those talents God gives. He gives certain gifts to some and withholds from others. Any person can, to some degree, develop skill in counseling, but I think the ability to truly have empathy and put yourself in another's place is a special gift.

Some ministers, as good as they are at preaching and praying, can never be true counselors. They can never quite see things from another person's perspective. Mr. Ort could. He gave you the feeling "I know exactly what you mean. Now let's talk about it. I really understand." That was the secret to his popularity with so many people.

John and Mort McMillan both remembered Uncle Ort for his sensitivity to others–a strong part of his makeup. The precise definition of *empathy*–the projection of one's personality into the personality of another, the ability to share in another's emotions or feelings–fit. I know because I myself sought out his listening ear, especially at the low points in my own life.

I was a sensitive teenager when the security of my home exploded. Over ten years later, my whole world crumbled when my husband and I separate and again my home was dissolved. At those crucial times

Uncle Ort's empathy and understanding were healing balm. It was not anything specific he did, but rather the way he was.

In the beginning, I asked John to be candid. "A person's frailties as well as admirable qualities go into a true portrait," I pointed out. "I simply have not come up with Uncle Ort's faults. I know he wasn't perfect, but my view is biased."

John complied. He told of a time after the Presbyterians sold the Shocco conference center and the Alabama Presbyterian Youth Conference convened on the Montevallo College campus.

> I recall Miss Tillie [my aunt] did not like some of the plans Mr. Ort was making for the conference. I do not remember the specifics, but they disagreed. Miss Tillie was as tall as he was. She stood in front of him and stared right at him and did not move–she stood her ground.
>
> "You are the stubbornest man alive," she said.
>
> "I have to be," he retorted.
>
> Miss Tillie turned to me. "That man, that man."

John laughed in the telling. He added, "But it wasn't anytime until Mr. Ort walked off smiling. He and Miss Tillie did not see eye to eye on everything. He was definitely on the cheerful side, but he could"–John searched for the proper word–"be quite stern."

> Mr. Ort would make his side known–plainly he spelled it out–but he was amenable to other points of view, except on something that involved principle. He was absolutely immovable if principle was involved. *Mr. Ort did not waver one inch from what he perceived to be right.*
>
> I can remember him at Bonnie Beach at a regional church meeting. Something came up that Mr. Ort did not agree with. He stood up straight and tall. There was no smile on his face. Almost as though he were hewn out of granite, he stood and made his position known. And that was that. As soon as the matter was settled, he went on being his usual self, the congenial fellow that he was.

John spoke repeatedly of how Uncle Ort got people to sing. John sat up straight on the edge of his chair and laughed as he waved his hands in the air to mimic Uncle Ort conducting a choir. "Mr. Ort never stood in one place. He put his whole self into it. He could pitch the songs in a key the majority of people could sing."

> The Men's Club was going strong when I came to Mobile. Mr. Ort was a charter member. He led the singing at the Men's Club, and I don't think anyone would believe that those men could sing as heartily as Mr. Ort could get them to sing.
>
> The people in the small congregation in Bromley had a love affair for Mr. Ort. The congregation had a lot of pride but couldn't afford their own minister. Once a month Mr. Ort drove the Reverend Cook, the Bay Minette minister, down to preach. One summer I preached revival services for them. There was no need for a choir; Mr. Ort led the singing. I shall always remember that Bromley meeting.
>
> Mr. Ort had respect for others. He was *Pres-by-ter-ian* through and through. He knew the *Book of Church Order*. I do not remember him quoting it–that would have been out of character for him–but he knew it. Occasionally he quoted the Bible at youth conferences–certain verses he liked. He loved the Psalms: they were meant to be sung.
>
> Miss Tillie was a good wife. She went right along with whatever he was doing. And sometimes she would calm him down a bit.

I pat my foot to that. She was a leveling influence. They were opposites: he was impulsive and quick, she slow and thoughtful. They compensated for each other.

> I was in Bay Minette for a family night supper when Mr. Ort showed his travel pictures, I think of Hawaii. The way he described something to you, you could just see and feel it. He was a delight_and his jokes!
>
> I do not remember a specific joke, but I do know he never told a joke or story that hurt anyone, one that was derogatory. He liked country jokes. "A man had an old hound dog" might be the way he'd begin. Then, after he'd told it, he'd laugh as though he'd just heard it for the first time himself.
>
> Christianity to him had its serious side, but it was to be lived and enjoyed. He was a joyous Christian gentleman!

Uncle Ort and I were close. Liking the same things–fishing, adventure, and good times–that is one thing. Another aspect of our special relationship was drastically different. This blossomed when I was in despair and agony. At such times my uncle popped up as a guardian angel. Like an antidote for poison, Uncle Ort enabled me to cope with my misfortune. No wonder he is the most unforgettable character I ever knew.

25

Trip of a Lifetime

His MOVE INTO RETIREMENT occurred as smoothly as the river runs into the bay. It began a few years after Walter and Eloise came to live in Bay Minette. With their new freedom they had plenty of things they wanted to do. Uncle Ort, the man who found rest in activity, was on the move.

In February 1949 he visited Aunt Ella and Uncle Warren in Lutz, Florida. The oranges and grapefruit fresh from their grove and fishing in their clear-water lake delighted him. He was happy to accommodate them by building a pier out into the lake. A few days after his return home, on March 5, his fourth grandchild, Donald, was born. While Donald and his mother were still in the hospital, he had a severe heart attack.

What an awful surprise and shock!

Recuperation included adjustment to a change of pace. To my knowledge he never questioned why it had happened but found plenty to be thankful for. He quickly realized he could have died. Gradually he regained his strength and slowed his pace. Life had an entirely new meaning.

He was happy to be alive. He felt financially secure, but the wealth he spoke about– almost bragged about–was not in his bank account. Rather it was his family, the church, his friends, and the confidence and trust people had in him.

For years Uncle Ort had read *Alaska Sportsman*, a publication from Ketchikan. The Alaskan Canadian highway, like the Panama Canal, was an outstanding engineering feat in the first part of the twentieth century. Bus tours over the highway appealed to him. He was itching to taste and see the northern wilderness. If it was the last trip he ever made, he wanted to go to Alaska. His 1950 travelogue begins:

> After a fishing trip to Northern Wisconsin in the Fall of 1949, I determined to go to Alaska next year. If finances permit, and health allows, I will go. I will take my wife with me, of course, to see that I behave myself.
>
> In the "Alaskan Sportman" I found a number of ads, that gave me a start. I wrote the Alaskan Railroad and the Alaskan Steamship Company and began making contacts, which later opened the entire list of concerns I needed to contact in order to complete the trip schedule.
>
> Since I was completing 50 years perfect Sunday School attendance I did not want to break the record, nor did I want to travel at night and miss any of the sights.
>
> With this in mind I proceeded to inform various companies. Every one of them proved eager to help and most willing to see that my every wish was met. So, after much writing and revising we finally worked out a schedule.
>
> Then, I secured the names of leading hotels in the towns where the itenary showed us stopping for the night and wrote each. These contacts responded quickly and reservations were arranged far in advance. [Hotel reservations were a security blanket for Uncle Ort; he wanted to know in advance where he was going to sleep.] The entire trip planned in such a manner that it was only necessary for us to follow through, beginning in August, at Seattle.

Uncle Ort and Aunt Tillie packed their black Ford, said a prayer and good-bye and left Bay Minette on Wednesday morning, July 19, 1950. A five-by-eight-inch Fidelity & Deposit Company spiral-bound datebook, an advertising gimmick for the New Orleans branch, provided a journal. On the inside front cover, Uncle Ort listed the names and addresses of friends who lived in the area where their itinerary took them–his way of keeping the names handy. All this organization and thrift was classic Ortishness.

They were eager for their first trip west of the Mississippi. When traveling by car, he figured how far they traveled from Bay Minette and how many miles they traveled each day. I am including his terse notes of their adventures by car, bus, train, and ship across the United States to Fairbanks and back.

Wednesday, July 19, left B.M. at 8:30, went to Reston, La. for the night in the Lincoln Town Motel.

Thursday, out at 7 a.m. Ran into water melon festival and parade in Minola, Texas. Cowboys, cowgirls eating melons–half an hour to get through town. North eastern Texas hilly with a few oil wells, not as many as I expected. Roads good, traveled 512 miles.

Northwestern Texas level for miles and miles, many wheat elevators, good many cattle, roads wide and good. Began to see cactus in west Texas. Set watches back on New Mexico border. Canvas water bags hang on the hoods of cars. Water evaporates, helps cool the motor, furnishes water for radiator–can be used to drink.

Friday arrived Albuquerque 1293 miles from Bay Minette, elevation 5000 feet. Spent happy hours with old schoolmate from Huntington, Ralph Burleigh, and his wife. Took a long ride into the mountains with them. Fine folks.

Ten thousand feet elevation in Jemes mountains, sage grass, evergreens dotted over mountains, Aspen trees at high altitude, Ponderosa pines, cactus with rose and yellow blooms and other wild flowers. Indian pueblos, adobe huts–build new one rather than repair old ones. Yards in Albuquerque surrounded with walls, protection against sand and wind storms. Reached Seattle a day ahead of our schedule, hotel could take care of us. Nice room.

Saturday morning picked up information and in the afternoon called on a business client. I purchased 50 acres of land in Baldwin County from a widow who inherited same from her deceased husband many years ago. The widow did not want to keep it any longer. [Uncle Ort's way of taking advantage of an opportunity.] Took four hour water tour in p.m. Saw Mt. Rainier 90 miles away, snow capped and pretty.

Sunday July 23 Got news of serious Korean situation which at one time threatened our trip. We drove out to the University Christian Church, the pastor is an old friend of ours, formerly of Huntington, Rev. John Paul Pack. Doing a great work. He appeared glad to see us. He introduced us to the teacher of the adult Sunday School class, Mrs. Johnson Boligee, at the Emmanuel Presbyterian Church. At closing time a man and woman came up to us and told us they knew someone from Bay Minette, Judge T. J. Mashburn, a ball player friend of mine.

Dinner at Old Town, drove to Santa Fe. Along the way curio shops run by Indians. No trees except in valley of Rio Grande. Flash floods. Saw Santa Fe twenty miles away. Navajo Museum with sand paintings, I recalled some of the sights about the rush to Santa Fe when I studied history. Saw house reputed to be the oldest in the U.S.

Monday, saw Pike's Peak, Colorado Springs, 14,100 feet. Mountains and scenery most colorful, arrived Denver 7:00 P.M., drove 437 miles today. Beautiful sunset on mountains–2653 miles from home. Fine meal at Golden Lantern.

Tuesday, scenery magnificent, gold mines, Idaho Springs, mink and cincilla farms, mines on mountain side, snow on highest peaks. Berthoud Pass 11,314 feet high, over the great divide. Columbine flower is state flower in Colorado. Great sheep country near Utah border, saw many of them.

Wednesday, arrived Salt Lake City 10:15 a.m., went to Temple square and were conducted through garden, chapel and Tabernacle. Attended organ concert at 12 noon. After lunch drove 15 miles out to Salt Lake, on to Tremonton, a lovely town in valley for night, 257 miles. Mountains all around.

Thursday, near Burley, Idaho sign says, WATCH FOR FLYING SAUCERS. Saw many mashed rabbits on road–33 in half a mile. Storage places covered with earth for keeping potatoes. Many fields of onions also dill. Sign between Mountain Home and Boise, NO FISHING WITHIN 300 YARDS. Seemed off, there was no water to fish in, that we could see. Traveled old Oregon Trail, spent night in Baker. Snow on mountains back of motel, 448 miles today, 3720 from home.

Friday, cold morning, beautiful scenery with trees, elevation 3800. Down curvy Dead Man's Pass, large wheat fields in valley close to

Pendleton, Oregon. Crossed Columbia River by ferry, into Washington state at 11:45 a.m. Saw lots of tumble weeds, large fields of hops, trellis 10 feet high, hop ranches. Snow peaked mountains in Chanute Pass, large pines, ten peaks visible with snow–Mt. Rainier National Park. Arrived Seattle 5:46, 4589 miles from Bay Minette.

Spent Saturday getting ticket, in evening had Smorgasbord supper.

Monday, all day around Seattle, saw vaudeville.

Tuesday Tour group left Seattle via bus for Spokane, arrived at 5, nice hotel.

Wednesday, August 2, left at 10 for Cranbrook, crossed border at 3 p.m. and to Mt. Baker Hotel in Cranbrook for the night. Set watches ahead one hour, cerfew blew at 9:30 (not dark until 9:00 p.m.). Rough trip through mountains all day.

Thursday, through Sinclair Gorge at 2:00, took pictures, radium hot springs at 2:30, temperature in swimming pool 120 degrees. Saw three moose run across road, also saw a deer and a number of beaver dams and homes. Arrived in Banff, cold enough for overcoats. Took lots of pictures and watched the clouds above mountain tops. Ten dollars of our money worth eleven in Canada.

Friday, breakfast with Culbertsons, took bus trip to Lake Louise, saw three mountain goats and one black bear. Lake beautiful, flanked in high rocky mountains, one of which is white with snow. Paddled around lake in canoe, dinner in hotel. Water in Lake Louise soapy blue, not clear. Saw poplar trees gnawed by deer and moose. Mosquitos bad and big. Eisenhouer Mountains majestic. Store sells many kinds of mountain climbing equipment and clothing worn for hiking, climbing, boating etc.

Saturday left Banff at 8, to Calgary then Edmonton and King Edward Hotel, Room 228. Raining in spots when we arrived–mountains behind us. About 40 miles out of Banff came into excellent wheat section. Many large granaries along railroad. Nine side by side in one town. Soil black and rolling, many cattle at Calgary. Mountains are named after missionaries or great men such as Eisenhouer and Rundel.

Sunday School at St. Andrews Presbyterian Church; 13 present. Visited the church built in 1871 by people of various denominations including Presbyterians. It is now the United McDougal Methodist Church. Slept and rested in the p.m. Chinese restaurant for dinner, neither of us cared for food. Really closed tight here on Sunday, no stores or picture show open.

August 6, up at 8, lazy. No paper published, national holiday. Around town all day, took street car loop, fish and chips supper, good cod. Saw baseball game at night–Eskimos vs. Dodgers–good game. No fat women in Canada, one or two fat men. In our party of about twenty and only two smoked, both were old women.

August 7, Tuesday, left at 8 for overnight trip to Dawson Creek, bus had flat at 11:00 p.m. Woke up at 5 a.m., breakfast at High Prairie, raining and lots of ugly mud. Reached Dawson Creek at 1:45 p.m., two hours late. Hotel O.K., streets hard mud, wooden side walks about town. Not a tree in the whole town. Needed top coat. Town dirty and muddy with a nasty sticky mud; five wheat elevators in town. Still daylight at 9 p.m.

Left Dawson Creek in rain and mud at 10:00 a.m. Thursday. Three hundred miles to Fort Nelson. Fair accommodations, lights went out at supper. Cool night, saw many pretty sights and two black bears along way. Harry Beatty, driver, is from Whitehorse, Yukon, Canada.

Friday left 9 a.m. for Lower Post. Two flat tires delayed us, took pictures and saw hot springs, reached Lower Post at 9:30 p.m. Had hilarious supper.

Saturday, nice trip to Whitehorse with the usual flat tire. Nice room in hotel, glad for reservation. Whitehorse is full of tourists so there was a scramble for rooms. Bus bunch had supper together. Attended lecture at Church Parish house.

No paved streets, people cross any place, not at corners, many board sidewalks, no newspapers. Yukon River flows past town–many curio shops. Softball game–daylight till 10:00. Set watches back another hour. Most buildings, even banks, are frame structure.

All around are big dogs, highly regarded by all. Saw stacks of ore loaded for equipment on the railroad. After 900 miles on the Alaskan Highway with no railroad crossing, we crossed over tracks.

What happened during the 10 to 12 hours on the bus each day may interest you, the reader. Having been together so much, we knew each other sufficiently well to begin pulling jokes and swapping yarns.

One day when some were about half asleep, I yelled at the top of my voice and woke every one with a start, even the bus driver jumped up on his seat and said, "For heaven's sake, don't ever do that again without warning me." Well, the next day I was about asleep and two of the "boys" stood right over me and yelled at the top of their voice and paid me back.

I read a take-off on a newspaper now and then in the hearing of all. Some of my choice jokes were thus pulled off. I had requests for another edition of the bus paper.

We also had lots of eats. Someone always managed to have a box of cookies, a bag of candy or something to nibble on. Once in a while some trapper or Indian or native would board the bus and ride a while.

We became one big family on the bus and the days of travel, stories told, tricks played and events which took place will remain in our memory.

That Sunday in the Yukon Territory he fudged! He bent his Sunday School attendance record. He tells us exactly what happened.

Yesterday I tried to find out where a Sunday School service would be held. Apparently there is none in White Horse in the summer. I did learn, however, that there would be early morning communion, so while my wife got her beauty sleep I slipped out of the hotel and found my place in the church. Went to Holy Communion at Christ Church, six present; 49 present at 11 o'clock service. Nice day.

Saw the mighty Yukon flowing past the town and three cars of lead ore on freight-passenger train. Great piles of wood everywhere for winter's use–no gardens as soil does not produce. Some soil imported to have flowers and small patches of vegetables. Fine fish dinner for $1.00.

August 14, up at 8, breakfast. "Beyond the Sunset" was playing on the juke box. In afternoon saw Indian cemetery, the Yukon rapids and other places of interest. Watched train with scoop buckets for gold. Many dredges loaded on barge. Nice in sun where cold north wind did not hit you. Spent the evening watching the steamer come up the Yukon. Mr. and Mrs. Walter Yeomans came and got us at 7:30 and took us over town and to their home for coffee–two lovely people we met on the bus. Managed to see three ball games in one evening. The players were all young and frisky folks. Saw northern lights at 11 p.m. then they faded, cool and clear night.

Tuesday, Heat turned on in room at 5:00. Next door noisy conference in room began at 5:30. Up at 6, reached Dry Creek at 8, in sight of big snow capped mountains most of the day. Saw several Indian towns and cemeteries.

Wednesday, August 16 frosty morning, beautiful snow capped

mountains all day, crossed into Alaska about 10:00 a.m., set watches back an hour. Government inspectors lined us up and asked a few questions. I managed to take a picture of Mrs. Ort pointing to the sign advising us that we were entering Alaska while an Indian with a papoose on her back, stood beside her.

Began to find more traffic and settlement around Fairbanks, saw vegetable gardens. Esther Earnest, from Eglin, A.F.B., was waiting for us when our bus pulled in to Fairbanks. She was our guide and toured us around Fairbanks like an old timer.

Thursday, went to post office for mail as only part of it had come to the hotel. I received a batch of movie films and personal mail. The post office is holding all the newspapers for me. Fairbanks is a dirty, dusty, drinking place; one street long. Plenty of saloons and sots. Went to the Alaskan College this p.m. and then to Ladd Field for supper with Esther. She showed us slides and we visited in her quarters. Small planes take off in snow.

Friday, left at 8:30 by rail for Mt. McKinley Park. Engine broke down and we were towed by freight car to the park, about three hours late. Nice room, beautiful modern hotels. Motion picture show at 8 p.m. a party climbing Mt. McKinley, took 80 days. No town here, just hotel and depot in national park. Sara Green traveling with us. [Teaming up with their traveling companions was an added pleasure for my aunt and uncle. Some became more than Christmas card friends.]

Saturday, to Mt. McKinley, a 62-mile trip with crooks, hills, and hollows, took pictures. Saw three bears, about 30 mountain sheep, one caribou and lots of ptarmigan [grouse]. Back to hotel, packed, hurried dinner and left. Found more settlements than in Canada.

Reached Anchorage at 11:30 p.m. Train one hour 20 minutes late. Women do all kinds of things on train–"butches," sweep coaches, wash windows, tend bar, manage and cook in Pullman diners. Hotel reservations O.K., nice room.

Sunday, up at 7:00, attended Presbyterian Church. Rev. Walkup, pastor. Duplicate services because of the crowds. Attended Sunday Club sponsored by the church. A negro, a Japanese and an Indian there, preacher asked us to shake hands all around, very friendly service. Will build a new church soon, good many strangers. Took books up after services. Potatoes take place of grits at meals. Grocery stores all open every day [a novelty back then].

Monday, bleak, windy day, left at 9 a.m. for Palmer. Dinner in a nice lodge on shore of the lake. Saw salmon working their way up a shallow stream. Spent p.m. addressing postcards. Supper with fellow travelers Sara and Mrs. Norton. Saw part of Ft. Richardson and many soldiers. Papers report big landslide on main railroad north of Anchorage. All train service suspended indefinitely until track rebuilt. Got through one day before slide.

Tuesday, noisy outside, up at 7:00, around town in a.m., packed up and left for train depot at 2 p.m. Left shaving kit in taxi and had to run taxi down to get it back. Slow train trip from Seward with pretty scenery–caribou, moose, Spencer Glacier and loop the loop track. Women "butches" selling things on the train. Arrived in Seward at 8:15 p.m. had lunch, boarded S.S. Alaska, left 9:30 p.m. Headed southward for the night. Smorgasbord on ship.

Tuesday, August 23, docked at Valdez, toured the town before dinner. Saw interesting Episcopal church, got cards and curios. Started to walk to glacier but did not get there, too far.

Wednesday, ship sailed at 3:45 for Cordova. Played bingo at night.

Thursday, up at 5 to see Cordova, left at 6:00 a.m. in misty weather. Gulf of Alaska very rough, got sea sick and all that goes with it.

Friday, seasick all day, nearly everyone else was took, reached quite water about dark.

Saturday, quiet water at Juneau, rained hard. Docked at 7 a.m. shopped in rain and left at 11:45 in rain. Business district very compact, nice. Hilly, old closed down mines. Ship loaded much halibut and other freight. Visited Petersburg, richest town in the world, per capita. Saw two seals, several porpoise and about 12 or 15 whales in all. Saw many canneries.

In his more amplified travelogue, Uncle Ort wrote of an encounter aboard ship. The Most Worthy Grand Matron, Order of the Eastern Star, was paying an official visit to Alaska. She was greeted at the ports by members of the local Eastern Star lodges, who presented her with flowers, gavels, and other mementos she could cherish. When she met my aunt and uncle, the Grand Matron asked whether they by any chance knew Mr. and Mrs. Joe Southall?

Did we know them? My gosh, we raised them! Mrs. Southall was the Worthy Grand Matron of Alabama.

These notables were also from Alabama. We were in their company long enough to discover why she had been elevated to her high office. She was most gracious, equal to all the responsibilities of the office. We would welcome a visit in our home of the Grand Matron and her husband; fine people.

Uncle Ort's trip diary continues:

Sunday, docked at Ketchikan at 8:30, left at 10, walked about town, visited the Presbyterian church.

The travelogue tells more about the events of that day:

We climbed a steep street to a water fall and there watched salmon on their way to the spawning grounds. We could see them resting in little eddies at the bottom of the falls then they made a run, a dash up the falling water, to a higher level. It was what we'd read about.

We went in the church and looked about, not a soul in sight. We coughed a time or two, and did everything but ring the bell, but no one showed up. Our time was limited so we eased back toward the boat and boarded just in time.

Before confirming our reservations, I had written the Alaskan Steamship Company to be sure there would be a religious service on Sunday. The purser arranged the Sabbath Service at 3 p.m. in the lounge.

The passenger he chose to conduct the service was coming to the states to study. He planned to be a missionary. Over half the travelers attended the service.

The surprise of the whole trip awaited me at dinner. Seems the people at our table tipped off the steward that this was my birthday. All things were made ready without my knowing. After we were seated I began looking over the menu to pick out the goodies for the tummy.

The steward, a most friendly and efficient officer, came and put his arm around me and congratulated me on my birthday. Just as I was about to blat out that it was not my birthday, friend wife kicked me on the shin, and pointed to the announcement at the top of the menu. Best Wishes and Happy Birthday to Ort H. Ertzinger from Capt. Burns and Crew. Now what would you do in this situation?

Well, some uneasy faces across the table and wife's kick told me to keep my mouth shut. I did. About this time the loud speaker announced to the diners that the captain was always happy to find someone aboard who was celebrating a birthday or anniversary. He called upon the diners to sing happy birthday to me. They did.

When I looked around there was a bottle of champagne in a bucket of ice directly in the center of the table, put there while I was standing to acknowledge the honor. I toasted to all and sat down hardly knowing what was going on.

Then the birthday cake came, a monster about 18 inches high and big enough to feed an army. The steward and the cooks really did a swell job on this cake. I cut the cake. Well, you can imagine what happened to the cake. I think all the crew, every officer and passenger had some. It lasted about as long as a snowball in Hades.

Completely flabbergasted I sat down to find out what really was going on. Then they told me. It seems a Sara Green from Ohio had been asked to find someone who had a birthday. She had been with us on the bus, train, and now the boat; she figured I could take a surprise.

Thereupon the whole plan took shape. All I did was keep my mouth shut and have fun. It really was hilarious. Hurrah, for my birthday aboard the S.S. Alaska. The first in 1950 was back in May.

A custom aboard ship was to have a talent show the last night out. We were roped into action. I sang as part of the Alaskan Octet and wife modeled some creation she called a hat. What a woman won't think up to win a prize just "aint." You should have seen the exhibit of hats.

The program, gotten up by a committee of passengers. The last day aboard they filtered out talent and chose people for the show. Their filter leaked, some got through that should have been filtered. Anyway it was a gala occasion!

I was the leader of the octet, the only guy who did not have a title. There was professor this and doctor that, but for me they were courteous enough to say mister. Our song went off in apple pie order that would have done honor to any barbershop quartette. The talent thing was a fitting climax to a wonderful trip.

Uncle Ort's trip diary records that on August 29 they "reached Seattle at 9 a.m. Got car, left at 11 and drove." They spent a night within hearing of the pouring water of Grand Coulee Dam.

That was the end of their loop-the-loop to Alaska and back, but not the end of their trip. From Grand Coulee Dam they drove east to

Yellowstone Park and on to Bismarck, North Dakota, where they visited cousins; thence to Chicago and Indiana for a couple of weeks, thence eastward through Youngstown along the Pennsylvania Turnpike to New York and Connecticut, and then home. They left Seattle on August 29 and arrived home on September 20, finding all well and happy.

Those who had wondered whether he was physically up to Alaska travel heaved a sigh of relief when Uncle Ort returned safely. Journal jottings from his 16,670-mile loop were the fodder for the thirty-nine-page single-spaced "Trip to Alaska" that he shared with family and friends. He closed with these words.

> A grand trip! When this log is finally mimeographed, the scrap book complete, and the movies culled and put on reels, we will have a record of a trip I have always wanted to make. It was a "trip of a lifetime."

26

A *Time to Reap*

THE TIME WAS RIGHT for Uncle Ort to reap some of what he had sowed. In 1953 a high school teacher sent him this note:

> Recently my students wrote themes about people. They were to describe the appearance, character, and personality of the person they admired. Giving the name of the person was not necessary.
>
> The enclosed paper was written by Fay Yarbough who, when I questioned her, admitted it was about you. I thought you would appreciate her estimate of your character. Many times most of the nice things are said after a person is gone.
>
> Ruth West

The enclosed paper reads as follows:

> There is a man about whom I could say, without hesitation, "He is one of the greatest men in Bay Minette." He is a very intellectual man and has worked hard all his life.
>
> By working he has gained wealth but he does not let this fact change his personality. He is a very dependable person and is active in almost all the organizations of the town. He is expecially active in his church. He is a great leader.
>
> He loves young people and there is hardly anything that he would

not do for them. He enjoys traveling and has been to many places in and out of the United States.

He is very good writer and has written many beautiful poems and songs, just for enjoyment. His church uses a song he wrote asking God to help them build a new church.

His most enjoyable pastime is fishing which he does often since his retirement. He is always on hand to give help when help is needed, especially in time of sorrow and grief.

Fay did not describe my uncle's appearance, and I too am derelict in this. Uncle Ort's manner and character overshadow his physical appearance in my mind's eye. As he grew older, I recall his thinning hair. He and my father kidded each other about that. His baseball hands, enlarged knuckles and lumps on his battered fingers, looked queer when he played the piano in his living room with firm touch and lively tempo.

Uncle Ort's fingers were always busy doing something–working crossword puzzles, picking out pecans in the fall, and typing the letters and poetry he wrote. He recorded his thoughts on any scrap of paper at hand. Some of these bits of paper he kept just as he wrote them; others were in poem form and typed, like this one.

> A ray of sunshine, man can't make,
>   A moonbeam, he can't buy.
> Nor can man put a twinkling star
>   Up in God's azure sky.
>
> Man cannot make a mountain range,
>   Nor drain the ocean deep;
> He can't arrange to have it snow
>   Nor make the heavens weep.
>
> Man can't produce a single tree,
>   Nor make a dead thing live;
> He can't create a breath of air
>   Nor one more heart beat give.
>
> Man cannot quench volcano's fire,
>   Nor still the ocean tide;
> He can't stop tornado's force
>   Nor cool the desert wide.

Man cannot melt the frozen north,
    Nor freeze the torrid zone;
Gravity's law he cannot break
    Nor live by bread alone.

So, what is man that he should boast
    Of any thing he's done.
God made the world and all therein
    E'er man's life had begun.

Without God's help, man cannot live
    On this old, earthly ball,
Thus man owes ev'ry thing to God,
    His life, his wealth, his all.

Ort H. Ertzinger, 1952

    My uncle's charitable, benevolent nature blossomed as he grew older. He was a philanthropist, tight-mouthed about the interest-free loans and gifts. Loans were a secret between him and the recipient. No record was kept of the thousands of dollars he loaned to individuals. He trusted the borrower to come forth voluntarily and repay; otherwise his death wiped out the debt.

    His joyous faith continued throughout his life, as did his poetry writing. The date on this poem is 1953.

Lives there a Christian, in our land,
    Whose life is in the Savior's hand;
Who never kneels in prayer to say,
    "Dear Lord, I thank you for this day?

Breathes there a man, from sin set free,
    Who finds no time, on bended knee,
To thank his Lord for life and health,
    For joys and hopes and earthly wealth?

Beats there a heart, within a man
    Who gathers all the wealth he can
That has grown cold with selfishness
    And shares no gold, to others bless?

Dies there a person, white or black,
    Who from the grave has e'er come back
To make atonement for his greed
    By giving gifts to those in need?

> No, God has given men one time
> In which to live a life sublime,
> And if he fails, and life is done,
> There's no reward, no glory won.
>
> Ort H. Ertzinger

The trip to Alaska only whetted Uncle Ort's appetite for travel. He wanted to see new places and meet new people. But would his heart allow it? Taking care of his body and health, Uncle Ort thought, was a mandate from God. A healthy mind is imperative to a healthy body. His heart ailment had not vanished; in fact, he had had several flare-ups.

His cardiologist in Mobile shocked him. Flying, he told my uncle, was sensible for long distances. Uncle Ort had never flown. I suspect, like most people then, he thought of it as risky and dangerous. The doctor explained and convinced my uncle that flying would be safer, less tiring, and more comfortable. Uncle Ort and Aunt Tillie investigated and decided the time was right for them to fly.

According to the travel folders, the leisurely pace of beautiful Hawaii was a good place to take it easy. While they were planning their Hawaiian trip, I was in Japan expecting orders to return to the United States. My tour with the 801st Air Evacuation Squadron, evacuating patients from Korea to Japan, was about over.

Exhilaration and anticipation surely accompanied Uncle Ort and Aunt Tillie as they drove west to Los Angeles. They were about to take their first flight, an overwater trip over the Pacific Ocean to the Hawaiian Islands.

While I was busy in Tachikawa selling my Jeep and buying gifts to take Stateside, I received Uncle Ort's letter including the June dates of their Hawaiian visit. He suggested that I contact them there if, by any chance, I traveled through while they were on Oahu. A few observations, fresh from his own penciled notes, detail their doings.

Saturday, June 9, 1951 Took off in U.S. Strato Cruiser at 10:30 a.m.–first third of the trip at 8,000 feet, and last two-thirds at 14,000 feet. Plane pressurized above 6,000 feet. Went along California coast for 50 miles and headed west over Pacific–53 passengers, two pilots, two co-pilots, one navigator and three stewardesses and two porters. Watched clouds below, fleecy and white. Dinner and something to drink and nibble on all day long. Set watch back three hours, at 8:30. Reached tiny island and landed without a jar. Beautiful fresh flower leis were thrown around our necks as soon as we got off the plane. Then a newspaper photographer paged us and took pictures. Reached Royal Hawaiian Hotel, welcomed with more leis. Dinner in formal attire. Saw hula show at night. Hotel grand, many notables here. Up until 11:30, then to Room 310, fresh pineapple prepared to eat awaited us.

Sunday, June 10 Breakfast at 8, then to old Hawaiian church; a big memorial service, 600 or more there. Royalty attended in uniform, capes with tribal insignias. Any kind of dress proved O.K. Choir sang Hallelujah Chorus without accompaniment. It was grand! Minister preached two sermons, one in Hawaiian and one in English. People of all colors worshipped here.

Dinner was served cafeteria style in the Surf Room, any kind of clothes do. [His careful scrutiny of other people's attire amuses me. His wife was a very meticulous dresser.]

Spent p.m. along Waikiki Beach watching the swimmers. Hula dancers danced in cocoanut grove–got a kiss from one of them. Saw outrigger races in ocean. Took pictures.

The prevailing notion about heart disease then was the value of rest, not exercise. Throughout the trip Uncle Ort stretched out and rested for an hour each day. He set a timer to be sure he did not cheat and get up too soon.

At their own easy pace they saw the sights of Oahu, the growing fields of poi, sugar cane, and pineapples, visited the Royal Japanese Temple and Pearl Harbor. They toured exotic Hawaiian places while I was completing my assignment in Japan.

Wonder of wonders, orders sending me Stateside granted me just what I wanted. My next station was to be with the School of Aviation Medicine in Montgomery, Alabama. I was to fly to California via Hickam AFB in Hawaii. Eu-re-ka!

Immediately I made a reservation on a Military Air Transport System (M.A.T.S.) flight to Hickam, near Honolulu. Next I sent a cable to Uncle Ort in Honolulu telling him when and where I would arrive.

Uncle Ort and Aunt Tillie adjusted their schedule to tour the islands and be back in Honolulu when I arrived.

Saturday, June 16. Flew to Hawaii today and landed at Hilo. The crew were most friendly. Florine Feikert, 2654 Campbell Avenue, Honolulu, hostess.

My relatives flew to the largest island, Hawaii, landing in Hilo. Uncle Ort wrote of unbelievable beauty and contrast. Orchid farms, ferns growing rampant and lush, startling in contrast to the cattle ranch and desert area overshadowed by the awesomely majestic snow-capped Mauna Loa.

Most spectacular to him was the volcanic crater and the 1950 lava flow, which was 17 miles long by half a mile wide and 15 to 59 feet deep. Astonishing contrast between the coral lava and coffee plantations. After a night on the edge of the sea at Kona, they toured the Dole pineapple plant, then flew back to Honolulu and the Royal Hawaiian Hotel.

Meanwhile, I was finalizing plans to meet them there. I will never forget the joys of that deadhead flight on a C-54 M.A.T.S. hospital plane. We flew eastward over the International Date Line at 20,000 feet in a pressurized cabin with a load of patients fresh from the Korean combat zone. The hospital plane was totally different from any I'd ever known–larger and better equipped, with a food preparation area, toilets and hand-washing facilities, and more.

The C-46 and C-47 combat cargo planes of the Fifth Air Force in the combat zone where I flew and cared for patients were simpler. We evacuated the wounded within the zone of the interior–Korea and Japan. At altitudes over 10,000 feet, we used oxygen masks for patients and ourselves and made do with precious little water in Thermos bottles.

More important, on the flight home, with about 50 patients and an adequate medical crew, I was a passenger. I had no official responsibilities, but a nurse is a nurse is a nurse. There was nothing to stop me from being friendly. We had much in common as we returned from war in a very strange land to our wonderful United States of America.

I did what I'd wanted to do a million times before—just listen to the men talk, to be a catalyst in their healing. Although it was not visible, their minds were often as wounded as their bodies.

I became so completely absorbed that my eagerness to see Uncle Ort and Aunt Tillie was pushed aside. The pilots had begun the descent before I realized that we had lost altitude and were about to land at Hickham Air Force Base in Honolulu. I hadn't paid attention to the procedure for deplaning. Suddenly I was cognizant that the wheels had touched terra firma where my relatives were waiting. The plane came to a halt, and the chocks were under the wheels, and my heart was going a mile a minute. The door at the back of the plane near where I sat was opened (I was accustomed to deplaning from the front), and I walked down the steps into the Hawaiian sunshine. I was about to burst in anticipation and excitement. Having relatives meet me at a military base was a totally new experience.

I saw Aunt Tillie and Uncle Ort, ran over and embraced them. As the three of us stood in a multiple-bear-hug flood of joy, a strong hand pulled at my shoulder. The touch was so firm that, even in my ecstasy, I paid attention. I turned to see a solemn-looking man with the insignia of the U.S. Customs Service pulling at my arm.

He was blunt. Customs came first, before Uncle Ort and Aunt Tillie. I was not even supposed to touch them. "What if you had a handful of illegal rubies? You could have slipped them in their pocket." Hawaii was not yet a state.

I expected to have customs examine my luggage. My ancient samurai sword was right on top of my trunk so that, if there was any question about my not having papers for it, the inspectors could easily remove the treasured sword. I was na_ve. I thought that respect for a U.S. Air Force officer would exempt her from inspection of her person. I was incensed. Uncle Ort and Aunt Tillie were stunned, too.

Not until I was registering at the very elegant Royal Hawaiian Hotel did it dawn on me that someone besides Uncle Sam would be expected to pay the bill. I'd been RON-ing (remaining overnight) in military billets for no charge for so long that I hadn't given it a thought. Now, like a bolt of thunder, it hit me that a room at this paradise must cost a pretty penny. Honolulu was a strangers-in-paradise experience for the three of us.

A U.S. fleet was in port, and the hotel was running over with handsome naval officers, smartly dressed in their summer uniforms. My name–Janice Warrene Feagin, AFNC, Flight Nurse, Korea–was on the hotel's roster of special guests, along with Alan Ladd and several other notables. I was treated accordingly by the hotel staff. The courtesies–having the hostess welcome me by name, receiving invitations to a hotel reception and dance–were a flattering surprise. Uncle Ort's tip to the proper people was responsible for my glamorous treatment.

My room was like a flower garden, with an array of exotic fruits, colorful blossoms, and wonderful aromas. With the encouragement of my aunt and uncle, I attended several functions and met exciting Navy men hungry for female companionship, but no one's company was as invigorating as Uncle Ort and Aunt Tillie's.

My country relatives were right at home in the fabulous surroundings of the poshest hotel on Oahu. Together on the terrace overlooking Waikiki Beach we talked. Their voices reflected the ecstasy of their first flight and their many new experiences.

While dining one evening, Uncle Ort spoke with the maitre d' about what he might take home to a special group of young people at his church back in Alabama. The headwaiter bowed and disappeared momentarily. He returned with a pound box of individually wrapped sugar cubes. "Royal Hawaiian Hotel" printed on the wrapper of each cube made this a nice souvenir.

We all three of us attended an authentic Hawaiian luau. The tables, decorated with gorgeous hibiscus (we were told there were over a hundred varieties), were arranged amid the palm trees near the Pacific Ocean. We watched the pigs being lifted from their cooking places–a large hole in the ground lined with ti leaves and filled with hot stones–then readied for the table. Whole pigs, wrapped in chicken wire to keep them from falling apart, had been lowered into these holes many hours earlier, then covered with tarpaulins. The meat cooked in its own juices. This pork was the delicious entree placed on the tables already laden with poi and fresh pineapple. After the meal, everyone sort of migrated to the beach a hundred yards away to see the net throwing contest.

We three spent the next morning at the Kodak show. The first time my aunt and uncle went to this entertainment, which was free to everyone, they found it so much to their liking that they returned to take me. Uncle Ort, a stockholder in the Eastman Kodak Company, speculated, "The Kodak film that spectators buy more than pays for the cost of putting on this show."

With the blue Pacific as a background and soft trade winds all around, native Hawaiian culture was on display. In their natural dress, natives sang as they gracefully swayed to the music of the Royal Hawaiian Serenaders. The Chamber of Commerce couldn't have fashioned a more effective advertising campaign. The dancers' hands told a story as they move rhythmically, and their shoulders kept in line; this was more than a hoochy-coochy dance.

Out of the blue, a smiling Hawaiian girl dancer walked directly over to Uncle Ort. Wearing a hula skirt made of fresh green leaves and fresh flower leis around her neck, this pretty girl gave us all a thrill. They recognized each other, for she had been the stewardess on their flight to the Island of Hawaii. Florine Feikert was her name. She explained that the dark green leaves of her skirt were from the ti plant and are used in making hula skirts for both men and women.

To cap off the show, big fat Hilo Hattie, dressed in a Hawaiian muumuu, corralled the men into the center ring. Some men refused, others acted shy and had to be coaxed, but not my uncle. Florine took Uncle Ort's hand, kissed him on the cheek, and led him willingly into the dance arena. But first he was sure Aunt Tillie had the movie camera poised to take his picture.

Several Hawaiian men dancers joined in to assure the men that hula dancing was for men, too. They demonstrated hip and body movement. Hilo Hattie with her loose joints and graceful movements captivated her audience. The men gradually got into the swing of it; as the music floated, the cameras clicked.

Of all the pictures of Hawaii, I most enjoyed the movies of Uncle Ort learning to hula. Amid the fifteen short and tall, fat and lean men, Uncle Ort is there, wearing fresh flower leis, smiling and swaying his body with the music. He is having the most fun of all.

To this day, when I hear "Kekali Nei Au" ("Lovely Hula Hands," or The Hawaiian Wedding Song) and other Hawaiian songs, I visualize Uncle Ort in Hawaii and recall the kiss of the trade winds. Memory invades my senses with contentment. Uncle Ort told me years later, after he'd traveled to many other countries, that his Hawaiian pictures were the ones he enjoyed seeing and showing the most.

Air travel opened the door of opportunity to the world for Uncle Ort and gave vent to a new focus–travel. It was time to end his twenty-six years as adult advisor to the young people. He and Aunt Tillie were eager for more first-hand experiences with people and places in other parts of Planet Earth.

The goodness of life improved with the years. For Uncle Ort, it was a time to reap.

27

Southern Exposure

WITH AN ITCHING FOOT,...

...getting more itchy all the time, I began casting about for some place to go, not too far, not too close. Some place out of the beaten path. We had been over the Alaskan Highway, had crossed the Pacific Ocean to the Hawaiian Islands. Next????

Looking through some material from the United Fruit Company led me to an instant decision. We will go to Panama and Guatemala for our next trip. It was settled just that easy, to Central America we will go.

I then wrote the Brownell Tourist Bureau, in Birmingham, Alabama, advising them of the dates we would like to fill with the trip and where we would like to go. I asked them to arrange the trip and advise the cost.

So Uncle Ort wrote about the preliminaries of his 1952 junket south. He continued:

Within a few days came a letter with a preliminary schedule and the approximate cost of the trip. Brownell was promptly instructed to proceed with the arrangements. In a matter of days, reservations were received, bills paid and our tickets in hand.

We will travel south on the speedy Chiriqui, a boat in the United Fruit Company's great white fleet. We are to depart from New Orleans and sail to Cristobal, cross the isthmus to Panama City, then fly to Guatemala, thence back to New Orleans and home. It looks like a most interesting trip and we were agog with arrangements. By "we," I mean wife and myself.

On Thursday, February 19, 1952, at 3 p.m., he and Aunt Tillie boarded the train in Bay Minette, heading for New Orleans. These are highlights from his journal.

We had a good night's rest in New Orleans, that most interesting southern city. Next day we reached the immigration office just as they opened. Goodie goodie, our passports were ready. Now we're all set for the trip so we grabbed a light lunch, closed out our hotel room and hired a taxi to the pier and boat.

Our papers let us go aboard the ship without delay. We did what everyone else does on a strange boat, wander about to see what it is all about and just get our bearings. On the stairway we ran head on into Rev. and Mrs. David Edington, formerly of Mobile now living in New Orleans. They were putting Dr. and Mrs. Warner Hall of South Carolina aboard. Good-friends aboard-we felt at home. We had known Dr. and Mrs. Hall through summer work with Presbyterian Conferences for the youth in Alabama. In the evening we met other folks from there and yonder. To bed at 9:40 as the great liner plowed its way into the Gulf of Mexico.

As we continued southward next day the gulf seemed unusually blue and pretty. But, the waves gave the boat a certain rock or pitch which turned the tummy in unusual angles. With some difficulty we made it to the dining room for all the meals, and then we ate with care so as not to feed the fish. We did not.

On the morning of February 24, just at dawn, the ship nosed into the harbor at Cristobal. Inspectors came aboard and checked us, looked over our papers and luggage and said we could go ashore. A tugboat came out and pushed our boat skillfully into the dock. Everything was hustle and bustle. The travel agency man helped us get through customs and soon we were put aboard a limousine and hastened across the isthmus to Panama City.

The twin cities of Cristobal and Colon are on the Atlantic side of the isthmus and west of Panama City located on the Pacific side. We went east 50 miles to get to the Pacific Ocean!!! Seems odd but that is the way it is.

Our driver informed us we had arrived during the Carnival Fiesta celebration. (A pre-Lenten observance like Mardi Gras.) He warned us we would see many funny fiesta sights; he did not exaggerate in the least.

The 330-room hotel which will be our home for the next seven days is about a mile from the center of town. Eight stories high with balconies, a crystal-clear swimming pool, a roof garden with a tile dance floor–the hotel was up to date. A six-piece band plays during dinner and for dances. The hotel employs an organist to play their own pipe organ.

We drove from the Atlantic to the Pacific Ocean in about an hour and 25 minutes. We still have trouble understanding why we go eastward to the Pacific, but we did. [A look at a map of that area of the world makes this quite clear.] Country roads, generally, are rough; farming operations are small and irregular. Much jungle vegetation grows there.

We paid $2.00 for the privilege of sitting on the balcony to watch the Spanish pollera [bolero?] dances. The dance is almost a no-contact affair; the man circles the lady. The brass band played noisy music until long after midnight.

Lady dancers wore long gowns in a beautiful color or with a flowered design, flared out at the bottom. Their ornament-bedecked hair shone in the light and quivered as the dancers moved about.

The men dancers' monuto shirt extended almost to their knees–beautifully made of coarse goods, on the order of burlap. The figured design matched their ladies' pollera gowns.

The dancers made a grand sight in their regalia. The man fans the lady with his hat, bows and curtsies and dances around her. One lady is supposed to outlast four men before the dance is completed.

Our first sightseeing tour took us through the country with little shops and stores along the highway. Many thatched huts and small houses dot the land; some have tin roofs. In the two-story buildings, the families reside upstairs. None of the houses seem strong enough to stand much wind or any kind of a storm. Banana and papaya trees with fruit in all stages of ripening grow nearby.

We noticed a good many lumps on the sides of the trees or among tree limbs. We inquired and our guide informed us that these lumps were termite nests. Termites play havoc with wooden homes; that is why new ones are being made of concrete block. The first concrete block factory is being constructed.

High in our air conditioned room we slept wonderfully each night and enjoyed a siesta every day. Our room looks down over the beautiful Pacific. We came to the Zone in the dry season, the best season of the year.

Our two-hour tour of the Canal Zone began promptly at nine o'clock and took us by many beautiful homes, the hospital, the schools, army headquarters, airport and other places of interest. The United States controls and manages a strip of land 5 miles on either side of the canal. Almost everything in the Zone is American built according to the needs of the tropics.

Seeing this engineering marvel in action impressed my uncle, who must have remembered 1913, when the canal was celebrated by President Wilson in Mobile.

We were informed there are two tides each day and each one has a rise and fall of 17 to 18 feet. The operation of the locks and handling of the ships is run to take full advantage of these tides. The ships can, however, go through nicely at any tide stage.

The climax of the canal tour was being able to stand on the concrete work of the Panama Canal itself, where we saw three boats and a tank barge pass through the locks. We were at the first lock coming from the Pacific. Between the locks the ships run on their own power.

Uncle Ort's interest in people was universal, so Scotty was big news the day they took a boat trip to Toboga Island.

On the 28th we were up pretty early; our taxi was waiting to take us to the boat. At the dock the driver introduced us to a fellow named Scotty, a character if we ever saw one. Someone is always ready to look after us. Scotty was, and did.

After arrival at Toboga, he piloted us all about town. Everyone knew Scotty; even the dogs and children seemed to like him. He helped us get our tickets, sat with us, and in his Scotch brogue gave us some information about Toboga Island.

He took us to a large veranda extending out so the ocean was under the hotel. I expressed a desire to fish. Within 10 minutes Scotty had a fishing trip arranged for us at 1:00 p.m. We watched the lobster fishermen as they eased through the low tide to look for the lobsters among the rocks. We saw them spear several and put them in the boat.

Toward noon the sky began to cloud up and the wind began to blow. The water in the ocean became rough; Scotty was worried lest it get too rough for fishing. We lounged about the veranda over the sea until nearly noon time. Definitely there was too much wind to fish as time wore on. Scotty announced it was time for lunch; he told us to follow.

We passed a Catholic church where Scotty lined up a bunch of native Indian children who were coming from school. With authority, he bossed them around and they appeared to regard him as their father. Willingly they obeyed him, posed nicely for a picture and did not ask for a tip. I got some good pictures of Scotty and Mrs. Ort.

The noon meal served in a screened-in dining room was tastily prepared. It consisted of fried Carbina, a delicious fish, and soup with yucca in it.

Scotty bemoaned the fact that no pineapple was available. Here on the island, he insisted, grew the sweetest and finest pineapple "pinya" [pi′ña] in the world. He just could not get over the lack of pineapples on the table. The people were too lazy, he complained, to climb up the hill to gather them for us to eat. Because they have a small black seed in them, their market value is low.

The wind got worse and the sky clouded up as though it would rain, so the fishing trip was canceled.

Uncle Ort and Aunt Tillie left Panama and flew north to Guatemala on Sunday.

We noticed that all the announcements about the planes were made first in English, then in Spanish. At 7 A.M. we boarded the Pan American World Airways four-motored air clipper and were whisked off the ground headed for Guatemala.

The take-off was smooth. We soon passed alongside of

DeMonotombo, a live volcano which was erupting in goodly quantities of smoke. We saw several smaller live volcanoes as we roared through the air; dozens of extinct volcanoes were also visible. Some mountains were deceiving; they had clouds over the summit which looked like erupting volcanoes, but were not.

At 11:30 we were in Guatemala, safe and sound. Luggage was placed on a long, low table and we were requested to open each bag. Once the bags were open, the head inspector ran his hand through our belongings, lifted up some of the clothing, gave us a sharp, piercing look and waved us to shut the baggage and get out.

Our cases were packed to the limit; getting them back together was rather an ordeal. It seemed some of the clothing was just bound to stick out. Finally we did get all things in order.

A guide stood outside the terminal with a slip of paper he held up, Mr. and Mrs. Ort Ertzinger. He looked us over and asked if the name belonged to us. [This novel way of identifying travelers amused him.] He took us over so completely, before we knew it, we were aboard a big limousine and headed to the Pan American Hotel. Our room was ready right over the main street.

The dining room waitresses were Indian women who wore long skirts with beautiful blouses and walked around in bare feet. Their long black hair was tied at the end with a bow.

In conversation with natives who could speak some English, we learned it was customary each day between the hours of 12 and 2 for everything in town to close up for siesta. One day I forgot and went to the Bank of England to exchange some money about 1:30. I had to wait until 2 o'clock for the bank to open.

I must devote some space to the sanitary system; wife says I must not. I MUST. If you are easily embarrassed skip this paragraph, possibly the next two. Your face might get red.

Just after daybreak, the church bells began ringing, calling the people to worship. Some four or five different bells rang at intervals until seven o'clock. One large bell seemed particularly anxious. I counted the rings: it rang 162 times before it stopped.

Rising early in Chichicastenango, as I always do, I looked out of the room window, across a little ravine toward a nice-looking Indian home. A woman came out of the house, walked to a banana tree, unwrapped her skirt and squatted on one knee. She was taking care of nature's early-morning call. She reached for a corn stalk and used it, tossed it aside, rewrapped her skirt and went back into the house.

A small boy came out of the front door and a small girl came out of the back door. They too followed the performance of their mother in the yard, then went back in the house. I was amazed and wonder, what next? As I watched, some buzzards from a nearby housetop flew to the three spots where the Indians had been, proceeded to remove the rubbish, then flew back to their perch on the housetop.

Hardly believing my eyes, I called Mrs. Ort to the window to watch with me. In a grassless field just next to the hotel we saw two men come out of the house. They went about halfway across the field and took care of nature's call. Immediately the buzzards appeared and cleaned up the place.

We learned later that the buzzards are regarded almost as a sacred bird. They are the town's garbage system and never fail to respond. We then understood why all drinking water had to be boiled, including that used in making ice.

We did not see a single toilet or privy in the whole town with an estimated population of 26,000, except in the hotel. The hotel was as modern as could be. All sanitary facilities available in the United States are available to its patrons. For this I am truly glad: my days of using the woods are over.

The markets are filled with an amazing array of goods. The sellers seat themselves on the ground and place the wares before them and wait for the customers. Wares to sell included onions; dried, smelly fish; garden vegetables of every kind; seeds for flowers; chickens; eggs; matches, candles, cigarettes, tobaccos; bags; bananas; woven goods of all kinds; pottery of every description; kitchen ware; chairs and even coffins. The meat market was screened from the many flies.

Meat from the carcass could be picked out by the purchaser, [and] then the merchant slashed off the desired portion. Two balanced pans provided the scale. A weight was placed in one pan, [and] the seller placed the meat in the other. After the meat was weighed, the buyer put it in a basket, lifted the basket to his or her head and usually went on to another part of the market to shop.

It would be unfair to think that Uncle Ort's detailed descriptions were derogatory. They were not intended to be. The buzzards are nature's disposal system. Undoubtedly my uncle realized the value of this natural way creatures on earth work together, although he found no satisfaction in the primitive living conditions for his brothers and sisters in the family of man. Undoubtedly this experience made him more appreciative of the standard of living we enjoy in the United States. This is the way his log ended:

> After passing customs, we boarded the plane for New Orleans, departing from the airport at 12:30 noon. We were in New Orleans at 5:05, boarded the plane for Mobile at 6:00, took the train for Bay Minette at 8:45 reaching home at 9:45 that evening. Evidently we had just been around the corner, the return trip was so fast we could hardly realize we were home. The trip was great.
>
> All the people with whom we traveled are grand people. Many we meet are common folk like ourselves, retired people with sufficient funds to enable them to run about without worry. Many are much more traveled than we. All are eager to help us find some new place to go or something new to see. One of the best parts of any trip is the grand folks we meet.

28

Western Arena

THEIR SLEEK BLACK FORD took Uncle Ort and Aunt Tillie on a 7,565-mile jaunt–San Antonio, Monterrey (Mexico), Carlsbad Caverns, Grand Canyon, Zion Park, Las Vegas, Hoover Dam, Camp Pendleton, San Diego, Long Beach, Los Angeles, Hollywood, Sequoia National Forest, Fresno, Yosemite, and Sacramento. On the inside cover of the Fidelity and Deposit datebook, in May 1953, Aunt Tillie wrote this list of places visited on their four-week journey. Uncle Ort added the Sierra Rockies.

The day after leaving Bay Minette, they arrived in San Antonio, Texas, where my husband and I lived. We were still a bride and groom, so there was a special delight in being host and hostess. The travelers followed our directions and found us at our base housing apartment on Randolph Air Force Base.

I was especially eager for them to see the School of Aviation Medicine. That is where my Air Force career had begun, where I had earned my Flight Nurse wings and later taught. Now, after duty in the Pacific Theater of Operations, I had returned to Randolph as an instructor in SAM. Association with the school allowed me to participate in aeromedical research, such as testing the effectiveness of the motion sickness medicine Dramamine.

The unpleasant weather did not deter my guests or dampen their spirits. After seeing the base, we did the usual San Antonio touristy things during their short visit. We took a saunter down the San Antonio Riverwalk amid the tall downtown buildings, saw the Alamo and a couple of other missions, and of course ate a Mexican dinner. We watched while the corn tortillas were cooked on hot stones, then ate enchiladas and guacamole salad.

The Officers' Club, Aunt Tillie thought, was an interesting place to celebrate her birthday. After dinner we were entertained by glamorous swimmers. The beautiful round club pool was the setting for a swimming extravaganza–an all-woman event with dozens of graceful swimmers. Uncle Ort always gave a lot of lip for pretty girls, as did my husband. Enjoying the show together was family fun.

Reminiscing about their visit as I put the guest sheets in the washing machine, I realized it was not what we'd done so much as their excitement and graciousness about everything. These ideal guests brought a good time with them and boosted my confidence as the lady of the house.

As usual while traveling, Uncle Ort made daily notations. One funny quirk in the datebook notes put me in a tailspin. Reading on each page went smoothly until the seventh day, when the puzzle began. He stopped writing in the middle of a thought in Monterrey, Mexico.

What in the world is going on? I asked myself. I finally figured out the thrifty "Ortish" system he had devised for situations when what he wanted to say would not fit on a given page. On May 7, for example, the space provided was insufficient, even when he wrote small and placed the lines close together. "As we walked along the narrow sidewalks," he wrote, "the taxi or horse and buggy men nearly dragged us into their shops. (see February 16)" Sure enough, sixty pages back, on the page dated February 16, the notations continued:

Bought postcards and candy. The clerk, a pretty Mexican, could not speak English. She wrote the prices on a slip of paper which she handed us. We visited a bank to get money exchanged. A Mexican peso is a piece of paper about the size of a dollar worth 12¢. Even kids know the exchange rate, which is posted everywhere.

Once I got the hang of it, no problem. Often, on that trip, it was necessary to extend writing space in this manner.

On a tour of Horsetail Falls 23 miles from town we went off the pavement over rocky dusty roads through several sprawling towns. Kids yelled greetings as we passed. We drove over ditches of fresh water babbling down the mountainside to the parched orange and pecan groves below.

We left our car at the gate, then for 3 pesos rented a burro to ride _ mile to the falls. We each mounted a puny-looking burro, [and] with a small boy to accompany us we headed up to the falls. Others were doing the same and we passed a good many men and women coming back. Our new friend from Texas had the burro trotting. She waved her boot when she saw us and yelled a great hurrah for Texas!

The burros were sure-footed and slowly wended their way along a rocky pathway nearly to the falls. We alit and climbed the rest of the way on boardwalks just below the falls. The spring up the mountains at the top of the falls is narrow, but gradually widens toward the bottom.

The elevation of the falls is 5100 feet, 3400 feet above the town. The water runs down the steep side, drops 150 feet, fans out and strikes the pool below, then converges into a narrow clear stream. The water spreads out like a horse's tail and is white all the way to the bottom, thus the name, Horsetail Falls.

I wanted to take some pictures overlooking the valley, so I'd picked out a place as we ascended. On the way down, we stopped by an adobe house in an olive tree grove and I took pictures.

As a traveler, he was a good American who adhered to the notion "When in Rome, do as the Romans do." He never expected others to do as he did, nor tried to impose his views on anyone else. His faithfulness should not be confused with narrowness; however, he was rigid about one lifetime habit–church attendance on the Sabbath.

Sunday May 17, breakfast at 8:30, drove by taxi to the Union Church of Monterrey. The minister acknowledged the visitors and read the home towns and denominations they represented—Bay Minette, Alabama; St. Louis, Texas; Boston, Massachusetts; Montreal, Canada; and several Mexican cities. Six denominations were represented.

The minister pointed out that some church members are more interested in their wealth than in their soul or the church. The Union Church is one of the few in town that had services in English. The church was full. The minister, a retired chaplain, has a wife who is from Birmingham, Alabama. The choir of 18 mature people with trained voices was half men and half women. [Likely Uncle Ort was envious; remember, in his church choir, he was the only male.] One lady sang two beautiful solos.

The afternoon performance they planned to attend was billed as a colorful pageant. That part of it escaped Uncle Ort. The Humane Society or SPCA would have agreed with him. I warn you, his descriptions are vivid, not written for the squeamish.

Bullfights are held only on Sunday afternoons. We went. The arena is a complete circle extending 15 to 20 tiers up and out, with seats for 5,000 people. Our seats were on the fourth row. We saw it ALL.

First the performers on horses proudly paraded out to much applause. They wore their shiny uniforms with stencil-spangled vests. The performers on foot were clad in tight-fitting garments; the bull could not possibly get his horn into their clothing.

After the parade, the performers retired into a second ring behind a five-foot wall, safe from the bull's charges. The signal to start is given with a tom-tom. The bull, usually black, came charging into the arena and the door closed behind them.

As the bull came through the door, a short stiletto with barbs was shot into the bull's back, just behind the shoulders. This remained in the flesh until the animal was dead. The shaft hung there to hurt the bull as it flopped up and down during his charges.

Men waving yellow cloths moved across to the arena. The bull charged but stopped before striking the boards. On the opposite side of the arena, another yellow cloth is flashed. The bull dashes madly back and forth, back and forth until he is winded.

The tom-toms and a horn signal two more riders on heavily padded ponies. Each is carrying 14-foot shafts with a short dagger on the end. They take their place opposite each other. By proper maneuvering the bull is egged into charging the horse. As he charges the rider pierces the hide of the bull with a long spear. The bull runs into the horse and occasionally throws the rider. As long as the bull continues to charge, the rider gouges the bull with a spear. The idea is to cut a hole in the bull, so the blood will stream out.

The numerous fighters do not let the bull have any rest. They keep him charging about until his tongue is hanging out in exhaustion. The bull becomes confused; he does not know which one to charge. HE ALWAYS CHARGES THE CLOTH, NOT THE MAN. Now and then the bull gets his horn or foot on the cloth, takes it away from the man. Seldom do the performers get gored or bleed. Five or six little openings around the arena with overlapping gateways make it easy for the fighter to dodge out of danger.

The tom-tom beats again, the horsemen leave, and the toreador enters with a bright red cloth, drapes it around his sword, and makes the tired bull charge.

As the bull passes, the toreador rears back and lets the bull graze his body, as a show of bravery, I guess. The matador adroitly steps to one side. By such maneuvering, he gets the enraged bull to charge his cloth as many as six times.

Now comes the thrust. All eyes are centered on the star of the show. The bull is weakened, but very much enraged. The toreador stands facing; the bull charges. Again he drives in his sword; it penetrates and is buried to the hilt.

One toreador stood before the bull too exhausted to charge. The toreador got down on one knee and finally on both knees right in front of the bull. The crowd cheered wildly! The toreador gallantly stepped aside to acknowledge the cheers of the crowd while the poor bull gasps for breath and bleeds from his many wounds.

When the toreador makes a particularly skillful thrust, he pierces the lungs. The blood streams from the bull's nostrils; the bull immediately falls to his knees dead. The toreador bows gallantly to all parts of the stands. If the spear does not immediately puncture the lungs, it takes longer.

While the crowd cheers, the toreador cuts off one of the bull's ears as a trophy. Hats, beer bottles, and seat cushions are thrown into the arena. Almost as soon as the bull hits the floor, men rushed in and pulled out as many of the barbed instruments as they can. A team of horses appeared dragging a double-tree and chain. The chain is fastened to the horns and the tortured bull dragged off.

The bull is doomed from the start and doesn't have a chance. Guards carried rifles and pistols to keep order. Passion among spectators was high as spectator fights enlivened the stands.

This had been an eventful day–the worship service, the fascinating but very distasteful bullfight–and there was more to come. Before they lay down to sleep, they experienced the promenade, a Mexican custom inherited from the Spanish.

On Sunday nights everyone goes to the city square, called the Parca. The older married men and women and children sit and watch as the younger boys and girls walk around the lovely lighted park. According to custom, this is the way they find their spouse. With their fans and in their coquettish ways, they flirt and eventually find a way to pair off.

Leaving Monterrey, they returned to the United States and headed for Grand Canyon Park. Uncle Ort described driving through spectacular beauty. With a clear sky they crossed the Continental Divide at Pie Town, New Mexico. Uncle Ort's movie camera was whirring; he took several reels of movies just in the canyon.

Coming out of Grand Canyon Park, within twelve miles of Cameron, the left tire went flat. He changed the tire, purchased a new tube and boot in Cameron, and they were back in business. Up at six the next day to discover that their camera was missing.

Searched car, room, and cafe. Found it in garage where we had tire fixed. Left it on fender, it fell off. The mechanic saw it fall and picked it up.

My aunt and uncle paid a surprise visit to Jack and his wife, Eva Mae, and son, Craig Michael. Jack was stationed at Camp Pendleton north of San Diego. They were expecting their second child. Kinfolks from back east were a special occasion for rejoicing. From Pendleton Uncle Ort drove to Los Angeles and then to Hollywood.

Greyline tour took us by many of the homes of movie stars, among others Lou Costello, Gregory Peck, and John Barrymore. Some of the homes were built on hills where only the fire department trucks were allowed to go, unless by invitation. The panoramic view of adjoining towns was beautiful.

Visited Republic motion picture studios and met a number of actors and actresses. Got some autographs. Met Captain Lillian Kinkella where Republic Studios was filming Flight Nurse. To see everything was done in proper Air Force manner, the studio employed Captain Kinkella, a U.S. Air Force nurse as consultant. Captain Kinkella knows Janice. They had flown in the same squadron in Japan and Korea. [Kinky and I had lived and worked together, and a picture of us together, side by side, had appeared in the *Air Force Times*.] Many actresses were in flight nurse garb, the kind Janice wears.

Getting out of L.A. is like unraveling a tough knot–terrible traffic for miles.

The final week of this westward excursion they drove north to Merced, where there were fruit orchards of many kinds–figs, grapes, and nice big juicy strawberries. Uncle Ort sent strawberries to Dr. McLeod in Bay Minette.

Going over the mountains they ran into plenty of snow, motored through the San Joaquin Valley, the Sierra Mountains, Lake Tahoe, Winnemucca, Nevada, and around Salt Lake City (their first trip to the Mormon capital).

Driving home by the northern route over the Continental Divide and mountains to Denver, then through Kansas, provided delightfully different scenery. They left Pine Bluff, Arkansas, at 6 a.m. for the last lap. Four hundred thirty-nine miles later, at 3:45 p.m., they reached Bay Minette.

Four weeks earlier, they had departed Bay Minette with 5,157 miles on their odometer. They returned with a dashboard reading of 12,722 miles–over seven thousand miles of traveling to fantastic places.

Hundreds of feet of movie film confirm their safari in the West. Uncle Ort's thirty-page travelogue sprouted from his scribbled notes. This exposure to the good ole United States gave him new pride in the majesty and wonder of his country.

29

Autobiography

IN HIS INDIVIDUAL STYLE, Uncle Ort wrote about what impressed him. The way people dressed, what they ate, and how they lived. His bias shows in his accounts of the buzzard sanitation in Guatemala and the bullfight in Mexico. These personal concerns, attitudes, and biases reflected in his travelogues make them, in a sense, autobiographical.

Uncle Ort trusted the slogan, "The World Is Yours with Brownell Tours," so in 1958 he and Aunt Tillie made a Grand Tour in Europe from May 28 to July 14 with Brownell.

> I had carried out my promises to myself to see our own country before tackling Europe. Mrs. Ort made up my mind that it was time for us to go to Europe. We had taken in Alaska, the Hawaiian Islands, Canada, Mexico, Guatemala, Central America–Panama, Cuba, Managua, Nicaragua; and about everything else we could hear about on the western side of the Atlantic.
>
> So we planned a trip to Europe. She does not care for flying as much as I do and would rather go by ship. We reached a compromise: we flew over and came back by ship. Their tour didn't cost too much, so with a variety of inviting travel leaflets, Europe, here we come.

They traveled from France to Italy, Austria, Switzerland, Germany,

Belgium, the Netherlands, Denmark, Sweden, England, and back to Belgium, where they sailed for New York. I have shaved down his account, leaving out the cathedrals, castles, museums, and history, which he meticulously wrote about. These are the especially Ortish segments of his seventy-six-page book.

> I took 31 reels of colored movies and many notes. When I returned to the hotel at night I wrote my observations, my listenings, and my understanding of what was told us by the various guides and interpreters.
>
> From Mobile to Newark, New Jersey, we flew by plane. May 28, 1958, was the date. We boarded a helicopter to fly over New York City but got halfway up when the 'copter settled back to the ground; for some unknown reason we could not get back in the air. Something was wrong, so they decided they'd better send us to the La Guardia by taxi. We were there in plenty of time for the 6:30 p.m. plane to Paris. It was a dandy flight all the way; we soared in the pressurized plane about 21,000 feet above the clouds.

I doubt that many passengers understood the direction they traveled or noticed the sun more carefully than Uncle Ort.

> The sun went down at 9 o'clock on the left side of the plane. The sun made the sky red again at 12:40 on the left-hand side of the plane and was shining brightly at 1:40. The course of our plane had been a big circle northward, eastward, and then southeasterly to Paris. Strange, the sun going down to our left and after only four hours of complete darkness coming up still on our left.
>
> The stewardess began serving breakfast about 3:30, our time. At 4:30 we were over Normandy. Shortly afterward we circled over Paris and landed, without a jolt.
>
> We were soon at the old St. Petersburg Hotel in the center of town. This old hotel is nicely kept and most convenient for our tours. The first morning in Paris our party was all on the bus before 9 o'clock, except us. Immediately we were aboard, off we went. We tried not to be last again.
>
> The group was from all parts of the United States [and] grew to know and like each other. We soon became more like a family than a tour party. [A photograph of the group is tucked inside the travelogue from which I took this.]
>
> The Brownell bus in Paris was a new one and very comfortable. A

delightfully charming French lady was our interpreter. Several nights we took in the Follies. Ugh. The elaborate shows with girls in the nude seem about the same. I still like women with their clothes on. Back to the hotel plenty tired. But we did not come to Europe to sleep, so, tired we'll be, but we'll see Europe.

Sunday afternoon, six or seven of us went to the Concord Square [Place de la Concorde], where we hoped to get some pictures of the Seine river. As we approached the square we saw armored cars and armed guards, which gave us an ominous feeling.

As we walked across the square toward the river, we passed the American Embassy with Old Glory flying. There were many other people around, so we felt pretty safe.

All of a sudden, a mob of some 150 or 200 men formed at the edge of the square in front of the Embassy. There was much shouting, throwing of hats in the air, and disturbance. The people hastily disappeared inside the buildings on the square, almost as the evaporation of a cloud. Only a few of us were left on the sidewalk.

Abruptly a number of armored cars drove up in front of the Embassy. Soldiers with their guns got out, marched into the rioting crowd, and dispersed them like a covey of quail. It was so efficient and instantaneously done that we were dumbfounded.

We decided it was time for us, too, to get off the square. We got back to the hotel thinking anything might happen.

Troubled seemed sure to break out. We were awakened about 3 o'clock. We could hear cars racing up and down the street, car doors slamming, men yelling, loud laughing. When we looked out, we saw they were only drunks making the racket, not a civilian-military disturbance. We went back to sleep, glad that we were to leave Paris the next day.

Departure time from Paris for Nice on June 4 was set at 9:30. After the turmoil of the night before, the members of the party were all on hand at 9:07, ready to leave France, so away we went. There was no use waiting; we were our own bosses. This only goes to prove that this group traveling together was a most exceptional one. The guide never had to spend an anxious moment over us.

Before boarding the train for Nice, let me comment about meals in Paris. Breakfast, known as "Continental breakfast," is a cup of coffee (ugh, what coffee) and a roll or bread. French rolls are about 5 inches long and about 2_ inches in diameter with crust hard enough to drive nails into. Mrs. Ort could not handle the crust, so she ate the middle and I ate the crust. My teeth can handle anything.

The normal drink with each meal is some sort of wine; since we did not drink the stuff, we wanted water. The request for water was interpreted as an insult, but after some insistence we got some.

Generally speaking, we liked Paris and would like to make another trip there. We left in the hope that the French government would be stabilized so these fine people again will become one of the world's great progressive nations.

At breakfast in Monte Carlo, we sat with a beautiful view of the palace which Grace Kelly now calls home. We asked for some water and the waiter brought hot water, thinking we intended to dilute our coffee. It needed diluting, all right, but we wanted drinking water. It was hard to make ourselves understood.

The coffee is served with hot milk. They pour the coffee in the cup on one side and with the other hand pour hot milk until it is supposed to be like you want it, but it never is.

Crossing into Italy, we rode through the rugged hill country known as the Italian Alps. We came upon flowers, flowers, and more flowers. Everywhere is adorned with flowers–apartment houses had flower boxes at the windows, plots of ground were covered, walls along the road were full of holes where flowers were planted and hanging down.

As we traveled on in the hilly country, we noticed something new. On the tops of some hills with sharp curves, mirrors were so placed that our driver could see around the curve. This was a big help in case another car was approaching from the opposite direction. Cars going either direction could use them to advantage.

Our bus driver for 13 days deserves a word of praise and commendation. He was not only a good driver, he was courteous, polite, and patient. He did not seem to get riled at slow or dense traffic and did not honk his horn at every delay or car that got too close. He handled the bus with great care and did not take any chances at crossings or narrow roadways.

The meals in Rome were much better than some we have had elsewhere. Breakfast included coffee, hot milk, rolls, eggs, bacon. If you wanted juice, this was an extra. Dinner was spaghetti in some form with a meat and dessert. For supper we were served a soup, meat course, ice cream, and fruit.

The waiters, all men, are adept at serving with the fork and spoon held in the same hand, used like tongs to place the food on your plate. They seem to enjoy waiting on Americans, though the waiters neither speak nor understand our language.

After a drive through the mountains, we finally came out on the shore of the Adriatic Sea. The sea was rough, with breakers beating on the beach as we skirted the shoreline for some 20 miles. When we left the seacoast and headed inland, we ran into extremely heavy traffic and a hard rain.

The driver was in the lowest gear ascending on the winding road to the Dominion of San Marino. We were expected at the hotel high on a hill. The women unloaded our baggage and carried it all to our rooms. No man was needed here.

Our next stop was Venice. On the great square [Piazza San Marco] stands the Tower of the Clock with Roman numerals. Two great iron men with sledges in their hands beat on a great bell which sounds the time. Built in 1499, this clock still operates right on the hour.

I stood in the rain to get a picture of the sledge wielders as they hammered out the hour of 10 o'clock. The clock also shows the phases of the moon and the movement of the sun across the Zodiac.

We left Innsbruck [Austria], where the people speak German, and drove westward. At once we were in the mountains, with farms as neat as a pin. The houses and barns looked old and were joined to each other because of the cold winters.

We began to see dairy farms and hay making. Everything was orderly; even the manure piles were in squares or circles. In many places concrete vats or square were built to hold this valuable fertilizer.

Our skilled bus driver left us in Lucerne. We bade him farewell in a language he could not understand, but with a hand clasp that assured him his driving for us was appreciated. It seemed as though we were losing a member of our family.

We motored to Wiesbaden, where we put up in the Klee hotel. Relatives of ours who were in Frankfurt on military duty called and took us to dinner. We enjoyed being with kinfolk, who showed us around and drove us to Frankfurt, where many Americans are stationed.

In Brussels, Belgium, the Golden Square in the center of town has a chess board painted on it. They play chess with life-sized wooden men. Most of the games are at night, when the board is brilliantly lighted. Hundreds of spectators gather to watch.

Brussels is the home of the famous Maneken Pis, where thousands of pictures have been taken of the statue pissing water. When we came upon this little squirt, he had clothes on. He was as nice and dry as anyone could be. The wetting hour had not yet come, and we did not think it worthwhile to wait to see this statue unclad.

In Amsterdam we saw the statue of the little boy who stuck his arm in the dike to keep it from flooding the land. He probably saved the lives and much land by this stunt.

At one of the famous Edam cheese factories in Holland we stopped long enough to go over the whole thing–house, barn, hay, cows, and factory–all are under one roof. It smelled more or less the same throughout the place. We sampled the cheese, ordered some sent home, and departed.

After a swing through the Scandinavian countries of Denmark and Sweden, they flew to London for a few days. Uncle Ort and Aunt Tillie had been looking forward to London for a very special reason. They hoped to see Ann Gardner (n_e Ann Zehner, who had grown up in his Bay Minette church) and Gale, her husband, who were vacationing there. Saturday, July 5, the four lunched and spent four happy hours together. They saw the usual tourist places–Westminster Abbey, Windsor Castle–and drove into Shakespeare country.

When they left London, they drove by the White Cliffs of Dover, made famous by the World War II song, then boarded a ship for Belgium. They sailed across the English Channel and docked in Ostend. After a good night's rest, they drove up the coast a few miles to the Belgian seaport of Zeebrugge. I will let Uncle Ort ring down the curtain on their entire forty-seven-day journey.

We reached the city of Zeebrugge about 8 a.m. but found that the S.S. *Atlantic* was not loaded and would not depart until 11 a.m. We got aboard, but the tide was low, so the boat could not be moved until the water was deeper.

We left the ship and walked over to watch the fishermen along the high sea wall. They fished for sole, which is about like our flounder, using worms, and threw their hooks as far as possible into the sea. I wanted to get a picture of a man landing a fish, but he told me to go away. He thought I was bad luck. I saw him miss getting two fish he hooked.

Two powerful tugs pulled our boat free from the mud. Finally at 5 o'clock in the afternoon they got us afloat, and we headed down the Channel to the Atlantic Ocean and out into the sea. Seven nights and six days later we were in New York. The lovely people on the ship, the fine meals, music, picture shows, and entertainment made the trip seem shorter than the days indicate.

We had trouble getting a taxi in New York but finally got one. Left Newark by plane at 5:30 and landed in Mobile at 9 o'clock, about 30 minutes late. Our loved ones met us, and we hurried home while we gushed out the story of our wonderful trip.

For Uncle Ort, the trip was not complete until he had written an account of his travels. Sharing what he saw and thought brought him great satisfaction.

30

Crescendo

All history is but the lengthened shadow of great men.
                                        −Ralph Waldo Emerson

THE NEW TOLL ROAD from Chicago to South Bend was something Uncle Ort and Aunt Tillie would tell folks back home about. Their fall trek to visit their birth state had gone as planned. Uncle Ort's diary sets the stage for the trip.

> *September 13, 1959* To Sunday School and church. Family ate dinner with us at our house−Swiss steak, David's favorite. Rained today, loaded car, David slept at our house tonight.
>
> *Monday, September 14* Up at 4, off for Memphis at 5. Arrived 2:30. Got David to college at 3 P.M. Nice day to travel, cloudy all day. Town Park Motel, Room 85 for night.

Driving David to college was a privilege his grandparents welcomed. Their oldest grandson unloaded all his baggage near his dorm and waved good-bye. He was beginning his second year at Southwestern at Memphis (now Rhodes College). My aunt and uncle continued their pilgrimage to Indiana.

The visit next day with Mamie Kahalley Pugh in Osceola, Arkansas, was a treat. My uncle had often bragged about Mamie's outstanding Christian character, brains, and ravishing beauty–fair skin and dark brown hair. He'd missed her leadership among the church youth group after she married and moved away. Taking time to stop and see her was their way of expressing their interest and caring.

Mamie's parents, natives of Syria, operated a very successful department store next to the Bay Minette post office. They owned the building and lived in a large apartment upstairs over the store. Uncle Ort's warmth and friendliness meant a lot to this family from another culture. Their trust and confidence in him was such that Uncle Ort was the executor of Mrs. Kahalley's will.

As they left Chicago and headed for Indiana, I imagine my aunt and uncle delighted in being able to return to familiar places. From the way I remember them talking, the ambiance of their childhood elicited a deep-down satisfaction. The two-story homes with cellars, roads laid out in squares and blocks outlining the farms and pasture land were just as they had been when Uncle Ort and Aunt Tillie were growing up. Quite a few of their friends were around, so they felt at home when they went back.

Huntington, Indiana, was a city without equal in Uncle Ort's past. This town on the Wabash was where he had first learned of God's love and developed his Sunday School habit. The Wabash River where he had learned to fish still flooded in the spring. His education in Huntington's public schools–how to read and write, how to play baseball, his musical training, and much more–was bedrock in his life.

Hearing Uncle Ort quote a poem written by the man who called people from Indiana Hoosiers impressed me. The author's name was James Whitcomb Riley. His poem molded my image of an ideal fall even though it did not exactly fit where I lived.

> They's somthing kindo' harty-like about the atmusfere
> When the heat of summer's over and the coolin' fall is here–
> Of course we miss the flowers, and the blossums on the trees,
> And the mumble of the hummin'birds and the buzzin' of the bees;
> But the air's so appetizin'; and the landscape through the haze
> Of a crisp and sunny morning of the airly autumn days.

Is a picture that no painter has the colorin' to mock–
When the frost is on the punkin and the fodder's in the shock.

Renewing lapsed friendships among Indiana relatives and friends was a pleasure for everyone. Indiana folk looked forward to the visit of their friends from the South, who were a catalyst for getting friends together. Ort and Ottilla were a barrel of fun to be around.

His friends knew and liked each other but never seemed to get together until Uncle Ort was there. I never figured out whether it was Uncle Ort's response to people that made him exuberant or whether, in an infectious sort of way, he was exuberant and made other people feel that way, too. In his diary he used the word "hilarious" when describing an evening with some of these friends.

People in Indiana were preparing for winter that September. Perhaps the here and now, the past and the present became one for these Ertzingers in the environment of his youth. I recall hearing Uncle Ort talk about his childhood in Huntington. I heard him talk of the chores of the autumn, when his family gathered and stored things for the icy winter ahead.

Their cellar was a very important place, and he was his mother's right-hand helper. She stored her homemade crocks of pickles and sauerkraut down cellar. He gathered baskets of apples and root vegetables–potatoes, carrots, and beets–and took them down to stay cool and dry. They furnished food for the family table all winter. Bartlett pears were wrapped individually and arranged to mellow and develop their special flavor and juice.

Uncle Ort had planned to build a cellar in the house he built for his bride, but the water table was too high, and he couldn't devise a way to dig a cellar that would not fill with water. This was one of the few things that I know of which he failed to do.

The enormous difference between fall in Huntington and fall in Baldwin County was like the difference in day and night. The bounty of the Indiana fall–harvesting fruits and vegetables–surpassed that in Alabama, as did the brilliant colors of the maple and elm trees.

Communities in southern Alabama and northern Indiana each had their own character, temperatures, and activities. Their differences were reflected in their agriculture, which gave my uncle an opportunity to show off. In Indiana he bragged about and showed off pecans, satsumas, and persimmons from Baldwin County. But he also gathered pumpkins, popcorn, and fancy gourds to take to Bay Minette, where he boasted about the wonderful goodness of an Indiana autumn.

These differences brought richness and variety. Early on, he and Mother imbued me with an attitude about the North and South that made me proud of their unique differences instead of considering one better than the other. Uncle Ort was the same wherever he went. He got a kick out of fishing, whether it was in the Wabash River or in Owl Creek. People on both sides of the Mason-Dixon Line were eager to hear his travel tales and see his pictures of life in other places. Wherever he was, Uncle Ort's exuberance about life and his love of people exploded.

This letter, published in the *Baldwin Times*, is testimony to what he thought about the South:

Dear friends:

Fifty years ago, June 29, 1909, I arrived in Bay Minette to make my future home. The years have sped swiftly and I have learned to love the town and her people.

When I was a minor I began my own business under the firm name of J. A. Ertzinger & Son. My first business experience was with my abstract company. This business is still in existence under the ownership and management of Walter M. Lindsey. A 50-year celebration is planned by him a little later in the year.

During the 50 years I lived in Bay Minette I have tried to contribute my share to the town's growth and activities. I hope the town has been a better place because I lived in it all these years.

The people throughout the county have been wonderful to me and have made my business career most fruitful and pleasant. The many friendships I have had happiness in forming, I consider my greatest asset. I want all to know that I am most appreciative of their friendship and of the business they entrusted to me through the years.

It is my intention to spend the rest of my life in Bay Minette. I know of no finer people to live with nor finer place to spend the remainder of my life.

Thanks to all.

Ort H. Ertzinger

He continued to write poems. For some reason, he seldom gave them titles. I was not thinking about growing old at the time he showed me this poem. I picked up on the humor more than on what it's like to be slowed down by age.

> How do I know my youth is all spent?
> Well, my get-up and go has got up and went.
>
> But in spite of it all I am able to grin
> When I think where my get-up has been.
>
> Old age is golden, so I've heard it said
> But somehow I wonder, as I get into bed.
>
> I am happy to say, as I close the door
> My friends are the same, only perhaps even more.
>
> When I was young, my slippers were red
> I could kick up my heels right over my head.
>
> Now, I am old, my slippers are black,
> I walk to the store and puff my way back.
>
> The reason I know my youth is all spent
> My get-up and go has got up and went.
>
> But I really don't mind when I think with a grin
> Of all the grand places my get-up has been.
>
> Since I retired from life's competition
> I busy myself with complete repetition.
>
> I get up each morning, dust off my wits,
> Pick up the paper and read the obits.
>
> My name is missing, I know I'm not dead
> So I eat a good breakfast, and thank God instead.

He slowed down, but he never let any grass grow under his feet. Right up to the time he went to Indiana, Uncle Ort was doing his thing in Bay Minette–serving for the umpteenth time as Worshipful Master of the Masons and being secretary-treasurer for the Hunt Club, an elder of the church, member of the board of directors of Baldwin County Savings and Loan, and I don't know what all.

Look at the way Uncle Ort moved. Monday he and his wife left Bay Minette at 5 a.m., deposited David in Memphis, and drove on. They visited Mamie in Arkansas, did business in Chicago, and arrived at Dorothy Dill's home in South Bend on Thursday afternoon, approximately 1200 miles later. Friday they spent the day at his cousin Dorothy's home catching up on the news; Uncle Ort called that "loafing."

Next day he had big plans. For years he'd wanted to sit in the bleachers and watch a major league baseball game. On Saturday he made a round trip to Chicago, a hundred miles away. They saw the Detroit Tigers beat the Chicago White Sox 5-4. This was his first major league game.

After church the following day with his friends Wendel and Rae, they drove north over the state line to Miles, Michigan, for a smorgasbord dinner at the Four Flags Hotel. A lady playing a piano with an organ attachment caught his fancy. It was similar to the one he had bought for the church back home.

One action-filled week after leaving home, on Monday, September 21, he and Aunt Tillie drove to Winona Lake, where they'd reserved a cottage. That way it was simple to maintain their personal routine and independence. Fishing couldn't have been more convenient.

He rented a boat by the week and tied it up to their pier a short walking distance from the front of their cottage. He had precisely the right kind of gear–lines, sinkers, lures, and so on. Fishing was good. On a typical morning he got twenty-six perch, so, even though the rains came, they fished morning and afternoon. Winona Lake was Uncle Ort's hog heaven.

Fishing did not occupy all their time, however. Almost every day they visited in the homes of their friends, sometimes sharing a meal. Good times and plenty of hearty laughter prevailed. Once he noted dividing the fish he'd caught into seven packages. He delivered each package to a friend. Truth to tell, fish never was Uncle Ort's favorite food. His greatest pleasure was in catching them and his next-greatest in giving them to someone.

On Sunday, October 7, they worshipped in Huntington at the church where he had been baptized–First Presbyterian. In the afternoon they drove to Manchester, sixty miles away, for a delightful evening with ten of his Indiana family. A chicken supper at the home of his niece Ruth and her husband, Joe Shanahan, was the centerpiece of this happy gathering. That night they returned to the lake; driving at night was no problem for them.

October 8, 5:45–fished at daylight and evening–the best bunch ever this p.m.,–39 bluegill and perch. To Dess's for dinner. World Series ended today. Los Angeles lost championship to Milwaukee.

October 9, Ottilla and I fished, cold, windy. Got 21, left at 2 for Whitmores'. They had swell supper–Betty, Pat, Bill Barbard, Linda, Dess and Hazel at supper. Grand time.

After going to bed that night, they heard youngsters making noise around the boats but thought nothing of it. Next morning, Saturday, their usual breakfast and devotional reading over, Uncle Ort looked out toward the lake and discovered that his boat was not where he had left it. Aunt Tillie agreed: the noisemakers must have tampered with the boats.

He took his poles and bait and walked down to the water; as he approached the water's edge, he spotted his boat. He had to move the other boats to get his to the pier.

Aunt Tillie was preparing to join him when she saw that something was wrong. He fell back from the water. While trying to get his boat, he had had a heart attack. He died instantly. His passing was Ortish–quick and without fanfare.

His life on earth escalated to a harmonious crescendo before he passed from this world to the next. Looking back, I have a hunch that Uncle Ort had a premonition of his death. He lived as though he had–every moment of every day in a love-God, love-your-neighbor mode. Rev. Robert Seidentopf put it this way:

Mr. Ort's funeral, which I conducted, gave me the most glorious opportunity I ever had to witness to Mr. Ort's faith and to God who inspires it. Mr. Ort left an imprint of God's love on many of us.

His sudden death grabbed those of us left behind like a tight steel vise. It hurt. His quick departure was agonizing, painful, and oh, so difficult to reconcile.

My aunt and uncle's best friends, Wayne and Bertha Rusher (whom Uncle Ort had just a few days earlier taken a package of his fresh-caught fish) were on the scene immediately. Making arrangements to get Uncle Ort's body to Bay Minette was expedited by these friends. They drove Uncle Ort's car and returned with Aunt Tillie to Bay Minette.

As I grieved, I kept thinking how tragic and unfair it was for my wonderful uncle to die so young. His body, other than his "ticker" (his favorite word when referring to his heart), was in good condition. He should have lived much longer. There was so much more he wanted to do.

People who knew him talk about him today with the same zest as they did when he was alive. A whole heap of people still spout forth their happy memories and funny stories when they hear Uncle Ort's name. The model he set, the faith he lived is priceless. He accepted life on its own terms, not his, with the firm belief that the hand of God was guiding it.

To me, his precepts are a living endowment, my own private inheritance from Uncle Ort, and one in which the interest and value continually increase. A heritage more precious than gold. No wonder he is the most unforgettable character in my life.

History is the essence of innumerable biographies. John Esten Cook said, "History lives in the men who make it. Individuals are the first study, not only as they appear in public, but much more as they are in private and when taken unaware." Uncle Ort is alive and well, an icon in history.

Epilogue

JUST SUPPOSE UNCLE ORT WAS HERE IN THE FLESH now. How great it would be if he pulled a Rip Van Winkle and woke up, all six feet, two inches of him, with his characteristic zest for living, his openness to new ideas. My jovial, caring uncle would be anxious to catch up on what was going on.

What would he say? What would he think about those things he held dear? What technology would impress him? How would he plug into today's world? Let me fantasize.

If my uncle reappeared after more than 30 years, he would be overjoyed with his family–in particular, the three great-granddaughters he'd never seen. Their accomplishments, character, and looks would delight him. The photos Heather made for a Rhodes College course; the close-up snapshot five-year-old Laura took of her cat; Meg, a star member of her high school basketball team.

Some things would not have changed very much. He and I would go fishing and talk things over. Again in the early morning we would enjoy the glory of the sun making its debut. But many changes would delight him.

He'd catch on quickly to modern devices. Soon he'd be enjoying a computer, compact disc player, cellular phone, and video camera. He would appreciate the twin-blade razor, sunscreen protection for his skin, and the interstate highway system.

Programs televised via satellite would better enable him to have a world view. The international Olympic Games would charm him. In his golden years, his enjoyment as a spectator would rival his active years as a participant. His interest in the church's mission work all over the world would continue.

The oil that geologists insist lies under Baldwin soil has still not been brought to the surface, but he'd find they are still trying. As he drove around the county, developments in tree farming he saw would please but not surprise him. Early on he realized that, given a chance, with proper drainage, pine trees grow naturally and quickly, but they need protective care. His belief in the value of the land was not ill founded.

The main campus of what is now Faulkner State Community College, located south of Bay Minette, would tickle him pink—offering as it does the opportunity for all high school graduates in Baldwin County to go to college right in Bay Minette. He'd enroll in some of the Continuing Education courses—or maybe teach the course on fishing!

Hot diggity dog, he'd discover a fishing place over by the Faulkner campus. Walter and Eloise had been good caretakers of his land there. They negotiated the damming of a stream to make a pond. Now there are fish and frogs and eels and all those creatures that belong in a Southern pond surrounded by trees. One would think it had always been there—a fishing spot so close to home.

He'd awake to find the reunited Presbyterian Church (USA), a reunion long overdue. The two groups were always one in the spirit according to Uncle Ort's way of thinking. The reunited church is now big, serving in *global* mission. Soon he'd find his niche there.

The strength and growth of the Chamber of Commerce would please him, both in Bay Minette and throughout Baldwin County. Watchdog members have done a pretty good job of staving off industry harmful to the environment. Overcrowding threatens a few specific areas of the county, and action needs to be taken now to curtail this. Uncle Ort would join with residents who want to maintain the quality of life they always knew, or keep the kind of community that attracted and brought them here in the first place.

Enlightened views on smoking would make him happy; he was ahead of his time in opposing the use of tobacco. One way or another he would support environmental programs such as People Opposing Pollution (POP).

He was a pioneer recycler, before the word came into common usage, with his Coke bottle collection. Now he would consider investment in companies that made a profit from recycling. The Environmental Protection Agency, with its controversial political role, would be something new to learn about. Was the EPA really doing what it was set up to do, or was it spending too much feathering its own nest as a burgeoning bureaucracy? Finding good causes to his liking would not be a problem.

On reentry Uncle Ort would be among the same kind of people he left: people with problems, people who needed his help. Law enforcement officers, mothers, grandmothers, bankers, and others who knew him would again seek out his listening ear. People continue to need someone who makes them feel good about themselves.

Ort Harmon Ertzinger lived from 1889 to 1959, the Harry Truman era. These two men had their own unique role in history.

The manuscript was prepared for computer
composition by Suzanne S. Barnhill, set up in
Palatino and Novarese types by Raimund Redlich
at Fairhope Creative and printed and bound by
Interstate/2 in Mobile, Alabama.